Jonathan Carver, John Coakley Lettsom

Three Years Travels through the Interior Parts of North-America

Vol. 2

Jonathan Carver, John Coakley Lettsom

Three Years Travels through the Interior Parts of North-America
Vol. 2

ISBN/EAN: 9783337345815

Printed in Europe, USA, Canada, Australia, Japan

Cover: Foto ©Andreas Hilbeck / pixelio.de

More available books at **www.hansebooks.com**

THROUGH THE

INTERIOR PARTS OF NORTH-AMERICA,

FOR MORE THAN

FIVE THOUSAND MILES,

CONTAINING,

An ACCOUNT of the great *Lakes,* and all the *Lakes,*
Iſlands, and R——, *Cataracts, Mountains, Minerals,*
Soil and *Vegetable Productions* of the *North-Weſt*
Regions of that *vaſt Continent;*

WITH A

DESCRIPTION *of the* BIRDS, BEASTS, REPTILES,
INSECTS, *and* FISHES *peculiar to the* COUNTRY.

TOGETHER WITH A CONCISE

HISTORY *of the* GENIUS, MANNERS, *and*
CUSTOMS *of the* INDIANS

Inhabiting the Lands that lie adjacent to the Heads and to the
Weſtward of the great *River Miſſiſſippi;*

AND AN

A P P E N D I X,

Deſcribing the uncultivated PARTS of AMERICA that are the
moſt proper for forming Settlements.

By CAPTAIN *JONATHAN CARVER,*
OF THE PROVINCIAL TROOPS IN AMERICA.

PHILADELPHIA:

PRINTED AND SOLD BY JOSEPH CRUKSHANK IN MARKET-STREET,
AND ROBERT BELL, IN THIRD-STREET.
M DCC LXXXIV.

TO

JOSEPH BANKS, Esq;

PRESIDENT

OF THE

ROYAL SOCIETY.

SIR,

WHEN the Public are informed that I have long had the Honour of your Acquaintance——that my Defign in publifhing the following Work has received your Sanction ——that the Compofition of it has ftood the Teft of your Judgment——and that it is by your Permiffion a Name fo defervedly eminent in the Literary World is prefixed to it, I need not be apprehenfive of its Succefs; as your

Patronage

Patronage will unqueſtionably give them Aſ-
ſurance of its Merit.

For this public Teſtimony of your Favour, in which I pride myſelf, accept, Sir, my moſt grateful Acknowledgments; and believe me to be, with great Reſpect,

Your obedient

humble Servant,

J. CARVER.

... *rt of Detroit*, - 71
- 72

AN
ADDRESS
TO THE
PUBLIC.
THE SECOND EDITION.

THE favourable reception this Work has met with, claims the Author's most grateful acknowledgments. A large edition having run off in a few months, and the sale appearing to be still unabated, a new impression is become necessary. On this occasion was he to conceal his feelings, and pass over, in silence, a distinction so beneficial and flattering, he would justly incur the imputation of ingratitude. That he might not do this, he takes the opportunity, which now presents itself, of conveying to the Public (though in terms inadequate to the warm emotions of his heart) the sense he entertains of their favour; and thus transmits to them his thanks.

In this new edition, care has been taken to rectify those errors which have unavoidably proceeded from the hurry of the press, and likewise any incorrectness in the language that has found its way into it.

The credibility of some of the incidents related in the following pages, and some of the stories introduced therein, having been questioned, particularly the prognostication of the Indian priest on the banks of Lake Superior, and the story of the Indian and his rattle snake, the author thinks it necessary to avail himself of the same opportunity, to endeavour to eradicate any impressions that might have been made on the minds of his readers, by the apparent improbability of these relations.

*A*s

Patronage will un related it just as it happened. Being an
s transaction (and, he flatters himself, at the
very trace of sceptical obstinacy or enthusiastic credulity) he was consequently able to describe every circumstance minutely and impartially. This he has done; but without endeavouring to account for the means by which it was accomplished. Whether the prediction was the result of prior observations, from which certain consequences were expected to follow by the sagacious priest, and the completion of it merely accidental; or whether he was really endowed with supernatural powers, the narrator left to the judgment of his readers; whose conclusions, he supposes, varied according as the mental faculties of each were disposed to admit or reject facts that cannot be accounted for by natural causes.

The story of the rattle snake was related to him by a French gentleman of undoubted veracity; and were the readers of this work as thoroughly acquainted with the sagacity and instinctive proceedings of that animal, as he is, they would be as well assured of the truth of it. It is well known, that those snakes which have survived through the summer the accidents reptiles are liable to, periodically retire to the woods, at the approach of winter; where each (as curious observers have remarked) takes possession of the cavity it had occupied the preceding year. As soon as the season is propitious, enlivened by the invigorating rays of the sun, they leave these retreats, and make their way to the same spot, though ever so distant, on which they before had found subsistence, and the means of propagating their species. Does it then require any extraordinary exertions of the mind to believe, that one of these regular creatures, after having been kindly treated by its master, should return to the box, in which it had usually been supplied with food, and had met with a comfortable abode, and that nearly about the time the Indian, from former experiments, was able to guess at? It certainly does not; nor will the liberal and ingenuous doubt the truth of a story so well authenticated, because the circumstances appear extraordinary in a country where the subject of it is scarcely known.

These explanations the author hopes will suffice to convince his readers, that he has not, as travellers are sometimes supposed to do, amused them with improbable tales, or wished to acquire importance by making his adventures favour of the marvellous.

CONTENTS.

	Page
INTRODUCTION,	17
The Author sets out from Boston on his Travels,	23
Description of Fort Michillimackinac,	ibid.
———— Fort Le Bay,	24
———— the Green Bay,	25
———— Lake Michigan,	27
Arrives at the Town of the Winnebagoes	28
Excursion of the Winnebagoes towards the Spanish Settlements,	29
Description of the Winnebago Lake,	30
Instance of Resolution of an Indian Woman,	31
Description of the Fox River,	ib.
Remarkable Story of a Rattle Snake,	32
The great Town of the Sackies,	33
Upper Town of the Ottagaumies,	34
Description of the Ouisconsin River,	ib.
Lower Town of the Ottagaumies, or La Prairie Le Chien,	ib.
An Attack by some Indian Plunderers,	35
Description of the Mississippi from the Mouth of the Ouisconsin to Lake Pepin,	36
———— Lake Pepin,	ib.
Remarkable Ruins of an ancient Fortification,	37
The River Bands of the Naudowessie Indians,	38
Adventure with a Party of these, and some of the Chipéways,	ib.

Description

Patronage will protected 't just as it happened. Being	39
Speech of the Prince of the Winnebagoes himself at the Falls of St. Anthony,	40
Description of the Falls,	41
Extent of the Author's Travels,	42
Description of the River St. Pierre,	43
Sources of the Four great Rivers of North America,	44
Reflections on their Affinity,	ib.
The Naudowessies of the Plains, with whom the Author wintered in the Year 1766,	45
The Author returns to the Mouth of the River St. Pierre,	47
Account of a violent Thunder storm,	ib.
Speech made by the Author in a Council held by the Naudowessies at the great Cave,	48
Adventure with a Party of Indians near Lake Pepin,	51
Description of the Country adjacent to the River St. Pierre,	53
Account of different Clays found near the Marble River,	ib.
Description of the Chipéway River,	ib.
Extraordinary Effects of a Hurricane,	54
The Author arrives at the Grand Portage, on the North-west Borders of Lake Superior,	55
Account of the Lakes lying farther to the North west: Lake Bourbon, Lake Winnepeek, Lake Du Bois, Lake La Pluye, Red Lake, &c.	ib.
Account of a Nation of Indians supposed to have been tributary to the Mexican Kings,	59
———— the shining Mountains,	60
A singular Prediction of the Chief Priest of the Killistinoes verified	61
Description of Lake Superior,	64
Story of the two Chipéways landing on the Island of Mauropas,	65
Account of great Quantities of Copper Ore,	67
Description of the Falls of St. Marie,	68
———— Lake Huron,	ib.
———— Saganaum and Thunder Bays,	69
Extraordinary Phænomenon in the Straights of Michillimackinac,	70
Description of Lake St. Claire,	71

Description

CONTENTS.

Description of the River, Town, and Fort of Detroit, — 71
Remarkable Rain at Detroit, — 72
Attack of Fort Detroit by Pontiac, — ib.
Description of Lake Erie, — 77
———— the River and Falls of Niagara, — 78
———— Lake Ontario, — ib.
———— the Oniada Lake, Lake Champlain, and Lake George, — 79
Account of a Tract of Land granted to Sir Ferdinando Gorges, and Captain John Mason, — 80
The Author's Motives for undertaking his Travels, — 81

CHAPTER I.

The Origin of the Indians, — 83
Sentiments of various Writers on this Point, — 84
———— Monsieur Charlevoix, — 87
———— James Adair, Esq; — 91
———— the Author of this Work, — 93
Corroboration of the latter by Doctor Robertson — 96

CHAPTER II.

Of the Persons, Dress, &c. of the Indians, — 97
An Account of those who have written on this Subject, — ib.
Description of the Persons of the Indians, — 99
———— their Dress, — 100
———— the Dress of the Ottagaumies, — 101
———— the Dress of the Naudowessies, — ib.
The Manner in which they build their Tents and Huts. — 102
Their Domestic Utensils, — ib.

B CHAPTER

CONTENTS.

CHAPTER III.

Of the Manners, Qualifications, &c. of the Indians, - 103
Peculiar Customs of the Women, - - - ib.
The circumspect and stoical Disposition of the Men, - 104
Their amazing Sagacity, - - - - 106
The Liberality of the Indians, and their Opinion respecting Money 107

CHAPTER IV.

Their Method of reckoning Time, &c. - - - 108
The Names by which they distinguish the Months, - 109
Their Idea of the Use of Figures, - - - ib.

CHAPTER V.

Of their Government, &c. - - - - 110
Their Division into Tribes, - - - - ib.
The Chiefs of their Bands, - - - - 111
The Members that compose their Councils, - - 112

CHAPTER VI.

Of their Feasts, - - - - - 113
Their usual Food, - - - - - ib.
Their Manner of dressing and eating their Victuals, - ib.

CHAPTER VII.

Of their Dances, - - - - - 114
The Manner in which they dance, - - - 115
The Pipe or Calumate Dance, - - - ib.
The War Dance, - - - - ib.

The

The Pawwaw Dance,	116
An uncommon Admission into a Society among the Naudowessies,	ib.
The Dance of the Indians on the Banks of the Mississippi, referred to in the Journal,	119
The Dance of the Sacrifice,	120

CHAPTER VIII.

Of their Hunting,	121
Their Preparation before they set out,	ib.
Their Manner of hunting the Bear,	122
——————————— Buffalo, Deer, &c.	ib.
——————————— Beaver,	123

CHAPTER IX.

Of their Manner of making War, &c.	125
The Indian Weapons,	ib.
Their Motives for making War,	126
Preparations before they take the Field,	128
The Manner in which they solicit other Nations to become their Auxiliaries,	129
Their Manner of declaring War,	130
The Method of engaging their Enemies,	131
An Instance of the Efficacy of it in the Defeat of General Braddock,	ib.
A Detail of the Massacre at Fort William-Henry in the Year 1757,	132
Acuteness and Alacrity of the Indians in pursuing their Enemies,	137
Their Manner of Scalping,	ib.
The Manner in which they retreat and carry off their Prisoners,	138
A remarkable Instance of Heroism in a Female Prisoner,	139
Treatment of their Prisoners,	140
The Origin of their selling Slaves,	144

CHAPTER

CONTENTS.

CHAPTER X.

Of their Manner of making Peace, &c. - - - 146
Account of an Engagement between the Iroquois and the Ottagaumies and Saukies, - - - - - ib.
Manner in which they conduct a Treaty of Peace, - - 148
Description of the Pipe of Peace, - - - - 149
——————— Belts of Wampum, - - - 150

CHAPTER XI.

Of their Games, - - - - - - - 150
The Game of the Ball, - - - - - 151
——————— Bowl or Platter, - - - ib.

CHAPTER XII.

Of their Marriage Ceremonies, - - - - 152
The Manner in which the Tribes near Canada celebrate their Marriages, - - - - - - - 153
The Form of Marriage among the Naudowessies, - - 154
Their Manner of carrying on an Intrigue, - - - 155
Of the Indian Names, - - - - - 156

CHAPTER XIII.

Of their Religion, - - - - - - 157
Their Ideas of a Supreme Being, - - - - ib.
——————— future State, - - - - 158
Of their Priests, - - - - - - ib.
The Sentiments of Others on the religious Principles of the Indians opposed, - - - - - 159

CHAPTER XIV.

Of their Diseases, &c. - - - - 160
The Complaints to which they are chiefly subject, - - 161
The

CONTENTS.

The Manner in which they construct their Sweating Stoves, 161
The Methods in which they treat their Diseases, ib.
An extraordinary Instance of the Judgment of an Indian Woman in a desperate Case, 163

CHAPTER XV.

The Manner in which they treat their Dead, 164
A Specimen of their Funeral Harangues, ib.
Their Method of burying the Dead, 165
A singular Instance of parental Affection in a Naudowessie Woman, 166

CHAPTER XVI.

A concise Character of the Indians, 167
Their personal and mental Qualifications, 168
Their public Character as Members of a Community, 169

CHAPTER XVII.

Of their Language, Hieroglyphicks, &c. 170
Of the Chipéway Tongue, ib.
Descriptive Specimen of their Hieroglyphicks, &c. 171
Vocabulary of the Chipéway Language, 172
———————— Naudowessie Language, 176

CHAPTER XVIII.

Of the Beasts, Birds, Fishes, Reptiles, and Insects, which are found in the Interior Parts of North America, 179

BEASTS.

The Tyger. The Bear, 179
The Wolf. The Fox, 180
Dogs. The Cat of the Mountain. The Buffalo, ib.
The Deer. The Elk. The Moose, 181

The

CONTENTS.

The Carrabou. The Carcajou. The Skunk,	182
The Porcupine. The Woodchuck. The Racoon,	183
The Martin. The Musquash. Squirrels,	184
The Beaver,	185
The Otter. The Mink,	187

BIRDS.

The Eagle. The Night Hawk,	188
The Fish Hawk. The Whipperwill,	ib.
The Owl. The Crane. Ducks. The Teal. The Loon,	189
The Partridge. The Woodpecker. The Wood Pigeon,	190
The Blue Jay. The Wakon Bird,	ib.
The Blackbird. The Redbird,	191
The Whetsaw. The King Bird. The Humming Bird,	ib.

FISHES.

The Sturgeon. The Cat Fish,	192
The Carp. The Chub,	193

SERPENTS.

The Rattle Snake,	193
The Long Black Snake. The Striped or Garter Snake. The Water Snake.	195
The Hissing Snake. The Green Snake. The Thorn-tail Snake. The Speckled Snake. The Ring Snake. The Two-headed Snake. The Tortoise or Land Turtle,	196

LIZARDS.

The Swift Lizard. The Slow Lizard. The Tree Toad,	196, 197

INSECTS.

The Silk Worm. The Tobacco Worm. The Bee,	197
The Lightning Bug or Fire Fly. The Water Bug. The Horned Bug. Locust,	198

CHAP-

CONTENTS.

CHAPTER XIX.

Of the Trees, Shrubs, Roots, Herbs, Flowers, — 199

TREES.

The Oak. The Pine Tree, - - - 199
The Maple. The Ash. The Hemlock Tree. The Bass or White Wood, - - - - - 200
The Wickopick or Suckwick. The Button Wood, — 201

NUT TREES.

The Butter or Oil Nut. The Beech Nut, - - 201
The Pecan Nut. The Hickory, - - - 202

FRUIT TREES.

The Vine. The Mulberry Tree. The Crab Apple Tree. The Plum Tree. The Cherry Tree, - - - 202
The Sweet Gum Tree, - - - - 203

SHRUBS.

The Willow. Shin Wood, - - - 203
The Sassafras. The Prickly Ash. The Moose Wood. The Spoon Wood. The Elder, - - - - 204
The Shrub Oak. The Witch Hazle. The Myrtle Wax Tree. Winter Green. The Fever Bush. The Cranberry Bush, 205
The Choak Berry, - - - - - 206

ROOTS and PLANTS.

Spikenard. Sarsaparilla. Ginsang, - - - 206
Gold Thread. Solomon's Seal. Devil's Bit. Blood Root, - 207

HERBS.

CONTENTS.

HERBS.

Sanicle. Rattle Snake Plantain, Poor Robin's Plantain. Toad Plantain. Rock Liverwort. Gargit or Skoke. Skunk Cabbage or Poke, - - - - - 208
Wake Robin. Wild Indigo. Cat Mint, - - 209

FLOWERS, - - - - - - - ib.

FARINACEOUS and LEGUMINOUS ROOTS, &c.

Maize or Indian Corn. Wild Rice, - - - 210
Beans. The Squash - - - - 211

APPENDIX.

The Probability of the interior Parts of North America becoming Commercial Colonies, - - - 212
The Means by which this might be effected. - - ib.
Tracts of Land pointed out, on which Colonies may be established with the greatest Advantage, - - - 213
Dissertation on the Discovery of a North-west Passage, - 216
The most certain Way of attaining it, - - - ib.
Plan proposed by Richard Whitworth, Esq; for making an Attempt from a Quarter hitherto unexplored, - - 217
The Reason of its being postponed, - - - ib.

INTRO-

INTRODUCTION.

NO sooner was the late War with France concluded, and Peace established by the Treaty of Versailles in the Year 1763, than I began to consider (having rendered my country some services during the war) how I might continue still serviceable, and contribute, as much as lay in my power, to make that vast acquisition of territory, gained by Great-Britain, in North America advantageous to it. It appeared to me indispensably needful, that Government should be acquainted in the first place with the true state of the dominions they were now become possessed of. To this purpose, I determined, as the next proof of my zeal, to explore the most unknown parts of them, and to spare no trouble or expence in acquiring a knowledge that promised to be so useful to my countrymen. I knew that many obstructions would arise to my scheme from the want of good Maps and Charts; for the French, whilst they retained their power in North America, had taken every artful method to keep all other nations, particularly the English, in ignorance of the concerns of the interior parts of it: and to accomplish this design with the greater certainty, they had published inaccurate maps and false accounts; calling the different nations of the Indians by nicknames they had given them, and not by those really appertaining to them. Whether the intention of the French in doing this, was to prevent these nations from being discovered and traded with, or to conceal their discourse, when they talked to each other of the Indian concerns, in their presence, I will not determine; but whatsoever was the cause from which it arose, it tended to mislead.

As a proof that the English had been greatly deceived by these accounts, and that their knowledge relative to Canada had usually been very confined;—before the conquest of Crown-Point in 1759, it had been esteemed an impregnable fortress: but no sooner was it taken, than we were convinced that it had acquired its greatest security from false reports, given out by its possessors, and might have been battered down with a few four pounders. Even its situation, which was represented to be so very advantageous, was found to owe its advantages to the same source. It cannot be denied but that some maps of these countries have been published by the French with an appearance of accuracy; but these are of so small a size and drawn on so minute a scale, that they are nearly inexplicable. The sources of the

Mississippi,

Miffiffippi, I can affert from my own experience, are greatly misplaced; for when I had explored them, and compared their situation with the French Charts, I found them very erroneously reprefented, and am fatisfied that thefe were only copied from the rude fketches of the Indians.

Even fo lately as their evacuation of Canada they continued their fchemes to deceive; leaving no traces by which any knowledge might accrue to their conquerors: for though they were well acquainted with all the Lakes, particularly with Lake Superior, having conftantly a veffel of confiderable burthen thereon, yet their plans of them are very incorrect. I difcovered many errors in the defcriptions given therein of its iflands and bays, during a progrefs of eleven hundred miles that I coafted it in canoes. They likewife, on giving up the poffeffion of them, took care to leave the places they had occupied in the fame uncultivated ftate they had found them; at the fame time deftroying all their naval force. I obferved myfelf part of the hulk of a very large veffel, burnt to the water's edge, juft at the opening from the Straits of St. Marie's into the Lake.

Thefe difficulties, however, were not fufficient to deter me from the undertaking, and I made preparations for fetting out. What I chiefly had in view, after gaining a knowledge of the manners, cuftoms, languages, foil, and natural productions of the different nations that inhabit the back of the Miffiffippi, was to afcertain the breadth of that vaft continent, which extends from the Atlantic to the Pacific Ocean, in its broadeft part between 43 and 46 degrees northern latitude. Had I been able to accomplifh this, I intended to have propofed to government to eftablifh a poft in fome of thofe parts about the Straits of Annian, which having been firft difcovered by Sir Francis Drake, of courfe belong to the Englifh. This I am convinced would greatly facilitate the difcovery of a Northweft Paffage, or a communication between Hudfon's Bay and the Pacific Ocean. An event fo defirable, and which has been fo often fought for, but without fuccefs. Befides this important end, a fettlement on that extremity of America would anfwer many good purpofes, and repay every expence the eftablifhment of it might occafion. For it would not only difclofe new fources of trade, and promote many ufeful difcoveries, but would open a paffage for conveying intelligence to China, and the Englifh fettlements in the Eaft Indies, with greater expedition than a tedious voyage by the Cape of Good Hope, or the Straits of Magellan will allow of.

How far the advantages arifing from fuch an enterprize may extend, can only be afcertained by the favourable concurrence of future events. But that the completion of the fcheme, I have had the honour of firft planning and attempting, will fome time or other be effected, I make no doubt. From the unhappy divifions that at prefent fubfift between Great Britain and America, it will probably be fome years before the attempt is repeated; but whenever it is, and the execution of it carried on with propriety,

priety, those who are so fortunate as to succeed, will reap, exclusive of the national advantages that must ensue, emoluments beyond their most sanguine expectations. And whilst their spirits are elated by their success, perhaps they may bestow some commendations and blessings on the person that first pointed out to them the way. These, though but a shadowy recompence for all my toil, I shall receive with pleasure.

To what power or authority this new world will become dependent, after it has arisen from its present uncultivated state, time alone can discover. But as the seat of Empire from time immemorial has been gradually progressive towards the West, there is no doubt but that at some future period, mighty kingdoms will emerge from these wildernesses, and stately palaces and solemn temples, with gilded spires reaching the skies, supplant the Indian huts, whose only decorations are the barbarous trophies of their vanquished enemies.

As some of the preceeding passages have already informed the reader that the plan I had laid down for penetrating to the Pacific Ocean, proved abortive, it is necessary to add, that this proceeded not from its impracticability (for the farther I went the more convinced I was that it could certainly be accomplished) but from unforeseen disappointments. However, I proceeded so far, that I was able to make such discoveries as will be useful in any future attempt, and prove a good foundation for some more fortunate successor to build upon. These I shall now lay before the public in the following pages; and am satisfied that the greatest part of them have never been published by any person that has hitherto treated of the interior nations of the Indians; particularly, the account I give of the Naudowessies, and the situation of the heads of the four great rivers that take their rise within a few leagues of each other, nearly about the centre of this great continent; viz. The River Bourbon, which empties itself into Hudson's Bay; the waters of Saint Lawrence; the Mississippi, and the River Oregon, or the River of the West, that falls into the Pacific Ocean, at the Straits of Annian.

The impediments that occasioned my returning, before I had accomplished my purposes, were these. On my arrival at Michillimackinac, the remotest English post, in September 1766, I applied to Mr. Rogers, who was then governor of it, to furnish me with a proper assortment of goods, as presents for the Indians who inhabit the track I intended to pursue. He did this only in part; but promised to supply me with such as were necessary, when I reached the Falls of Saint Anthony. I afterwards learned that the governor fulfilled his promise in ordering the goods to be delivered to me; but those to whose care he intrusted them, instead of conforming to his orders, disposed of them elsewhere.

Disappointed in my expectations from this quarter, I thought it necessary to return to La Prairie Le Chien; for it was impossible to proceed any further without presents to ensure me a favourable

vourable reception. This I did in the beginning of the year 1767, and finding my progress to the westward thus retarded, I determined to direct my course northward. I took this step with a view of finding a communication from the Heads of the Mississippi into Lake Superior, in order to meet, at the grand Portage on the North-west side of that lake, the traders that usually come, about this season, from Michillimackinac. Of these I intended to purchase goods, and then to pursue my journey from that quarter by way of the lakes de Pluye, Dubois, and Ounipique to the Heads of the river of the West, which, as I have said before, falls into the Straits of Annian, the termination of my intended progress.

I accomplished the former part of my design, and reached Lake Superior in proper time; but unluckily the traders I met there acquainted me, that they had no goods to spare; those they had with them being barely sufficient to answer their own demands in these remote parts. Thus disappointed a second time, I found myself obliged to return to the place from whence I began my expedition, which I did after continuing some months on the north and east borders of Lake Superior, and exploring the bays and rivers that empty themselves into this large body of water.

As it may be expected that I should lay before the public the reasons that these discoveries, of so much importance to every one who has any connections with America, have not been imparted to them before, notwithstanding they were made upwards of ten years ago, I will give them to the world in a plain and candid manner, and without mingling with them any complaints on account of the ill treatment I have received.

On my arrival in England, I presented a petition to his Majesty in council, praying for a reimbursement of those sums I had expended in the service of government. This was referred to the Lords Commissioners of Trade and Plantations. Their Lordships from the tenor of it thought the intelligence I could give of so much importance to the nation, that they ordered me to appear before the Board. This message I obeyed, and underwent a long examination; much I believe to the satisfaction of every Lord present. When it was finished, I requested to know what I should do with my papers; without hesitation the first Lord replied, That I might publish them whenever I pleased. In consequence of this permission, I disposed of them to a bookseller: but when they were nearly ready for the press, an order was issued from the council board, requiring me to deliver, without delay, into the Plantation Office, all my Charts and Journals, with every paper relative to the discoveries I had made. In order to obey this command, I was obliged to re-purchase them from the bookseller at a very great expence, and deliver them up. This fresh disbursement I endeavoured to get annexed to the account I had already delivered in; but the request was denied me, notwithstanding I had only acted, in the disposal of my

papers,

papers, conformably to the permiffion I had received from the Board of Trade. This lofs, which amounted to a very confiderable fum, I was obliged to bear, and to reft fatisfied with an indemnification for my other expences.

Thus fituated, my only expectations are from the favour of a generous public; to whom I fhall now communicate my plans, journals, and obfervations, of which I luckily kept copies, when I delivered the originals into the Plantation Office. And this I do the more readily, as I hear they are miflaid; and there is no probability of their ever being publifhed. To thofe who are interefted in the concerns of the interior parts of North America, from the contiguity of their poffeffions, or commercial engagements, they will be extremely ufeful, and fully repay the fum at which they are purchafed. To thofe, who, from a laudable curiofity, wifh to be acqainted with the manners and cuftoms of every inhabitant of this globe, the accounts here given of the various nations that inhabit fo vaft a tract of it, a country hitherto almoft unexplored, will furnifh an ample fund of amufement and gratify their moft curious expectations. And I flatter myfelf they will be as favourably received by the public, as defcriptions of iflands, which afford no other entertainment than what arifes from their novelty; and difcoveries, that feem to promife very few advantages to this country, though acquired at an immenfe expence.

To make the following work as comprehenfible and entertaining as poffible, I fhall firft give my readers an account of the route I purfued over this immenfe continent, and as I pafs on, defcribe the number of inhabitants, the fituation of the rivers and lakes, and the productions of the country. Having done this, I fhall treat, in diftinct chapters, of the manners, cuftoms, and languages of the Indians and to complete the whole, add a vocabulary of the words moftly in ufe among them.

And here it is neceffary to befpeak the candour of the learned part of my readers in the perufal of it, as it is the production of a perfon unufed, from oppofite avocations, to literary purfuits. He therefore begs they would not examine it with too critical an eyes efpecially when he affures them that his attention has been more employed on giving a juft defcription of a country that promifes, in fome future period, to be an inexhauftible fource of riches to that people who fhall be fo fortunate as to poffefs it, than on the ftyle or compofition; and more careful to render his language intelligible and explicit, than fmooth and florid.

A

A JOURNAL OF THE TRAVELS,

WITH A

DESCRIPTION

OF THE

COUNTRY, LAKES, &c.

IN June 1766, I sat out from Boston, and proceeded by way of Albany and Niagara, to Michillimackinac; a fort situated between the Lakes Huron and Michigan, and distant from Boston 1300 miles. This being the uttermost of our factories towards the north-west, I considered it as the most convenient place from whence I could begin my intended progress, and enter at once into the regions I designed to explore.

Referring my readers to the publications already extant for an account of those parts of North America, that, from lying adjacent to the back settlements, have been frequently described, I shall confine myself to a description of the more interior parts of it, which having been but seldom visited, are consequently but little known. In doing this, I shall in no instance exceed the bounds of truth, or have recourse to those useless and extravagant exaggerations too often made use of by travellers, to excite the curiosity of the public, or to increase their own importance. Nor shall I insert any observations, but such as I have made myself, or, from the credibility of those by whom they were related, am enabled to vouch for their authenticity.

Michillimackinac, from whence I began my travels, is a fort composed of a strong stockade, and is usually defended by a garrison of one hundred men. It contains about thirty houses, one of which belongs to the governor, and another to the commissary. Several traders also dwell within its fortifications, who find it a convenient situation to traffic with the neighbouring nations. Michillimackinac, in the language of the Chipéway Indians, signifies a Tortoise; and the place is supposed to receive its name from an island, lying about six or seven miles to the north-east, within sight of the fort, which has the appearance of that animal.

During

During the Indian war that followed soon after the conquest of Canada in the year 1763, and which was carried on by an army of confederate nations composed of the Hurons, Miamies, Chipéways, Ottowaws, Pontowattimies, Miffiſſauges, and ſome other tribes, under the direction of Pontiac, a celebrated Indian warrior, who had always been in the French intereſt, it was taken by ſurprize in the following manner: The Indians having ſettled their plan, drew near the fort, and began a game at ball, a paſtime much uſed among them, and not unlike tennis. In the height of their game, at which ſome of the Engliſh officers, not ſuſpecting any deceit, ſtood looking on, they ſtruck the ball, as if by accident, over the ſtockade; this they repeated two or three times, to make the deception more complete; till at length, having by this means lulled every ſuſpicion of the centry at the ſouth gate, a party ruſhed by him; and the reſt ſoon following, they took poſſeſſion of the fort, without meeting with any oppoſition. Having accompliſhed their deſign, the Indians had the humanity to ſpare the lives of the greateſt part of the garriſon and traders, but they made them all priſoners, and carried them off. However ſome time after they took them to Montreal, where they were redeemed at a good price. The fort alſo was given up again to the Engliſh at the peace made with Pontiac, by the commander of Detroit the year following.

Having here made the neceſſary diſpoſitions for purſuing my travels, and obtained a credit from Mr. Rogers, the governor, on ſome Engliſh and Canadian traders who were going to trade on the Miſſiſſippi, and received alſo from him a promiſe of a freſh ſupply of goods when I reached the falls of Saint Anthony, I left the fort on the 3d of September, in company with theſe traders. It was agreed that they ſhould furniſh me with ſuch goods as I might want, for preſents to the Indian chiefs, during my continuance with them, agreeable to the governor's order. But when I arrived at the extent of their route, to find other guides, and to depend on the goods the governor had promiſed to ſupply me with.

We accordingly ſet out together, and on the 18th arrived at Fort La Bay. This fort is ſituated on the ſouthern extremity of a bay in Lake Michigan, termed by the French the Bay of Puants; but which, ſince the Engliſh have gained poſſeſſion of all the ſettlements on this part of the continent, is called by them the Green Bay. The reaſon of its being thus denominated, is from its appearance; for on leaving Michillimackinac in the ſpring ſeaſon, though the trees there have not even put forth their buds, yet you find the country around La Bay, notwithſtanding the paſſage has not exceeded fourteen days, covered with the fineſt verdure, and vegetation as forward as it could be were it ſummer.

This fort alſo is only ſurrounded by a ſtockade, and being much decayed is ſcarcely defenſible againſt ſmall arms. It was built by the French for the protection of their trade, ſome time before

before they were forced to relinquish it; and when Canada and its dependencies were surrendered to the English, it was immediately garrisoned with an officer and thirty men. These were made prisoners by the Menomonies soon after the surprise of Michillimackinac, and the fort has neither been garrisoned or kept in repair since.

The bay is about ninety miles long, but differs much in its breadth; being in some places only fifteen miles, in others from twenty to thirty. It lies nearly from north-east to south-west. At the entrance of it from the lake are a string of islands, extending from north to south, called the Grand Traverse. These are about thirty miles in length, and serve to facilitate the passage of canoes, as they shelter them from the winds, which sometimes come with violence across the Lake. On the side that lies to the south-east is the nearest and best navigation.

The islands of the Grand Traverse are mostly small and rocky. Many of the rocks are of an amazing size, and appear as if they had been fashioned by the hands of artists. On the largest and best of these islands stands a town of the Ottowaws, at which I found one of the most considerable chiefs of that nation, who received me with every honour he could possibly show to a stranger. But what appeared extremely singular to me at the time, and must do so to every person unacquainted with the customs of the Indians, was the reception I met with on landing. As our canoes approached the shore, and had reached within about three score rods of it, the Indians began a feu-de-joy; in which they fired their pieces loaded with balls; but at the same time they took care to discharge them in such a manner as to fly a few yards above our heads: during this they ran from one tree or stump to another, shouting and behaving as if they were in the heat of battle. At first I was greatly surprised, and was on the point of ordering my attendants to return their fire, concluding their intentions were hostile; but being undeceived by some of the traders, who informed me that this was their usual method of receiving the chiefs of other nations, I considered it in its true light, and was pleased with the respect thus paid me.

I remained here one night. Among the presents I made the chiefs, were some spirituous liquors; with which they made themselves merry, and all joined in a dance, that lasted the greatest part of the night. In the morning when I departed, the chief attended me to the shore, and, as soon as I had embarked, offered up, in an audible voice, and with great solemnity, a fervent prayer in my behalf. He prayed "that the Great Spirit would favour me with a prosperous voyage; that he would give me an unclouded sky, and smooth waters, by day, and that I might lie down, by night, on a beaver blanket, enjoying uninterrupted sleep, and pleasant dreams; and also that I might find continual protection under the great pipe of peace." In this manner he continued his petitions till I could no longer hear them.

D

I must

I muſt here obſerve, that notwithſtanding the inhabitants of Europe are apt to entertain horrid ideas of the ferocity of theſe ſavages, as they are termed, I received from every tribe of them in the interior parts, the moſt hoſpitable and courteous treatment; and am convinced, that till they are contaminated by the example and ſpirituous liquors of their more refined neighbours, they retain this friendly and inoffenſive conduct towards ſtrangers. Their inveteracy and cruelty to their enemies I acknowledge to be a great abatement of the favourable opinion I would wiſh to entertain of them; but this failing is hereditary, and having received the ſanction of immemorial cuſtom, has taken too deep root in their minds to be ever extirpated.

Among this people I eat of a very uncommon kind of bread. The Indians, in general, uſe but little of this nutritious food: whilſt their corn is in the milk, as they term it, that is, juſt before it begins to ripen, they ſlice off the kernels from the cob to which they grow, and knead them into a paſte. This they are enabled to do without the addition of any liquid, by the milk that flows from them; and when it is effected, they parcel it out into cakes, and incloſing them in leaves of the baſſwood tree, place them in hot embers, where they are ſoon baked. And better flavoured bread I never eat in any country.

This place is only a ſmall village containing about twenty-five houſes and ſixty or ſeventy warriors. I found nothing there worthy of further remark.

The land on the ſouth-eaſt ſide of the Green Bay is but very indifferent, being overſpread with a heavy growth of hemlock, pine, ſpruce and fir trees. The communication between Lake Michigan and the Green Bay has been reported by ſome to be impracticable for the paſſage of any veſſels larger than canoes or boats, on account of the ſhoals that lie between the iſlands in the Grand Traverſe; but on ſounding it I found ſufficient depth for a veſſel of ſixty tons, and the breadth proportionable.

The land adjoining to the bottom of this bay is very fertile, the country in general level, and the perſpective view of it pleaſing and extenſive.

A few families live in the fort, which lies on the weſt-ſide of the Fox-River, and oppoſite to it, on the eaſt-ſide of its entrance, are ſome French ſettlers who cultivate the land, and appear to live very comfortably.

The Green Bay or Bay of Puants is one of thoſe places to which the French, as I have mentioned in the introduction, have given nicknames. It is termed by the inhabitants of its coaſts, the Menomonie Bay; but why the French have denominated it the Puant or Stinking Bay I know not. The reaſon they themſelves give for it is, that it was not with a view to miſlead ſtrangers, but that by adopting this method they could converſe with each other, concerning the Indians, in their preſence, without being underſtood by them. For it was remarked by the perſons who firſt traded among them, that when they were ſpeaking to each

each other about them, and mentioned their proper name, they instantly grew suspicious, and concluded that their visiters were either speaking ill of them, or plotting their destruction. To remedy this they gave them some other name. The only bad consequence arising from the practice then introduced is, that English and French Geographers, in their plans of the interior parts of America, give different names to the same people, and thereby perplex those who have occasion to refer to them.

Lake Michigan, of which the Green Bay is a part, is divided on the north-east from Lake Huron by the Straits of Michillimackinac; and is situated between forty-two and forty-six degrees of latitude, and between eighty-four and eighty-seven degrees of west-longitude. Its greatest length is two hundred and eighty miles, its breadth about forty, and its circumference nearly six hundred. There is a remarkable string of small islands, beginning over against Askin's Farm, and running about thirty miles south-west into the Lake. These are called the Beaver Islands. Their situation is very pleasant, but the soil is bare. However they afford a beautiful prospect.

On the north-west parts of this lake the waters branch out into two bays. That which lies towards the north is the Bay of Noquets, and the other the Green Bay just described.

The waters of this as well as the other great lakes are clear and wholesome, and of sufficient depth for the navigation of large ships. Half the space of the country that lies to the east, and extends to Lake Huron, belongs to the Ottowaw Indians. The line that divides their territories from the Chipéways, runs nearly north and south, and reaches almost from the southern extremity of this lake, across the high lands, to Michillimackinac, through the centre of which it passes. So that when these two tribes happen to meet at the factory, they each encamp on their own dominions, at a few yards distance from the stockade.

The country adjacent either to the east or west side of this lake is composed but of an indifferent soil, except where small brooks or rivers empty themselves into it; on the banks of these it is extremely fertile. Near the borders of the lake grow a great number of sand cherries, which are not less remarkable for their manner of growth, than for their exquisite flavour. They grow upon a small shrub, not more than four feet high, the boughs of which are so loaded that they lie in clusters on the sand. As they grow only on the sand, the warmth of which probably contributes to bring them to such perfection; they are called by the French, cherries de sable, or sand cherries. The size of them does not exceed that of a small musket ball, but they are reckoned superior to any other sort for the purpose of steeping in spirits. There also grow around the lake gooseberries, black currants, and an abundance of juniper, bearing great quantities of berries of the finest sort.

Sumack likewise grows here in great plenty; the leaf of which, gathered at Michaelmas when it turns red, is much esteemed by

the

the natives. They mix about an equal quantity of it with their tobacco, which causes it to smoke pleasantly. Near this lake, and indeed about all the great lakes, is found a kind of willow, termed by the French, bois rouge, in English red wood. Its bark, when only of one year's growth, is of a fine scarlet colour, and appears very beautiful; but as it grows older, it changes into a mixture of grey and red. The stalks of this shrub grow many of them together, and rise to the height of six or eight feet, the largest not exceeding an inch diameter. The bark being scraped from the sticks, and dried and powdered, is also mixed by the Indians with their tobacco, and is held by them in the highest estimation for their winter smoaking. A weed that grows near the great lakes, in rocky places, they use in the summer season. It is called by the Indians, Segockimac, and creeps like a vine on the ground, sometimes extending to eight or ten feet, and bearing a leaf about the size of silver penny, nearly round; it is of the substance and colour of the laurel, and is, like the tree it resembles, an evergreen. These leaves, dried and powdered, they likewise mix with their tobacco; and, as said before, smoak it only during the summer. By these three succedaneums the pipes of the Indians are well supplied through every season of the year; and as they are great smoakers, they are very careful in properly gathering and preparing them.

On the 20th of September I left the Green Bay, and proceeded up Fox River, still in company with the traders and some Indians. On the 25th I arrived at the great town of the Winnebagoes, situated on a small island, just as you enter the east end of Lake Winnebago. Here the queen who presided over this tribe instead of a Sachem, received me with great civility, and entertained me in a very distinguished manner, during the four days I continued with her.

The day after my arrival I held a council with the chiefs, of whom I asked permission to pass through their country, in my way to more remote nations, on business of importance. This was readily granted me, the request being esteemed by them as a great compliment paid to their tribe. The queen sat in the council, but only asked a few questions, or gave some trifling directions in matters relative to the state; for women are never allowed to sit in their councils, except they happen to be invested with the supreme authority, and then it is not customary for them to make any formal speeches as the chiefs do. She was a very ancient woman, small in stature, and not much distinguished by her dress from several young women that attended her. These her attendants seemed greatly pleased whenever I showed any tokens of respect to their queen, particularly when I saluted her, which I frequently did to acquire her favour. On these occasions the good old lady endeavoured to assume a juvenile gaiety, and by her smiles showed she was equally pleased with the attention I paid her.

The

The time I tarried here, I employed in making the best observations possible on the country, and in collecting the most certain intelligence I could of the origin, language, and customs of this people. From these enquiries I have reason to conclude, that the Winnebagoes originally resided in some of the provinces belonging to New Mexico; and being driven from their native country, either by intestine divisions, or by the extensions of the Spanish conquests, they took refuge in these more northern parts about a century ago.

My reason for adopting this supposition, are, first from their unalienable attachment to the Naudowessie Indians (who, they say, gave them the earliest succours during their emigration) notwithstanding their present residence is more than six hundred miles distant from that people.

Secondly, that their dialect totally differs from every other Indian nation yet discovered; it being a very uncouth guttural jargon, which none of their neighbours will attempt to learn. They converse with other nations in the Chipéway tongue, which is the prevailing language throughout all the tribes, from the Mohawks of Canada, to those who inhabit the borders of the Mississippi, and from the Hurons and Illinois to such a dwell near Hudson's Bay.

Thirdly, from their inveterate hatred to the Spaniards. Some of them informed me that they had many excursions to the southwest, which took up several moons. An elderly chief more particularly acquainted me, that about forty-six winters ago, he marched at the head of fifty warriors, toward the south-west, for three moons. That during this expedition, whilst they were crossing a plain, they discovered a body of men on horseback, who belonged to the Black People; for so they call the Spaniards. As soon as they perceived them, they proceeded with caution, and concealed themselves till night came on; when they drew so near as to be able to discern the number and situation of their enemies. Finding they were not able to cope with so great a superiority by day-light, they waited till they had retired to rest; when they rushed upon them, and, after having killed the greatest part of the men, took eighty horses loaded with what they termed white stone. This I suppose to have been silver, as he told me the horses were shod with it, and that their bridles were ornamented with the same. When they had satiated their revenge, they carried off their spoil, and being got so far as to be out of the reach of the Spaniards that had escaped their fury, they left the useless and ponderous burthen, with which the horses were loaded, in the woods, and mounting themselves, in this manner returned to their friends. The party they had thus defeated, I conclude to be the caravan that annually conveys to Mexico, the silver which the Spaniards find in great quautities on the mountains lying near the heads of the Coloredo River: and the plains where the attack was made, probably, some they were obliged to pass over in their way to

the

the heads of the River St. Fee, or Rio del Nord, which falls into the Gulph of Mexico, to the weſt of the Miſſiſſippi.

The Winnebagoes can raiſe about two hundred warriors. Their town contains about fifty houſes, which are ſtrongly built with paliſades, and the iſland on which it is ſituated nearly fifty acres. It lies thirty-five miles, reckoning according to the courſe of the river, from the Green Bay.

The river, for about four or five miles from the bay, has a gentle current; after that ſpace, till you arrive at the Winnebago Lake, it is full of rocks and very rapid. At many places we were obliged to land our canoes, and carry them a conſiderable way. Its breath, in general, from the Green Bay to the Winnebago Lake, is between ſeventy and a hundred yards: the land on its borders very good, and thinly wooded with hickery, oak, and hazel.

The Winnebago Lake is about fifteen miles long from eaſt to weſt, and ſix miles wide. At its ſouth-eaſt corner, a river falls into it that takes its riſe near ſome of the northern branches of the Illinois River. This I called the Crocodile River, in conſequence of a ſtory that prevails among the Indians, of their having deſtroyed, in ſome part of it, an animal, which from their deſcription muſt be a crocodile or an alligator.

The land adjacent to the Lake is very fertile, abounding with grapes, plums, and other fruits, which grow ſpontaneouſly. The Winnebagoes raiſe on it a great quantity of Indian corn, beans, pumpkins, ſquaſh, and water melons, with ſome tobacco. The lake itſelf abounds with fiſh, and in the fall of the year, with geeſe, ducks, and teal. The latter, which reſort to it in great numbers, are remarkably good and extremely fat, and are much better flavoured than thoſe that are found near the ſea, as they acquire their exceſſive fatneſs by feeding on the wild rice, which grow ſo plentifully in theſe parts.

Having made ſome acceptable preſents to the good old queen, and received her bleſſing, I left the town of the Winnebagoes on the 29th of September, and about twelve miles from it arrived at the place where the Fox River enters the Lake on the north ſide of it. We proceeded up this river, and on the 7th of October reached the great Carrying Place, which divides it from the Ouiſconſin.

The Fox River, from the Green Bay to the Carrying Place, is about one hundred and eighty miles. From the Winnebago Lake to the Carrying Place the current is gentle, and the depth of it conſiderable; notwithſtanding which, it is in ſome places with difficulty that cannoes can paſs, through the obſtructions they meet with from the rice ſtalks, which are very large and thick, and grow here in great abundance. The country around it is very fertile and proper in the higheſt degree for cultivation, excepting in ſome places near the river, where it is rather too low. It is in no part very woody, and yet can ſupply ſufficient to anſwer the demands of any number of inhabitants. This

river

river is the greatest resort for wild fowl of every kind that I met with in the whole courfe of my travels; frequently the fun would be obfcured by them for fome minutes together.

About forty miles up this river, from the great town of the Winnebagoes, ftands a fmaller town belonging to that nation.

Deer and bears are very numerous in thefe parts, and a great many beavers and other furs are taken on the ftreams that empty themfelves into this river.

The river I am treating of, is remarkable for having been, about eighty years ago, the refidence of the united bands of the Ottigaumies and the Saukies, whom the French had nicknamed, according to their wonted cuftom, Des Sacs and Des Reynards, the Sacks and the Foxes, of whom the following anecdote was related to me by an Indian.

About fixty years ago, the French miffionaries and traders having received many infults from thefe people, a party of French and Indians, under the command of Captain Morand marched to revenge their wrongs. The Captain fet out from the Green Bay in the winter, when they were unfufpicious of a vifit of this kind, and purfuing his route over the fnow to their villages, which lay about fifty miles up the Fox River, came upon them by furprize. Unprepared as they were, he found them an eafy conqueft, and confequently killed or took prifoners the greateft part of them. On the return of the French to the Green Bay, one of the Indian chiefs in alliance with them, who had a confiderable band of the prifoners under his care, ftopped to drink at a brook; in the mean time his companions went on: which being obferved by one of the women whom they had made captive, fhe fuddenla feized him with both her hands, whilft he ftooped to drink, by an exquifitely fufceptible part, and held him faft till he expired on the fpot. As the chief, from the extreme torture he fuffered, was unable to call out to his friends, or to give any alarm, they paffed on without knowing what had happened; and the woman having cut the bands of thofe of her fellow prifoners who were in the rear, with them made her efcape. This heroine was ever after treated by her nation as their deliverer, and made a chiefefs in her own right, with liberty to entail the fame honour on her defcendants: an unufual diftinction, and permitted only on extraordinary occafions.

About twelve miles before I reached the Carrying Place, I obferved feveral fmall mountains which extended quite to it. Thefe indeed would only be efteemed as molehills when compared with thofe on the back of the colonies, but as they were the firft I had feen fince my leaving Niagara, a track of nearly eleven hundred miles, I could not leave them unnoticed.

The Fox River, where it enters the Winnebago Lake, is about fifty yards wide, but it gradually decreafes to the Carrying Place, where it is no more than five yards over, except in a few places where it widens into fmall lakes, though ftill of a confiderable depth. I cannot recollect any thing elfe that is remarkable

markable in this river, except that it is so serpentine for five miles, as only to gain in that place one quarter of a mile.

The Carrying Place between the Fox and Ouisconsin Rivers is in breadth not more than a mile and three quarters, though in some maps it is so delineated as to appear to be ten miles. And here I cannot help remarking, that all the maps of these parts, I have ever seen, are very erroneous. The rivers in general are described as running in different directions from what they really do; and many branches of them, particularly of the Missippi, omitted. The distances of places, likewise, are greatly misrepresented. Whether this is done by the French geographers (for the English maps are all copied from theirs) through design, or for want of a just knowledge of the country, I cannot say; but I am satisfied that travellers who depend upon them in the parts I visited, will find themselves much at a loss.

Near one half of the way, between the rivers, is a morass overgrown with a kind of long grass, the rest of it a plain with some few oak and pine trees growing thereon. I observed here a great number of rattle-snakes. Monf. Pinnisance, a French trader, told me a remarkable story concerning one of these reptiles, of which, he said, he was an eye-witness. An Indian, belonging to the Menomonie nation, having taken one of them, found means to tame it; and when he had done this, treated it as a Deity t his Great Father, and carrying it with him in a box w ; went. This the Indian had done for several summe . Monf. Pinnisance accidentally met with him at this C..., ng Place, just as he was setting off for a winter's hunt. The French gentleman was surprized, one day, to see the Indian place the box which contained his god on the ground, and opening the door give him his liberty; telling him, whilst he did it, to be sure and return by the time he himself should come back, which was to be in the month of May following. As this was but October, Monsieur told the Indian, whose simplicity astonished him, that he fancied he might wait long enough when May arrived, for the arrival of his great father- The Indian was so confident of his creature's obedience, that he offered to lay the Frenchman a wager of two gallons of rum, that at the time appointed he would come and crawl into his box. This was agreed on, and the second week in May following fixed for the determination of the wager. At that period they both met there again; when the Indian set down his box, and called for his great father. The snake heard him not; and the time being now expired, he acknowledged that he had lost. However, without seeming to be discouraged, he offered to double the bett if his great father came not within two days more. This was further agreed on; when behold on the second day, about one o'clock, the snake arrived, and, of his own accord crawled into the box, which was placed ready for him. The French gentleman vouched for the truth of this story, and

from

from the accounts I have often received of the docility of thofe creatures, I fee no reafon to doubt his veracity.

I obferved that the main body of the Fox River came from the fouth-weft, that of the Ouifconfin from the north-eaft; and alfo that fome of the fmall branches of thefe two rivers, in defcending into them, doubled, within a few feet of each other, a little to the fouth of the Carrying Place. That two fuch rivers fhould take their rife fo near each other, and after running fuch different courfes, empty themfelves into the fea, at a diftance fo amazing (for the former having paffed through feveral great lakes, and run upwards of two thoufand miles, falls into the Gulf of St. Lawrence, and the other, after joining the Miffiffippi, and having run an equal number of miles, difembogues itfelf into the Gulf of Mexico) is an inftance fcarcely to be met in the extenfive continent of North-America. I had an opportunity the year following, of making the fame obfervations on the affinity of various head branches of the waters of the St. Lawrence and the Miffiffippi to each other; and now bring them as a proof, that the opinion of thofe geographers, who affert, that rivers taking their rife fo near each other, muft fpring from the fame fource, is erroneous. For I perceived a vifibly diftinct feparation in all of them, notwithftanding, in fome places, they approached fo near, that I could have ——ed from one to the other.

On the 8th of October we got our cano Ouifconfin River, which at this place is more than a yards wide; and the next day arrived at the Great Town of the Saukies. This is the largeft and beft built Indian town I ever faw. It contains about ninety houfes, each large enough for feveral families. Thefe are built of hewn plank, neatly jointed, and covered with bark fo compactly as to keep out the moft penetrating rains. Before the doors are placed comfortable fheds, in which the inhabitants fit, when the weather will permit, and fmoak their pipes. The ftreets are regular and fpacious; fo that it appears more like a civilized town than the abode of favages. The land near the town is very good. In their plantations, which lie adjacent to their houfes, and which are neatly laid out, they raife great quantities of Indian corn, beans, melons, &c. fo that this place is efteemed the beft market for traders to furnifh themfelves with provifions, of any within eight hundred miles of it.

The Saukies can raife about three hundred warriors, who are generally employed every fummer in making incurfions into the territories of the Illinois and Pawnee nations, from whence they return with a great number of flaves. But thofe people frequently retaliate, and, in their turn, deftroy many of the Saukies, which I judge to be the reafon that they increafe no fafter.

Whilft I ftaid here, I took a view of fome mountains that lie about fifteen miles to the fouthward, and abound in lead ore. I afcended on one of the higheft of thefe, and had an extenfive view

view of the country. For many miles nothing was to be seen but lesser mountains, which appeared at a distance like haycocks, they being free from trees. Only a few groves of hickery, and stunted oaks, covered some of the vallies. So plentiful is lead here, that I saw large quantities of it lying about the streets in the town belonging to the Saukies, and it seemed to be as good as the produce of other countries.

On the 10th of October we proceeded down the river, and the next day reached the first town of the Ottigaumies. This town contained about fifty houses, but we found most of them deserted, on account of an epidemical disorder that had lately raged among them, and carried off more than one half of the inhabitants. The greater part of those who survived had retired into the woods, to avoid the contagion.

On the 15th we entered that extensive river the Mississippi. The Ouisconsin, from the Carrying Place to the part where it falls into the Mississippi, flows with a smooth but strong current; the water of it is exceedingly clear, and through it you may perceive a fine and sandy bottom, tolerably free from rocks. In it are a few islands, the soil of which appeared to be good, though somewhat woody. The land near the river also seemed to be, in general, excellent; but that at a distance is very full of mountains, where it is said there are many lead mines.

About five miles from the junction of the rivers, I observed the ruins of a large town in a very pleasing situation. On enquiring of the neighbouring Indians why it was thus deserted, I was informed, that about thirty years ago, the Great Spirit had appeared on the top of a pyramid of rocks, which lay at a little distance from it, towards the west, and warned them to quit their habitations; for the land on which they were built belonged to him, and he had occasion for it. As a proof that he, who gave them these orders, was really the Great Spirit, he further told them, that the grass should immediately spring up on those very rocks from whence he now addressed them, which they knew to be bare and barren. The Indians obeyed, and soon after discovered that this miraculous alteration had taken place. They shewed me the spot, but the growth of the grass appeared to be no ways supernatural. I apprehend this to have been a stratagem of the French or Spaniards to answer some selfish view; but in what manner they effected their purposes I know not.

This people, soon after their removal, built a town on the bank of the Mississippi, near the mouth of the Ouisconsin, at a place called by the French La Prairies les Chiens, which signifies the Dog Plains; it is a large town, and contains about three hundred families; the houses are well built after the Indian manner, and pleasantly situated on a very rich soil, from which they raise every necessary of life in great abundance. I saw here many horses of a good size and shape. This town is the great mart where all the adjacent tribes, and even those who inhabit the most remote branches of the Mississippi, annually assemble

about

about the latter end of May, bringing with them their furs to difpofe of to the traders. But it is not always that they conclude their fale here; this is determined by a general council of the chiefs, who confult whether it would be more conducive to their intereft, to fell their goods at this place, or carry them on to Louifiana, or Michillimackinac. According to the decifion of this council they either proceed further, or return to their different homes.

The Miffiffippi, at the entrance of the Ouifconfin, near which ftands a mountain of confiderable height, is about half a mile over; but oppofite to the laft mentioned town it appears to be more than a mile wide, and full of iflands, the foil of which is extraordinary rich, and but thinly wooded.

A little farther to the weft, on the contrary fide, a fmall river falls into the Miffiffippi, which the French call Le Jaun Riviere, or the Yellow River. Here the traders who had accompanied me hitherto, took up their refidence for the winter. I then bought a canoe, and with two fervants, one a French Canadian, and the other a Mohawk of Canada, on the 19th proceeded up the Miffiffippi.

About ten days after I had parted from the traders, I landed as I ufually did every evening, and having pitched my tent, I ordered my men, when night came on, to lay themfelves down to fleep. By a light that I kept burning I then fat down to copy the minutes I had taken in the courfe of the preceeding day. About ten o'clock, having juft finifhed my memorandums, I ftepped out of my tent to fee what weather it was. As I caft my eyes towards the bank of the river, I thought I faw by the light of the ftars, which fhone bright, fomething that had the appearance of a herd of beafts coming down a defcent at fome diftance; whilft I was wondering what they could be, one of the number fuddenly fprung up, and difcovered to me the form of a man. In an inftant they were all on their legs, and I could count about ten or twelve of them running towards me. I immediately re-entered the tent, and having awakened my men, ordered them to take their arms, and follow me. As my firft apprehenfions were for my canoe, I ran to the water's fide, and found a party of Indians (for fuch I now difcovered them to be) on the point of plundering it. Before I reached them I commanded my men not to fire till I had given the word, being unwilling to begin hoftilities unlefs occafion abfolutely required. I accordingly advanced with refolution, clofe to the points of their fpears, they had no other weapons, and brandifhing my hanger, afked them with a ftern voice, what they wanted? They were ftaggered at this, and perceiving they were like to meet with a warm reception, turned about and precipitately retreated. We purfued them to an adjacent wood, which they entered, and we faw no more of them. However, for fear of their return, we watched alternately during the remainder of the night. The next day my fervants were under great apprehenfions, and earneftly entreat-
ed

ed me to return to the traders we had lately left. But I told them, that if they would not be esteemed old women (a term of the greatest reproach among the Indians) they must follow me; for I was determined to pursue my intended route, as an Englishman, when once engaged in an adventure, never retreated. On this they got into the canoe, and I walked on the shore to guard them from any further attack. The party of Indians who had thus intended to plunder me, I afterwards found to be some of those straggling bands, that having been driven from among the different tribes to which they belonged for various crimes, now associated themselves together, and, living by plunder, prove very troublesome to travellers who pass this way; nor are even Indians of every tribe spared by them. The traders had before cautioned me to be upon my guard against them, and I would repeat the same caution to those whose business might call them into these parts.

On the first of November I arrived at Lake Pepin, which is rather an extended part of the River Mississippi, that the French have thus denominated, about two hundred miles from the Ouisconsin. The Mississippi below this Lake flows with a gentle current, but the breadth of it is very uncertain, in some places it being upwards of a mile, in others not more than a quarter. This river has a range of mountains on each side throughout the whole of the way; which in particular parts approach near to it, in others lie at a greater distance. The land betwixt the mountains, and on their sides, is generally covered with grass with a few groves of trees interspersed, near which large droves of deer and elk are frequently seen feeding.

In many places pyramids of rocks appeared, resembling old ruinous towers; at others amazing precipices; and what is very remarkable, whilst this scene presented itself on one side, the opposite side of the same mountain was covered with the finest herbage, which gradually ascended to its summit. From thence the most beautiful and extensive prospect that imagination can form opens to your view. Verdant plains, fruitful meadows, numerous islands, and all these abounding with a variety of trees that yield amazing quantities of fruit, without care or cultivation; such as the nut-tree, the maple which produces sugar, vines loaded with rich grapes, and plum-trees bending under their blooming burdens, but above all, the fine river flowing gently beneath, and reaching as far as the eye can extend, by turns attract your admiration and excite your wonder.

The Lake is about twenty miles long, and near six in breadth; in some places it is very deep, and abounds with various kinds of fish. Great numbers of fowl frequent also this Lake and rivers adjacent; such as storks, swans, geese, brants, and ducks; and in the groves are found great plenty of turkeys and partridges. On the plains are the largest buffaloes of any in America. Here I observed the ruins of a French factory, where it

is

is faid Captain St. Pierre refided, and carried on a very great trade with the Naudoweffies, before the reduction of Canada.

About fixty miles below this Lake is a mountain remarkably fituated; for it ftands by itfelf exactly in the middle of the River, and looks as if it had flidden from the adjacent fhore into the ftream. It cannot be termed an ifland, as it rifes immediately from the brink of the water to a confiderable height. Both the Indians and the French call it the Mountain in the River.

One day having landed on the fhore of the Miffiffippi, fome miles below Lake Pepin, whilft my attendants were preparing my dinner, I walked out to take a view of the adjacent country. I had not proceeded far, before I came to a fine, level, open plain, on which I perceived at a little diftance, a partial elevation that had the appearance of an intrenchment. On a nearer infpection I had greater reafon to fuppofe that it had really been intended for this many centuries ago. Notwithftanding it was now covered with grafs, I could plainly difcern that it had once been a breaft-work of about four feet in height, extending the beft part of a mile, and fufficiently capacious to cover five thoufand men. Its form was fomewhat circular, and its flanks reached to the River. Though much defaced by time, every angle was diftinguifhable, and appeared as regular, and fafhioned with as much military skill, as if planned by Vauban himfelf. The ditch was not vifible, but I thought on examining more curioufly, that I could perceive there certainly had been one. From its fituation alfo, I am convinced that it muft have been defigned for this purpofe. It fronted the country, and the rear was covered by the River; nor was there any rifing ground for a confiderable way that commanded it; a few ftraggling oaks were alone to be feen near it. In many places fmall tracts were worn acrofs it by the feet of the elks and deer, and from the depth of the bed of earth by which it was covered, I was able to draw certain conclufions of its great antiquity. I examined all the angles and every part with great attention, and have often blamed myfelf fince, for not encamping on the fpot, and drawing an exact plan of it. To fhew that this defcription is not the offspring of a heated imagination, or the chimerical tale of a miftaken traveller, I find on enquiry fince my return, that Monf. St. Pierre and feveral traders have, at different times, taken notice of fimilar appearances on which they have formed the fame conjectures, but without examining them fo minutely as I did. How a work of this kind could exift in a country that has hitherto (according to the general received opinion) been the feat of war to untutored Indians alone, whofe whole ftock of military knowledge has only, till within two centuries, amounted to drawing the bow, and whofe only breaft-work even at prefent is the thicket, I know not. I have given as exact an account as poffible of this fingular appearance, and

and leave to future explorers of these distant regions to discover whether it is a production of nature or art.

Perhaps the hints I have here given might lead to a more perfect investigation of it, and give us very different ideas of the ancient state of realms that we at present believe to have been from the earliest period only the habitations of savages.

The Mississippi, as far as the entrance of the River St. Croix, thirty miles above Lake Pepin, is very full of islands; some of which are of a considerable length. On these, also, grow great numbers of the maple or sugar tree, and around them vines loaded with grapes creeping to their very tops. From the Lake upwards few mountains are to be seen, and those but small. Near the River St. Croix reside three bands of the Naudowessie Indians, called the River Bands.

This nation is composed, at present, of eleven bands. They were originally twelve; but the Assinipoils some years ago revolting, and separating themselves from the others, there remain only at this time eleven. Those I met here are termed the River Bands; because they chiefly dwell near the banks of this River: the other eight are generally distinguished by the title Naudowessies of the Plains, and inhabit a country that lies more to the westward. The names of the former are the Nehogatawonahs, the Mawtawbauntowahs, and the Shahsweentowahs, and consist of about four hundred warriors.

A little before I met with these three bands, I fell in with a party of the Mawtawbauntowahs, amounting to forty warriors and their families. With these I resided a day or two, during which time five or six of their number, who had been out on an excursion, returned in great haste, and acquainted their companions that a large party of the Chipéway warriors, " enough," as they expressed themselves, " to swallow them " all up," were close at their heels, and on the point of attacking their little camp. The chiefs applied to me, and desired I would put myself at their head, and lead them out to oppose their enemies. As I was a stranger, and unwilling to excite the anger of either nation, I knew not how to act; and never found myself in a greater dilemma. Had I refused to assist the Naudowessies I should have drawn on myself their displeasure, or had I met the Chipéways with hostile intentions, I should have made that people my foes, and had I been fortunate enough to have escaped their arrows at this time, on some future occasion should probably have experienced the severity of their revenge. In this extremity I chose the middle course, and desired that the Naudowessies would suffer me to meet them, that I might endeavour to avert their fury. To this they reluctantly assented, being persuaded, from the inveteracy which had long prevailed between them, that my remonstrances would be in vain.

Taking my Frenchman with me, who could speak their language, I hastened towards the place where the Chipéways were supposed to be. The Naudowessies during this kept at a distance

stance behind. As I approached them with the pipe of peace, a small party of their chiefs, consisting of about eight or ten, came in a friendly manner towards me; with whom, by the means of my interpreter, I held a long conversation; the result of which was, that their rancour being by my persuasions in some measure mollified, they agreed to return back without accomplishing their savage purposes. During our discourse I could perceive, as they lay scattered about, that the party was very numerous, and many of them armed with muskets.

Having happily succeeded in my undertaking, I returned without delay to the Naudowessies, and desired they would instantly remove their camp to some other part of the country, lest their enemies should repent of the promise they had given, and put their intentions in execution. They accordingly followed my advice, and immediately prepared to strike their tents. Whilst they were doing this, they loaded me with thanks; and when I had seen them on board their canoes I pursued my route.

To this adventure I was chiefly indebted for the friendly reception I afterwards met with from the Naudowessies of the Plains, and for the respect and honours I received during my abode among them. And when I arrived many months after at the Chipéway village, near the Ottowaw lakes, I found that my fame had reached that place before me. The chiefs received me with great cordiality, and the elder part of them thanked me for the mischief I had prevented. They informed me, that the war between their nation and the Naudowessies had continued without interruption for more than forty winters. That they had long wished to put an end to it, but this was generally prevented by the young warriors of either nation, who could not restrain their ardour when they met. They said, they should be happy if some chief of the same pacific disposition as myself, and who possessed an equal degree of resolution and coolness, would settle in the country between the two nations; for by the interference of such a person, an accommodation, which on their parts they sincerely desired, might be brought about. As I did not meet any of the Naudowessies afterwards, I had not an opportunity of forwarding so good a work.

About thirty miles below the Falls of St. Anthony, at which I arrived the tenth day after I left Lake Pepin, is a remarkable cave of an amazing depth. The Indians term it Wakon-teebe, that is, the Dwelling of the Great Spirit. The entrance into it is about ten feet wide, the height of it five feet. The arch within is near fifteen feet high and about thirty feet broad. The bottom of it consists of fine clear sand. About twenty feet from the entrance begins a lake, the water of which is transparent, and extends to an unsearchable distance; for the darkness of the cave prevents all attempts to acquire a knowledge of it. I threw a small pebble towards the interior parts of it with my utmost strength: I could hear that it fell into the water, and notwithstanding it was of so small a size, it caused an astonish-

ing

ing and horrible noise that reverberated through all those gloomy regions. I found in this cave many Indian hieroglyphicks, which appeared very ancient, for time had nearly covered them with moss, so that it was with difficulty I could trace them. They were cut in a rude manner upon the inside of the walls, which were composed of a stone so extremely soft that it might easily be penetrated with a knife: a stone every where to be found near the Missisippi. The cave is only accessible by ascending a narrow, steep passage that lies near the brink of the river.

At a little distance from this dreary cavern is the burying-place of several bands of the Naudowessie Indians: though these people have no fixed residence, living in tents, and abiding but a few months on one spot, yet they always bring the bones of their dead to this place; which they take the opportunity of doing when the chiefs meet to hold their councils, and to settle all public affairs for the ensuing summer.

Ten miles below the Falls of St. Anthony the River St. Pierre, called by the natives the Waddapawmenesotor, falls into the Missisippi from the West. It is not mentioned by Father Hennipin, although a large fair river: this omission I conclude, must have proceeded from a small island that is situated exactly at its entrance, by which the sight of it is intercepted. I should not have discovered this river myself, had I not taken a view, when I was searching for it, from the high lands opposite, which rise to a great height.

Nearly over against this river I was obliged to leave my canoe, on account of the ice, and travel by land to the Falls of St. Anthony, where I arrived on the 17th of November. The Missisippi from the St. Pierre to this place is rather more rapid than I had hitherto found it, and without islands of any consideration.

Before I left my canoe I overtook a young prince of the Winnebago Indians, who was going on an embassy to some of the bands of the Naudowessies. Finding that I intended to take a view of the Falls, he agreed to accompany me, his curiosity having been often excited by the accounts he had received from some of his chiefs: he accordingly left his family (for the Indians never travel without their households) at this place, under the care of my Mohawk servant, and we proceeded together by land, attended only by my Frenchman, to this celebrated place.

We could distinctly hear the noise of the water full fifteen miles before we reached the falls; and I was greatly pleased and surprized, when I approached this astonishing work of nature: but I was not long at liberty to indulge these emotions, my attention being called off by the behaviour of my companion.

The prince had no sooner gained the point that overlooks this wonderful cascade, than he began with an audible voice to
address

address the Great Spirit, one of whose places of residence he imagined this to be. He told him that he had come a long way to pay his adorations to him, and now would make him the best offerings in his power. He accordingly first threw his pipe into the stream; then the roll that contained his tobacco; after these, the bracelets he wore on his arms and wrists; next an ornament that encircled his neck, composed of beads and wires; and at last the ear-rings from his ears; in short, he presented to his god every part of his dress that was valuable: during this he frequently smote his breast with great violence, threw his arms about, and appeared to be much agitated.

All this while he continued his adorations and at length concluded them with fervent petitions that the Great Spirit would constantly afford us his protection on our travels, giving us a bright sun, a blue sky, and clear untroubled waters: nor would he leave the place till we had smoaked together with my pipe in honour of the Great Spirit.

I was greatly surprized at beholding an instance of such elevated devotion in so young an Indian, and instead of ridiculing the ceremonies attending it, as I observed my catholic servant tacitly did, I looked on the prince with a greater degree of respect for these sincere proofs he gave of his piety; and I doubt not but that his offerings and prayers were as acceptable to the universal Parent of mankind, as if they had been made with greater pomp, or in a consecrated place.

Indeed, the whole conduct of this young prince at once amazed and charmed me. During the few days we were together his attention seemed totally to be employed in yielding me every assistance in his power; and even in so short a time he gave me innumerable proofs of the most generous and disinterested friendship; so that on our return I parted from him with great reluctance. Whilst I beheld the artless, yet engaging manners of this unpolished savage, I could not help drawing a comparison between him and some of the more refined inhabitants of civilized countries, not much, I own, in favour of the latter.

The Falls of St. Anthony received their name from Father Louis Hennipin, a French missionary, who travelled into these parts about the year 1680, and was the first European ever seen by the natives. This amazing body of waters, which are above 250 yards over, form a most pleasing cataract; they fall perpendicularly about thirty feet, and the rapids below, in the space of 300 yards more, render the descent considerably greater; so that when viewed at a distance they appear to be much higher than they really are. The above-mentioned traveller has laid them down at above sixty feet; but he has made a greater error in calculating the height of the Falls of Niagara; which he asserts to be 600 feet; whereas from latter observations accurately made, it is well known that it does not exceed 140 feet. But the good father I fear too often had no other foundation for his accounts than report, or, at best, a slight inspection.

In the middle of the Falls stands a small island, about forty feet broad and somewhat longer, on which grow a few cragged hemlock and spruce trees; and about half way between this island and the eastern shore is a rock, lying at the very edge of the Fall, in an oblique position, that appeared to be about five or six feet broad, and thirty or forty long. These Falls vary much from all the others I have seen, as you may approach close to them without finding the least obstruction from any intervening hill or precipice.

The country around them is extremely beautiful. It is not an uninterrupted plain where the eye finds no relief, but composed of many gentle ascents, which in the summer are covered with the finest verdure, and interspersed with little groves, that give a pleasing variety to the prospect. On the whole, when the Falls are included, which may be seen at the distance of four miles, a more pleasing and picturesque view cannot, I believe, be found throughout the universe. I could have wished that I had happened to enjoy this glorious sight at a more seasonable time of the year, whilst the trees and hillocks were clad in nature's gayest livery, as this must have greatly added to the pleasure I received; however, even then it exceeded my warmest expectations. I have endeavoured to give the reader as just an idea of this enchanting spot as possible; but all description, whether of the pencil or the pen, must fall infinitely short of the original.

At a little distance below the Falls stands a small island, of about an acre and an half, on which grow a great number of oak trees, every branch of which, able to support the weight, was full of eagles nests. The reason that this kind of birds resort in such numbers to this spot, is that they are here secure from the attacks either of man or beast, their retreat being guarded by the rapids, which the Indians never attempt to pass. Another reason is, that they find a constant supply of food for themselves and their young, from the animals and fish which are dashed to pieces by the falls, and driven on the adjacent shore.

Having satisfied my curiosity, as far as the eye of man can be satisfied, I proceeded on, still accompanied by my young friend, till I had reached the River St. Francis, near sixty miles above the Falls. To this river Father Hennipin gave the name of St. Francis, and this was the extent of his travels, as well as mine, towards the north-west. As the season was so advanced, and the weather extremely cold, I was not able to make so many observations on these parts as I otherwise should have done.

It might however, perhaps, be necessary to observe, that in the little tour I made about the Falls, after travelling fourteen miles, by the side of the Mississippi, I came to a river nearly twenty yards wide, which ran from the north-east, called Rum-River. And on the 20th of November came to another termed

Goose-

Goose-River, about twelve yards wide. On the 21st I arrived at the St. Francis, which is about thirty yards wide. Here the Mississippi itself grows narrow, being not more than ninety yards over; and appears to be chiefly composed of small branches. The ice prevented me from noticing the depth of any of these three rivers.

The country in some places is hilly, but without large mountains; and the land is tolerably good. I observed here many deer and carriboos, some elk, with abundance of beavers, otters, and other furs. A little above this, to the north-east, are a number of small lakes called the Thousand Lakes; the parts about which, though but little frequented, are the best within many miles for hunting, as the hunter never fails of returning loaded beyond his expectations.

The Mississippi has never been explored higher up than the River St. Francis, and only by Father Hennipin and myself thus far. So that we are obliged solely to the Indians, for all the intelligence we are able to give relative to the more northern parts. As this River is not navigable from the sea for vessels of any considerable burthen, much higher up than the Forks of the Ohio, and even that is accomplished with great difficulty, owing to the rapidity of the current, and the windings of the river, those settlements that may be made on the interior branches of it, must be indisputably secure from the attacks of any maritime power. But at the same time the settlers will have the advantage of being able to convey their produce to the sea-ports with great facility, the current of the river from its source to its entrance into the Gulph of Mexico, being extremely favourable for doing this in small craft. This might also in time be facilitated by canals or shorter cuts; and a communication opened by water with New York, Canada, &c. by way of the lakes. The Forks of the Ohio are about nine hundred miles from the mouth of the Mississippi, following the course of the river; and the Messorie two hundred miles above these. From the latter it is about twenty miles to the Illinois River, and from that to the Ouisconsin, which I have given an account of about eight hundred more.

On the 25th I returned to my canoe, which I had left at the mouth of the River St. Pierre; and here I parted with regret from my young friend the prince of the Winnebagoes. This river being clear of ice by reason of its southern situation, I found nothing to obstruct my passage. On the 28th, being advanced about forty miles, I arrived at a small branch that fell into it from the north; to which, as it had no name that I could distinguish it by, I gave my own. About forty miles higher up I came to the Forks of Verd and Red Marble Rivers, which join at some little distance before they enter the St. Pierre.

The River St. Pierre, at its junction with the Mississippi, is about a hundred yards broad, and continues that breadth nearly all the way I sailed upon it. It has a great depth of water,

and

and in some places runs very briskly. About fifty miles from its mouth are some rapids, and much higher up there are many others.

I proceeded up this river about two hundred miles to the country of the Naudoweſſies of the Plains, which lies a little above the Forks formed by the Verd and Red Marble Rivers, just mentioned, where a branch from the south nearly joins the Meſſorie River. By the accounts I received from the Indians, I have reaſon to believe that the River St. Pierre and the Meſſorie, though they enter the Miſſiſſippi twelve hundred miles from each other, take their riſe in the ſame neighbourhood; and this within the ſpace of a mile.

The River St. Pierre's northern branch rifes from a number of lakes near the ſhining mountains; and it is from ſome of theſe, alſo, that a capital branch of the River Bourbon, which runs into Hudſon's Bay, has its ſources.

From the intelligence I gained from the Naudoweſſie Indians, among whom I arrived the 7th of December, and whoſe language I perfectly acquired during a reſidence of five months; and alſo from the accounts I afterwards obtained from the Aſſinipoils, who ſpeak the ſame tongue, being a revolted band of the Naudoweſſies; and from the Killiſtinoes, neighbours of the Aſſinipoils, who ſpeak the Chipéway language, and inhabit the heads of the River Bourbon; I ſay from theſe nations, together with my own obſervations, I have learned that the four moſt capital rivers on the Continent of North America, viz. the St. Lawrence, the Miſſiſſippi, the river Bourbon, and the Oregon of the river of the Weſt (as I hinted in my Introduction) have their ſources in the ſame neighbourhood. The waters of the three former are within thirty miles of each other; the latter, however, is rather farther weſt.

This ſhews that theſe parts are the higheſt lands in North America; and it is an inſtance not to be paralleled on the other three quarters of the globe, that four rivers of ſuch magnitude ſhould take their rife together, and each, after running ſeparate courſes, diſcharge their waters into different oceans at the diſtance of two thouſand miles from their ſources. For in their paſſage from this ſpot to the bay of St. Lawrence, eaſt, to the bay of Mexico, ſouth, to Hudſon's Bay, north, and to the bay at the Straights of Annian, weſt, each of theſe traverſe upwards of two thouſand miles.

I ſhall here give my Readers ſuch reflections as occurred to me, when I had received this intereſting information, and had by numberleſs enquiries, aſcertained the truth of it; that is, as far as it was poſſible to arrive at a certainty without a perſonal inveſtigation.

It is well known that the Colonies, particularly thoſe of New-England and Canada, are greatly affected, about the time their winter ſets in, by a north-weſt wind, which continues for ſeveral months, and renders the cold much more intenſe there than it is in the interior parts of America. This I can, from my own knowledge, affert, as I found the winter, that I paffed to the weftward of the Miffiffippi, far from fevere; and the north-weft wind blowing on thofe countries confiderably more temperate than I have often experienced it to be nearer the coaft. And that this did not arife from an uncertainty of the feafons, but was annually the cafe, I conclude, both from the fmall quantity of fnow that then fell, and a total difufe of fnow fhoes by thefe Indians, without which none of the more eaftern nations can poffibly travel during the winter.

As naturalifts obferve, that air refembles water in many refpects, particularly by often flowing in a compact body; and that this is generally remarked to be with the current of large ftreams, and feldom acrofs them, may not the winds that fet violently into the Bay of Mexico about the latter end of the year, take their courfe over the continent in the fame direction as the Miffiffippi does; till meeting with the north winds (that from a fimilar caufe blow up the Bourbon from Hudfon's Bay) they are forced acrofs the great lakes, down the current of the waters of the St. Lawrence, and united, commit thofe ravages, and occafion thofe fevere winters, experienced in the before-mentioned countries? During their progrefs over the lakes they become expanded, and confequently affect a greater tract of land than they otherwife would do.

According to my fcanty knowledge of natural philofophy, this does not appear improbable. Whether it is agreeable to the laws eftablifhed by naturalifts to account for the operations of that element, I know not. However, the defcription here given of the fituation of thofe vaft bodies of water, and their near approach to each other, with my own undigefted fuppofitions of their effect on the winds, may prove perhaps, in abler hands, the means of leading to many ufeful difcoveries.

On the 7th of December, I arrived (as I faid before) at the utmoft extent of my travels towards the weft; where I met with a large party of the Naudoweffie Indians, among whom I refided feven months. Thefe conftituted a part of the eight bands of the Naudoweffies of the Plains; and are termed the Wawpeentowahs, the Tintons, the Afrahcootans, the Mawhaws, and the Schians. The other three bands, whofe names are the Schianefe, the Chongoufceton, and the Waddapawjeftin, dwell higher up, to the weft of the River St. Pierre, on plains that, according to their account, are unbounded; and probably terminate on the coaft of the Pacific Ocean. The Naudoweffie nation, when united, confifts of more than two thoufand warriors. The Affinipoils, who revolted from them, amount to about three hundred; and leagued with the Killiftinoes, live in a continual ftate of enmity with the other eleven bands.

As I proceeded up the River St. Pierre, and had nearly reached the place where thefe people were encamped, I obferved two or three canoes coming down the ftream; but no fooner had

had the Indians that were on board them difcovered us, than they rowed toward the land, and leaping afhore with precipitation, left their canoes to float as the current drove them. In a few minutes I perceived fome others; who, as foon as they came in fight, followed, with equal fpeed, the example of their countrymen.

I now thought it neceffary to proceed with caution; and therefore kept on the fide of the river oppofite to that on which the Indians had landed. However, I ftill continued my courfe, fatisfied that the pipe of peace, which was fixed at the head of my canoe, and the Englifh colours that were flying at the ftern, would prove my fecurity. After rowing about half a mile farther, in turning a point, I difcovered a great number of tents, and more than a thoufand Indians, at a little diftance from the fhore. Being now nearly oppofite to them, I ordered my men to pull directly over, as I was willing to convince the Indians by fuch a ftep, that I placed fome confidence in them.

As foon as I had reached the land, two of the chiefs prefented their hands to me, and led me, amidft the aftonifhed multitude, who had moft of them never feen a white man before, to a tent. Into this we entered, and according to the cuftom that univerfally prevails among every Indian nation, began to fmoke the pipe of peace. We had not fat long before the crowd became fo great, both around, and upon the tent, that we were in danger of being crufhed by its fall. On this we returned to the plain, where, having gratified the curiofity of the common people, their wonder abated, and ever after they treated me with great refpect.

From the chiefs I met with the moft friendly and hofpitable reception; which induced me, as the feafon was fo far advanced, to take up my refidence among them during the winter. To render my ftay as comfortable as poffible, I firft endeavoured to learn their language. This I foon did, fo as to make myfelf perfectly intelligible, having before acquired fome flight knowledge of the language of thofe Indians that live on the back of the fettlements; and in confequence met with every accommodation their manner of living would afford. Nor did I want for fuch amufements as tended to make fo long a period pafs cheerfully away. I frequently hunted with them; and at other times beheld with pleafure their recreations and paftimes, which I fhall defcribe hereafter.

Sometimes I fat with the chiefs, and whilft we fmoked the friendly pipe, entertained them, in return for the accounts they gave me of their wars and excurfions, with a narrative of my own adventures, and a defcription of all the battles fought between the Englifh and the French in America, in many of which I had a perfonal fhare. They always paid great attention to my details, and asked many pertinent queftions relative to the European methods of making war.

I held thefe converfations with them in a great meafure to procure

procure from them some information relative to the chief point I had constantly in view, that of gaining a knowledge of the situation and produce, both of their own country, and those that lay to the westward of them. Nor was I disappointed in my designs; for I procured from them much useful intelligence. They likewise drew for me plans of all the countries with which they were acquainted; but as I entertained no great opinion of their geographical knowledge, I placed not much dependence on them, and therefore think it unnecessary to give them to the public. They draw with a piece of burnt coal, taken from the hearth, upon the inside bark of the birch tree; which is as smooth as paper, and answers the same purposes, notwithstanding it is of a yellow cast. Their sketches are made in a rude manner, but they seem to give us as just an idea of a country, although the plan is not so exact, as more experienced draughtsmen could do.

I left the habitations of these hospitable Indians the latter end of April 1767; but did not part from them for several days, as I was accompanied on my journey by near three hundred of them, among whom were many chiefs, to the mouth of the River St. Pierre. At this season, these bands annually go to the Great Cave, before mentioned, to hold a grand council with all the other bands; wherein they settle their operations for the ensuing year. At the same time they carry with them their dead for interment, bound up in buffaloes skins. Besides those that accompanied me, others were gone before, and the rest were to follow.

Never did I travel with so cheerful and happy a company. But their mirth met with a sudden and temporary allay from a violent storm that overtook us one day on our passage. We had just landed, and were preparing to set up our tents for the night, when a heavy cloud overspread the heavens, and the most dreadful thunder, lightning, and rain issued from it, that ever I beheld.

The Indians were greatly terrified, and ran to such shelter as they could find; for only a few tents were as yet erected. Apprehensive of the danger that might ensue from standing near any thing which could serve for a conductor, as the cloud appeared to contain such an uncommon quantity of electrical fluid, I took my stand as far as possible from any covering; chusing rather to be exposed to the peltings of the storm, than to receive a fatal stroke. At this the Indians were greatly surprized, and drew conclusions from it not unfavourable to the opinion they already entertained of my resolution. Yet I acknowledge that I was never more affected in my life; for nothing scarcely could exceed the terrific scene. The peals of thunder were so loud that they shook the earth; and the lightning flashed along the ground in streams of sulphur; so that the Indian chiefs themselves, although their courage in war is usually invincible, could not help trembling at the horrid combustion. As soon as the storm was over, they flocked around me, and informed me, that it was a

proof

proof of the anger of the evil spirits, whom they were apprehensive that they had highly offended.

When we arrived at the Great Cave, and the Indians had deposited the remains of their deceased friends in the burial-place that stands adjacent to it, they held their great council, into which I was admitted, and at the same time had the honour to be installed or adopted a chief of their bands. On this occasion I made the following speech, which I insert to give my readers a specimen of the language and manner in which it is necessary to address the Indians, so as to engage their attention, and to render the speaker's expressions consonant to their ideas. It was delivered on the first day of May 1767.

" My brothers, chiefs of the numerous and powerful Naudowessies! I rejoice that through my long abode with you, I can now speak to you (though after an imperfect manner) in your own tongue, like one of your own children. I rejoice also that I have had an opportunity so frequently to inform you of the glory and power of the Great King that reigns over the English and other nations; who is descended from a very ancient race of sovereigns, as old as the earth and waters; whose feet stand on two great islands, larger than any you have ever seen, amidst the greatest waters in the world; whose head reaches to the sun, and whose arms encircle the whole earth. The number of whose warriors are equal to the trees in the vallies, the stalks of rice in yonder marshes, or the blades of grafs on your great plains. Who has hundreds of canoes of his own, of such amazing bigness, that all the waters in your country would not suffice for one of them to swim in; each of which have guns, not small like mine, which you see before you, but of such magnitude, that an hundred of your stoutest young men would with difficulty be able to carry one. And these are equally surprizing in their operation against the great kings enemies when engaged in battle; the terror they carry with them your language wants words to express. You may remember the other day when we were encamping, at Wadawpawmenesoter, the black clouds, the wind, the fire, the stupendous noise, the horrible cracks, and the trembling of the earth, which then alarmed you, and gave you reason to think your gods were angry with you; not unlike these are the warlike implements of the English, when they are fighting the battles of their great King.

" Several of the chiefs of your bands have often told me, in times past, when I dwelt with you in your tents, that they much wished to be counted among the children and allies of the great King my master. You may remember how often you have desired me, when I return again to my own country, to acquaint the great King of your good disposition towards him and his subjects, and that you wished for traders from the English to come among you.

" Being now about to take my leave of you, and to return
" to

" to my own country, a long way towards the rising sun, I
" again ask you to tell me whether you continue of the same
" mind as when I spoke to you in council last winter; and as
" there are now several of your chiefs here, who came from
" the great plains towards the setting of the sun, whom I have
" never spoke with in council before, I ask you to let me know
" if you are all willing to acknowledge yourselves the children
" of my great master the King of the English and other nati-
" ons, as I shall take the first opportunity to acquaint him of
" your desires and good intentions.

" I charge you not to give heed to bad reports; for there
" are wicked birds flying about among the neighbouring nati-
" ons, who may whisper evil things in your ears against the
" English, contrary to what I have told you; you must not be-
" lieve them, for I have told you the truth.

" And as for the chiefs that are about to go to Michillimack-
" inac, I shall take care to make for them and their suite, a
" straight road, smooth waters, and a clear sky; that they may
" go there, and smoke the pipe of Peace, and rest secure on a
" beaver blanket under the shade of the great tree of Peace.
" Farewell!"

To this speech I received the following answer, from the mouth of the principal chief:

" Good brother! I am now about to speak to you with the
" mouths of these my brothers, chiefs of the eight bands of
" the powerful nation of the Naudowessies. We believe and
" are well satisfied in the truth of every thing you have told
" us about your great nation, and the Great King our greatest
" father; for whom we spread this beaver blanket, that his
" fatherly protection may ever rest easy and safe amongst us his
" children: your colours and your arms agree with the accounts
" you have given us about your great nation. We desire that
" when you return, you will acquaint the Great King how
" much the Naudowessies wish to be counted among his good
" children.

" You may believe us when we tell you that we will not open
" our ears to any who may dare to speak evil of our Great Fa-
" ther the King of the English and other nations.

" We thank you for what you have done for us in making
" peace between the Naudowessies and the Chipéways, and hope
" when you return to us again, that you will complete this
" good work; and quite dispelling the clouds that intervene,
" open the blue sky of peace, and cause the bloody hatchet to
" be deep buried under the roots of the great tree of peace.

" We wish you to remember to represent to our Great Fa-
" ther, how much we desire that traders may be sent to abide
" among us, with such things as we need, that the hearts of
" our young men, our wives, and children may be made glad.
" And may peace subsist between us, so long as the sun, the
" moon,

" moon, the earth, and the waters shall endure. Fare-
" well!"

I thought it necessary to caution the Indians against giving heed to any bad reports that may reach them from the neighbouring nations to the disadvantage of the English, as I had heard, at different places through which I passed, that emissaries were still employed by the French to detach those who were friendly to the English from their interest. And I saw, myself, several belts of Wampum that had been delivered for this purpose to some of the tribes I was among. On the delivery of each of these a Talk was held, wherein the Indians were told that the English, who were but a petty people, had stolen that country from their Great Father the king of France whilst he was asleep; but that he would soon awake, and take them again under his protection. These I found were sent from Canada by persons who appeared to be well affected towards the government under which they lived.

Whilst I tarried at the mouth of the River St. Pierre with these friendly Indians, I endeavoured to gain intelligence whether any goods had been sent towards the Falls of St. Anthony for my use, agreeable to the promise I had received from the governor when I left Michillimackinac. But finding from some Indians, who passed by in their return from those parts, that this agreement had not been fulfilled, I was obliged to give up all thoughts of proceeding farther to the north-west by this route, according to my original plan. I therefore returned to La Prairie le Chien, where I procured as many goods from the traders I left there the preceeding year as they could spare.

As these however were not sufficient to enable me to renew my first design, I determined to endeavour to make my way across the country of the Chipéways to Lake Superior; in hopes of meeting at the Grand Portage on the north side of it, the traders that annually go from Michillimackinac to the north-west; of whom I doubted not but that I should be able to procure goods enough to answer my purpose, and also to penetrate through those more northern parts to the Straights of Annian.

And I the more readily returned to La Prairie le Chien, as I could by that means the better fulfil the engagement I had made to the party of Naudowessies mentioned at the conclusion of my speech.

During my abode with this people, wishing to secure them entirely in the interest of the English, I had advised some of the chiefs to go to Michillimackinac, where they would have an opportunity of trading, and of hearing the accounts that I had entertained them with of my countrymen, confirmed. At the same time I had furnished them with a recommendation to the governor, and given them every direction necessary for their voyage.

In consequence of this, one of the principal chiefs, and twenty-five of an inferior rank, agreed to go the ensuing summer

mer. This they took an opportunity of doing, when they came with the reſt of their band to attend the grand council at the mouth of the River St. Pierre. Being obliged, on account of the diſappointment I had juſt been informed of, to return ſo far down the Miſſiſſippi, I could from thence the more eaſily ſet them on their journey.

As the intermediate parts of this river are much frequented by the Chipéways, with whom the Naudoweſſies are continually at war, they thought it more prudent, being but a ſmall party, to take the advantage of the night, than to travel with me by day; accordingly no ſooner was the grand council broke up, than I took a friendly leave of theſe people, from whom I had received innumerable civilities, and purſued once more my voyage.

I reached the eaſtern ſide of Lake Pepin the ſame night, where I went aſhore and encamped as uſual. The next morning, when I had proceeded ſome miles farther, I perceived at a diſtance before me a ſmoke, which denoted that ſome Indians were near; and in a ſhort time diſcovered ten or twelve tents not far from the bank of the river. As I was apprehenſive that this was a party of the Rovers I had before met with, I knew not what courſe to purſue. My attendants perſuaded me to endeavour to paſs by them on the oppoſite ſide of the river; but as I had hitherto found that the beſt way to enſure a friendly reception from the Indians, is to meet them boldly, and without ſhewing any tokens of fear, I would by no means conſent to their propoſal. Inſtead of this I croſſed directly over, and landed in the midſt of them, for by this time the greateſt part of them were ſtanding on the ſhore.

The firſt I accoſted were Chipéways inhabiting near the Ottowaw Lakes; who received me with great cordiality, and ſhook me by the hand in token of friendſhip. At ſome little diſtance behind theſe ſtood a chief remarkably tall and well made, but of ſo ſtern an aſpect, that the moſt undaunted perſon could not behold him without feeling ſome degree of terror. He ſeemed to have paſſed the meridian of life, and by the mode in which he was painted and tatowed, I diſcovered that he was of high rank. However, I approached him in a courteous manner, and expected to have met with the ſame reception I had done from the others: but to my great ſurprize, he with-held his hand, and looking fiercely at me, ſaid in the Chipéway tongue, "Cawin niſhiſhin ſaganoſh," that is, "The Engliſh are no good." As he had his tomahawk in his hand, I expected that this laconick ſentence would have been followed by a blow; to prevent which, I drew a piſtol from my belt, and, holding it in a careleſs poſition, paſſed cloſe by him, to let him ſee I was not afraid of him.

I learned ſoon after from the other Indians, that this was a chief, called by the French the Grand Sautor, or the Great Chipéway Chief, for they denominate the Chipéways Sautors. They

likewiſe

likewise told me that he had been always a steady friend to that people, and when they delivered up Michillimackinac to the English on their evacuation of Canada, the Grand Sautor had sworn that he would ever remain the avowed enemy of its new possessors, as the territories on which the fort is built belonged to him.

Finding him thus disposed, I took care to be constantly upon my guard whilst I staid; but that he might not suppose I was driven away by his frowns. I took up my abode there for the night. I pitched my tent at some distance from the Indians, and had no sooner laid myself down to rest, than I was awakened by my French servant. Having been alarmed by the sound of Indian music, he had run to the outside of the tent, where he beheld a party of the young savages dancing towards us in an extraordinary manner, each carrying in his hand a torch fixed on the top of a long pole. But I shall defer any further account of this uncommon entertainment, which at once surprized and alarmed me till I treat of the Indian dances.

The next morning I continued my voyage, and before night reached La Prarie le Chien; at which place the party of Naudowessies soon overtook me. Not long after the Grand Sautor also arrived, and before the Naudowessies left that place to continue their journey to Michillimackinac, he found means, in conjunction with some French traders from Louisiana, to draw from me about ten of the Naudowessie chiefs, whom he prevailed upon to go towards those parts.

The remainder proceeded, according to my directions, to the English fort; from whence I afterwards heard that they returned to their own country without any unfortunate accident befalling them, and greatly pleased with the reception they had met with. Whilst not more than half of those who went to the southward, through the difference of that southern climate from their own, lived to reach their abode. And since I came to England I have been informed, that the Grand Sautor having rendered himself more and more disgustful to the English, by his inveterate enmity towards them, was at length stabbed in his tent, as he encamped near Michillimackinac, by a trader to whom I had related the foregoing story.

I should have remarked, that whatever Indians happen to meet at La Prairie le Chien the great mart to which all who inhabit the adjacent countries resort, though the nations to which they belong are at war with each other, yet they are obliged to restrain their enmity, and to forbear all hostile acts during their stay there. This regulation has been long established among them for their mutual convenience, as without it no trade could be carried on. The same rule is observed also at the Red Mountain (afterwards described) from whence they get the stone of which they make their pipes: these being indispensable to the accommodation of every neighbouring tribe, a similar restriction becomes needful, and is of public utility.

The

The River St. Pierre, which runs through the territories of the Naudowessies, flows through a most delightful country, abounding with all the necessaries of life, that grow spontaneously; and with a little cultivation it might be made to produce even the luxuries of life. Wild rice grows here in great abundance; and every part is filled with trees bending under their loads of fruits, such as plums, grapes, and apples; the meadows are covered with hops, and many sorts of vegetables; whilst the ground is stored with useful roots, with angelica, spikenard, and ground-nuts as large as hens eggs. At a little distance from the sides of the river are eminences, from which you have views that cannot be exceeded even by the most beautiful of those I have already described; amidst these are delightful groves, and such amazing quantities of maples, that they would produce sugar sufficient for any number of inhabitants.

A little way from the mouth of this river, on the north side of it, stands a hill, one part of which, that towards the Mississippi, is composed entirely of white stone, of the same soft nature as that I have before described; for such, indeed, is all the stone in this country. But what appears remarkable is, that the colour of it is as white as the driven snow. The outward part of it was crumbled by the wind and weather into heaps of sand, of which a beautiful composition might be made; or, I am of opinion that, when properly treated, the stone itself would grow harder by time, and have a very noble effect in architecture.

Near that branch which is termed the Marble River, is a mountain, from whence the Indians get a sort of red stone, out of which they hew the bowls of their pipes. In some of these parts is found a black hard clay, or rather stone, of which the Naudowessies make their family utensils. This country likewise abounds with a milk-white clay, of which China ware might be made equal in goodness to the Asiatic; and also with a blue clay that serves the Indians for paint, with this last they contrive, by mixing it with the red stone powdered, to paint themselves of different colours. Those that can get the blue clay here mentioned, paint themselves very much with it; particularly when they are about to begin their sports and pastimes. It is also esteemed by them a mark of peace, as it has a resemblance of a blue sky, which with them is a symbol of it, and made use of in their speeches as a figurative expression to denote peace. When they wish to shew that their inclinations are pacific towards other tribes, they greatly ornament both themselves and their belts with it.

Having concluded my business at La Prairie le Chien, I proceeded once more up the Mississippi, as far as the place where the Chipéway River enters it a little below Lake Pepin. Here, having engaged an Indian pilot, I directed him to steer towards the Ottawaw Lakes, which lie near the head of this river. This he did, and I arrived at them the beginning of July.

The Chipéway River, at its junction with the Mississippi, is about eighty yards wide, but is much wider as you advance into it. Near thirty miles up it separates into two branches, and I took my course through that which lies to the eastward.

The country adjoining to the river, for about sixty miles, is very level, and on its banks lie fine meadows, where larger droves of buffaloes and elks were feeding, than I had observed in any other part of my travels. The track between the two branches of this river is termed the Road of War between the Chipeway and Naudoweſſie Indians.

The country to the Falls is almost without any timber, and above that very uneven and rugged, and closely wooded with pines, beach, maple and birch. Here a most remarkable and astoniſhing sight presented itself to my view. In a wood, on the east of the river, which was about three quarters of a mile in length, and in depth farther than my eye could reach, I observed that every tree, many of which were more than six feet in circumference, was lying flat on the ground, torn up by the roots. This appeared to have been done by some extraordinary hurricane, that came from the west some years ago; but how many I could not learn, as I found no inhabitants near it, of whom I could gain information. The country on the west side of the river, from being less woody, had escaped in a great measure this havock, as only a few trees were blown down.

Near the heads of this river is a town of the Chipéways, from whence it takes its name. It is situated on each side of the river (which at this place is of no considerable breadth) and lies adjacent to the banks of a small lake. This town contains about forty houses, and can send out upwards of one hundred warriors, many of whom were fine stout young men. The houses of it are built after the Indian manner, and have neat plantations behind them; but the inhabitants, in general, seemed to be the nastiest people I had ever been among. I observed that the women and children indulged themselves in a custom, which though common, in some degree, throughout every Indian nation, appears to be, according to our ideas, of the most nauseous and indelicate nature; that of searching each other's head, and eating the prey caught therein.

In July I left this town, and having crossed a number of small lakes and carrying places that intervened, came to a head branch of the River St. Croix. This branch I descended to a fork, and then ascended another to its source. On both these rivers I discovered several mines of virgin copper, which was as pure as that found in any other country.

Here I came to a small brook, which my guide thought might be joined at some distance by streams that would at length render it navigable. The water at first was so scanty, that my canoe would by no means swim in it; but having stopped up several old beaver dams, which had been broken down by the hunters, I was enabled to proceed for some miles, till by the conjunction of a few brooks, these aids became no longer necessary. In a short time the water increased to a most rapid

pid river, which we defcended till it entered into Lake Superior. This river I named after a gentleman that defired to accompany me from the town of the Ottagaumies to the Carrying Place on Lake Superior, Goddard's River.

To the weft of this is another fmall river, which alfo empties itfelf into the Lake. This I termed Strawberry River, from the great number of ftrawberries of a good fize and flavour that grew on its banks.

The country from the Ottawaw Lakes to Lake Superior is in general very uneven and thickly covered with woods. The foil in fome places is tolerably good, in others but indifferent. In the heads of the St. Croix and the Chipeways Rivers are exceeding fine fturgeon. All the wildernefs between the Miffiffippi and Lake Superior is called by the Indians the Mofchettoe country, and I thought it moft juftly named; for, it being then their feafon, I never faw or felt fo many of thofe infects in my life.

The latter end of July I arrived, after having coafted through Weft Bay, at the Grand Portage, which lies on the northweft borders of Lake Superior. Here thofe who go on the north-weft trade, to the Lakes De Pluye, Dubois, &c. carry over their canoes and baggage about nine miles, till they come to a number of fmall lakes, the waters of fome of which defcend into Lake Superior, and others into the River Bourbon. Lake Superior from Weft Bay to this place is bounded by rocks, except towards the fouth-weft part of the Bay where I firft entered it, there it was tolerably level.

At the Grand Portage is a fmall bay, before the entrance of which lies an ifland that intercepts the dreary and uninterrupted view over the Lake which otherwife would have prefented itfelf, and makes the bay ferene and pleafant. Here I met a large party of the Killiftinoe and Affinipoil Indians, with their refpective kings and their families. They were come to this place in order to meet the traders from Michillimackinac, who make this their road to the north-weft. From them I received the following account of the Lakes that lie to the north-weft of Lake Superior.

Lake Bourbon, the moft northern of thefe yet difcovered, received its name from the French traders who accompanied a party of Indians to Hudfon's Bay fome years ago ; and was thus denominated by them in honour of the royal family of France. It is compofed of the waters of the Bourbon River, which, as I have before obferved, rifes a great way to the fouthward, not far from the northern heads of the Miffiffippi.

This lake is about eighty miles in length, north and fouth, and is nearly circular. It has no very large iflands on it. The land on the eaftern fide is very good; and to the fouth-weft there are fome mountains: in many other parts there are barren plains, bogs and moraffes. Its latitude is between fifty-two and fifty-four degrees north, and it lies nearly fouth-weft from Hud-

fon's

son's Bay. As through its northern situation the weather there is extremely cold, only a few animals are to be found in the country that borders on it. They gave me but an indifferent account either of the beasts, birds, or fishes. There are indeed some buffaloes of a small size which are fat and good about the latter end of summer, with a few moose and carribboo deer; however this deficiency is made up by the furs of every sort that are to be met with in great plenty around the lake. The timber growing here is chiefly fir, cedar, spruce, and some maple.

Lake Winnepeek, or as the French write it Lac Ouinipique, which lies nearest to the foregoing, is composed of the same waters. It is in length about two hundred miles north and south; its breadth has never been properly ascertained, but is supposed to be about one hundred miles in its widest part. This lake is very full of islands; these are, however, of no great magnitude. Many considerable rivers empty themselves into it, which, as yet, are not distinguished by any names. The waters are stored with fish, such as trout and sturgeon, and also with others of a smaller kind peculiar to these lakes.

The land on the south-west part of it is very good, especially about the entrance of a large branch of the River Bourbon, which flows from the south-west. On this river there is a factory that was built by the French, called Fort la Reine, to which the traders from Michillimackinac resort to trade with the Assinipoils and Killistinoes. To this place the Mahahs, who inhabit a country two hundred and fifty miles south-west, come also to trade with them; and bring great quantities of Indian corn, to exchange for knives, tomahawks, and other articles. Those people are supposed to dwell on some of the branches of the River of the West.

Lake Winnepeek has on the north-east some mountains, and on the east many barren plains. The maple or sugar tree grows here in great plenty, and there is likewise gathered an amazing quantity of rice, which proves that grain will flourish in these northern climates as well as in warmer. Buffaloes, carriboo, and moose deer, are numerous in these parts. The buffaloes of this country differ from those that are found more to the south only in size; the former being much smaller: just as the black cattle of the northern parts of Great-Britain differ from English oxen.

On the waters that fall into this Lake, the neighbouring nations take great numbers of excellent furs. Some of these they carry to the factories and settlements belonging to the Hudson's Bay Company, situated above the entrance of the Bourbon River; but this they do with reluctance on several accounts; for some of the Assinipoils and Killistinoes, who usually traded with the Company's servants, told me, that if they could be sure of a constant supply of goods from Michillimackinac, they would not trade any where else. They shewed me some cloth and other

articles

articles that they had purchased at Hudson's Bay, with which they were much dissatisfied, thinking they had been greatly imposed upon in the barter.

Allowing that their accounts were true, I could not help joining in their opinion. But this dissatisfaction might probably proceed, in a great measure, from the intrigues of the Canadian traders: for whilst the French were in possession of Michillimackinac, having acquired a thorough knowledge of the trade of the north-west countries, they were employed on that account, after the reduction of Canada, by the English traders there, in the establishment of this trade with which they were themselves quite unacquainted. One of the methods they took to withdraw these Indians from their attachment to the Hudson's Bay Company, and to engage their good opinion in behalf of their new employers, was by depreciating on all occasions the Company's goods, and magnifying the advantages that would arise to them from trafficking entirely with the Canadian traders. In this they too well succeeded, and from this, doubtless, did the dissatisfaction the Assinipoils and Killistinoes expressed to me, partly proceed. But another reason augmented it; and this was the length of their journey to the Hudson's Bay factories, which, they informed me, took them up three months, during the summer heats to go and return, and from the smallness of their canoes they could not carry more than a third of the beavers they killed. So that it is not to be wondered at, that these Indians should wish to have traders come to reside among them. It is true that the parts they inhabit are within the limits of the Hudson's Bay territories; but the Company must be under the necessity of winking at an encroachment of this kind, as the Indians would without doubt protect the traders when among them. Besides, the passports granted to the traders that go from Michillimackinac give them liberty to trade to the north-west about Lake Superior; by which is meant Fort La Reine, Lake Winnepeek, or any other parts of the waters of the Bourbon River, where the Couriers de Bois, or Traders, may make it most convenient to reside.

Lac du Bois is commonly termed by the French in their maps, or in English the Lake of the Wood, is so called from the multiplicity of wood growing on its banks; such as oaks, pines, firs, spruce, &c. This Lake lies still higher upon a branch of the River Bourbon, and nearly east from the south end of Lake Winnepeek. It is of great depth in some places. Its length from east to west about seventy miles, and its greatest breadth about forty miles. It has but few islands, and these of no great magnitude. The fishes, fowls, and quadrupeds that are found near it, vary but little from those of the other two lakes. A few of the Killistinoe Indians sometimes encamp on the borders of it to fish and hunt.

This Lake lies in the communication between Lake Superior, and the Lakes Winnepeek and Bourbon. Its waters are not esteemed

esteemed quite so pure as those of the other lakes, it having, in many places, a muddy bottom.

Lac La Pluye, so called by the French, in English the Rainy Lake, is supposed to have acquired this name from the first travellers, that passed over it, meeting with an uncommon deal of rain; or, as some have affirmed, from a mist like rain, occasioned by a perpendicular water-fall that empties itself into a river which lies to the south-west.

This Lake appears to be divided by an isthmus, near the middle, into two parts: the west part is called the Great Rainy Lake, the east, the Little Rainy Lake, as being the least division. It lies a few miles farther to the eastward, on the same branch of the Bourbon, than the last-mentioned Lake. It is in general very shallow in its depth. The broadest part of it is not more than twenty miles, its length, including both, about three hundred miles. In the west part the water is very clear and good; and some excellent fish are taken in it. A great many fowl resort here at the fall of the year. Moose deer are to be found in great plenty, and likewise the carriboo; whose skin for breeches or gloves exceeds by far any other to be met with in North-America. The land on the borders of this Lake is esteemed in some places very good, but rather too thickly covered with wood. Here reside a considerable band of the Chipéways.

Eastward from this Lake lie several small ones, which extend in a string to the great carrying place, and from thence into Lake Superior. Between these little Lakes are several carrying places, which renders the trade to the north-west difficult to accomplish, and exceedingly tedious, as it takes two years to make one voyage from Michillimackinac to these parts.

Red Lake is a comparatively small lake at the head of a branch of the Bourbon River, which is called by some Red River. Its form is nearly round, and about sixty miles in circumference. On one side of it is a tolerable large island, close by which a small river enters. It bears almost south-east both from Lake Winnepeek and from Lake du Bois. The parts adjacent are very little known, or frequented, even by the savages themselves.

Not far from this Lake, a little to the south-west, is another called White Bear Lake, which is nearly about the size of the last mentioned. The waters that compose this Lake are the most northern of any that supply the Mississippi, and may be called with propriety its most remote source. It is fed by two or three small rivers, or rather large brooks.

A few miles from it, to the south-east, are a great number of small lakes, none of which are more than ten miles in circumference, that are called the Thousand Lakes In the adjacent country is reckoned the finest hunting for furs of any on this continent; the Indians who hunt here seldom returning without having their canoes loaded as deep as they can swim.

Having

Having juſt before obſerved that this Lake is the utmoſt northern ſource of the Miſſiſſippi, I ſhall here further remark, that before this river enters the Gulph of Mexico, it has not run leſs, through all its meanderings, than three thouſand miles; or, in a ſtrait line from north to ſouth, about twenty degrees, which is nearly fourteen hundred Engliſh miles.

Theſe Indians informed me, that to the north-weſt of Lake Winnepeek lies another, whoſe circumference vaſtly exceeded any they had given me an account of. They deſcribe it as much larger than Lake Superior. But as it appears to be ſo far to the north-weſt, I ſhould imagine that it was not a lake, but rather the Archipelago or broken waters that form the communication between Hudſon's Bay and the northern parts of the Pacific Ocean.

There are an infinite number of ſmall lakes, on the more weſtern parts of the weſtern head-branches of the Miſſiſſippi, as well between theſe and Lake Winnepeck, but none of them are large enough to ſuppoſe either of them to be the lake or waters meant by the Indians.

They likewiſe informed me, that ſome of the northern branches of the Meſſorie and the ſouthern branches of the St. Pierre have a communication with each other, except for a mile; over which they carry their canoes. And by what I could learn from them, this is the road they take when their war parties make their excurſions upon the Pawnees' and Pawnawnees, nations inhabiting ſome branches of the Meſſorie River. In the country belonging to theſe people it is ſaid, that Mandrakes are frequently found, a ſpecies of root reſembling human beings of both ſexes; and that theſe are more perfect than ſuch as are diſcovered about the Nile in Nether-Ethiopia.

A little to the north-weſt of the heads of the Meſſorie and the St. Pierre, the Indians further told me, that there was a nation rather ſmaller and whiter than the neighbouring tribes, who cultivate the ground, and, (as far as I could gather from their expreſſions) in ſome meaſure, the arts. To this account they added that ſome of the nations, who inhabit thoſe parts that lie to the weſt of the Shining Mountains, have gold ſo plenty among them that they make their moſt common utenſils of it. Theſe mountains (which I ſhall deſcribe more particularly hereafter) divide the waters that fall into the South Sea from thoſe that run into the Atlantic.

The people dwelling near them are ſuppoſed to be ſome of the different tribes that were tributary to the Mexican kings, and who fled from their native country, to ſeek an aſylum in theſe parts, about the time of the conqueſt of Mexico by the Spaniards, more than two centuries ago.

As ſome confirmation of this ſuppoſition it is remarked, that they have choſen the moſt interior parts for their retreat, being ſtill prepoſſeſſed with a notion that the ſea-coaſts have been infeſted ever ſince with monſters vomiting fire, and hurling about

thunder

thunder and lightning; from whose bowels issued men, who, with unseen instruments, or by the power of magick, killed the harmless Indians at an astonishing distance. From such as these, their fore-fathers (according to a tradition among them that still remains unimpaired) fled to the retired abodes they now inhabit. For as they found that the floating monsters, which had thus terrified them could not approach the land, and that those who had descended from their sides did not care to make excursions to any considerable distance from them, they formed a resolution to betake themselves to some country, that lay far from the sea-coasts, where only they could be secure from such diabolical enemies. They accordingly set out with their families, and after a long peregrination, settled themselves near these mountains, where they concluded they had found a place of perfect security.

The Winnebagoes, dwelling on the Fox River (whom I have already treated of) are likewise supposed to be some strolling band from the Mexican countries. But they are able to give only an imperfect account of their original residence. They say they formerly came a great way from the westward, and were driven by wars to take refuge among the Naudowessies; but as they are entirely ignorant of the arts, or of the value of gold, it is rather to be supposed, that they were driven from their ancient settlements by the above-mentioned emigrants, as they passed on towards their present habitation.

These suppositions, however, may want confirmation; for the smaller tribes of Indians are subject to such various alterations in their places of abode, from the wars they are continually engaged in, that it is almost impossible to ascertain, after half a century, the original situation of any of them.

That range of mountains, of which the Shining Mountains are a part, begin at Mexico, and continuing northward on the back, or to the east of California, separate the waters of those numerous rivers that fall either into the Gulph of Mexico, or the Gulph of California. From thence continuing their course still northward, between the sources of the Missisippi and the rivers that run into the South Sea, they appear to end in about forty-seven or forty-eight degrees of north-latitude; where a number of rivers arise, and empty themselves either into the South Sea, into Hudson's Bay, or into the waters that communicate between these two seas.

Among these mountains, those that lie to the west of the River St. Pierre, are called the Shining Mountains, from an infinite number of chrystal stones, of an amazing size, with which they are covered, and which, when the sun shines full upon them, sparkle so as to be seen at a very great distance.

This extraordinary range of mountains is calculated to be more than three thousand miles in length, without any very considerable intervals, which I believe surpasses any thing of the kind in the other quarters of the globe. Probably in future ages

ages they may be found to contain more riches in their bowels, than those of Indostan and Malabar, or that are produced on the golden coast of Guinea; nor will I except even the Peruvian mines. To the west of these mountains, when explored by future Columbuses or Raleighs, may be found other lakes, rivers, and countries, full fraught with all the necessaries or luxuries of life; and where future generations may find an asylum, whether driven from their country by the ravages of lawless tyrants, or by religious persecutions, or reluctantly leaving it to remedy the inconveniences arising from a superabundant increase of inhabitants; whether, I say, impelled by these, or allured by hopes of commercial advantages, there is little doubt but their expectations will be fully gratified in these rich and unexhausted climes.

But to return to the Assinipoils and Killistinoes, whom I left at the Grand Portage, and from whom I received the foregoing account of the lakes that lie to the north-west of this place.

The traders we expected being later this season than usual, and our numbers very considerable, for there were more than three hundred of us, the stock of provisions we had brought with us was nearly exhausted, and we waited with impatience for their arrival.

One day, whilst we were all expressing our wishes for this desirable event, and looking from an eminence in hopes of seeing them come over the lake, the chief priest belonging to the band of the Killistinoes told us, that he would endeavour to obtain a conference with the Great Spirit, and know from him when the traders would arrive. I paid little attention to this declaration, supposing that it would be productive of some juggling trick, just sufficiently covered to deceive the ignorant Indians. But the king of that tribe telling me that this was chiefly undertaken by the priest to alleviate my anxiety, and at the same time to convince me how much interest he had with the Great Spirit I thought it necessary to restrain my animadversions on his design.

The following evening was fixed upon for this spiritual conference. When every thing had been properly prepared, the king came to me and led me to a capacious tent, the covering of which was drawn up, so as to render what was transacting within visible to those who stood without. We found the tent surrounded by a great number of the Indians, but we readily gained admission, and seated ourselves on skins laid on the ground for that purpose.

In the center I observed that there was a place of an oblong shape, which was composed of stakes stuck in the ground, with intervals between, so as to form a kind of chest or coffin, large enough to contain the body of a man. These were of a middle size, and placed at such a distance from each other, that whatever lay within them was readily to be discerned. The tent was perfectly illuminated by a great number of torches made splinters cut from the pine or birch tree, which the Indians held in their hands.

In a few minutes the prieſt entered; when an amazing large elk's skin being ſpread on the ground, juſt at my feet, he laid himſelf down upon it, after having ſtript himſelf of every garment except that which he wore cloſe about his middle. Being now proſtrate on his back, he firſt laid hold of one ſide of the skin, and folded it over him, and then the other; leaving only his head uncovered. This was no ſooner done, than two of the young men who ſtood by, took about forty yards of ſtrong cord, made alſo of an elk's hide, and rolled it tight round his body, ſo that he was completely ſwathed within the skin Being thus bound up like an Egyptian Mummy, one took him by the heels, and the other by the head and lifted him over the pales into the incloſure. I could alſo now diſcern him as plain as I had hitherto done, and I took care not to turn my eyes a moment from the object before me, that I might the more readily detect the artifice; for ſuch I doubted not but that it would turn out to be.

The prieſt had not lain in this ſituation more than a few ſeconds, when he began to mutter. This he continued to do for ſome time, and then by degrees grew louder and louder, till at length he ſpoke articulately; however what he uttered was in ſuch a mixed jargon of the Chipeway, Ottowaw, and Killiſtinoe languages, that I could underſtand but very little of it. Having continued in this tone for a conſiderable while, he at laſt exerted his voice to its utmoſt pitch, ſometimes raving, and ſometimes praying, till he had worked himſelf into ſuch an agitation, that he foamed at his mouth.

After having remained near three quarters of an hour in the place, and continued his vociferation with unabated vigor, he ſeemed to be quite exhauſted, and remained ſpeechleſs. But in an inſtant he ſprung upon his feet, notwithſtanding at the time he was put in, it appeared impoſſible for him to move either his legs or arms, and ſhaking off his covering, as quick as if the bands with which it had been bound were burned aſunder, he began to addreſs thoſe who ſtood around, in a firm and audible voice. " My brothers," ſaid he, " the Great Spirit has deign-
" ed to hold a Talk with his ſervant at my earneſt requeſt. He
" has not, indeed, told me when the perſons we expect, will be
" here; but to-morrow, ſoon after the ſun has reached his
" higheſt point in the heavens, a canoe will arrive, and the
" people in that will inform us when the traders will come."

Having ſaid this, he ſtepped out of the incloſure, and after he had put on his robes, diſmiſſed the aſſembly. I own I was greatly aſtoniſhed at what I had ſeen; but as I obſeved that every eye in the company was fixed on me with a view to diſcover my ſentiments, I carefully concealed every emotion.

The next day the ſun ſhone bright, and long before noon all the Indians were gathered together on the eminence that overlooked

looked the lake. The old king came to me and asked me, whether I had so much confidence in what the priest had foretold, as to join his people on the hill, and wait for the completion of it? I told him I was at a loss what opinion to form of the prediction, but that I would readily attend him. On this we walked together to the place where the others were assembled. Every eye was again fixed by turns on me and on the lake; when just as the sun had reached his zenith, agreeable to what the priest had foretold, a canoe came round a point of land about a league distant. The Indians no sooner beheld it, than they set up an universal shout, and by their looks seemed to triumph in the interest their priest thus evidently had with the Great Spirit.

In less than an hour the canoe reached the shore, when I attended the king and chiefs to receive those who were on board. As soon as the men were landed, we walked all together to the king's tent, when, according to their invariable custom, we began to smoke; and this we did, notwithstanding our impatience to know the tidings they brought, without asking any questions; for the Indians are the most deliberate people in the world. However, after some trivial conversation, the king enquired of them, whether they had seen any thing of the traders? The men replied that they had parted from them a few days before, and that they proposed being here the second day from the present. They accordingly arrived at that time greatly to our satisfaction, but more particularly so to that of the Indians, who found by this event the importance both of their priest and of their nation, greatly augmented in the sight of a stranger.

This story I acknowledge appears to carry with it marks of great credulity in the relator. But no one is less tinctured with that weakness than myself. The circumstances of it, I own, are of a very extraordinary nature; however, as I can vouch for their being free from either exaggeration or misrepresentation, being myself a cool and dispassionate observer of them all, I thought it necessary to give them to the public. And this I do without wishing to mislead the judgment of my readers, or to make any superstitious impressions on their minds, but leaving them to draw from it what conclusions they please.

I have already observed that the Assinipoils, with a part of whom I met here, are a revolted band of the Naudowessies; who on account of some real or imagined grievances, for the Indians in general are very tenacious of their liberty, had separated themselves from their countrymen, and fought for freedom at the expence of their ease. For the country they now inhabit about the borders of Lake Winnepeek, being much farther north, is not near so fertile or agreeable as that they have relinquished. They still retain the language and manners of their former associates.

The Killistinoes, now the neighbours and allies of the Assinipoils, for they also dwell near the same lake, and on the waters

ters of the River Bourbon, appear to have been originally a tribe of the Chipéways, as they speak their language, though in a different dialect. Their nation confifts of about three or four hundred warriors, and they feem to be a hardy brave people. I have already given an account of their country when I treated of Lake Winnepeek. As they refide within the limits of Hudfon's Bay, they generally trade at the factories which belong to that company, but, for the reafons mentioned before, they frequently come to the place where I happened to join them, in order to meet the traders from Michillimackinac.

The anxiety I had felt on account of the traders delay, was not much alleviated by their arrival. I again found my expectations difappointed, for I was not able to procure the goods I wanted from any of them. I was therefore obliged to give over my defigns, and return to the place from whence I firft began my extenfive circuit. I accordingly took leave of the old king of the Killiftinoes, with the chiefs of both bands, and departed. This prince was upwards of fixty years of age, tall and flightly made, but he carried himfelf very erect. He was of a courteous, affable difpofition, and treated me, as did all the chiefs, with great civility.

I obferved that this people ftill continued a cuftom, that appeared to have been univerfal before any of them became acquainted with the manners of the Europeans, that of complimenting ftrangers with the company of their wives; and this is not only practifed by the lower ranks, but by the chiefs themfelves, who efteem it the greateft proof of courtefy they can give a ftranger.

The beginning of October, after having coafted round the north and eaft borders of Lake Superior, I arrived at Cadot's Fort, which adjoins to the Falls of St. Marie, and is fituated near the fouth-weft corner of it.

Lake Superior, formerly termed the Upper Lake from its northern fituation, is fo called on account of its being fuperior in magnitude,to any of the Lakes on that vaft continent. It might juftly be termed the Cafpian of America, and is fuppofed to be the largeft body of frefh water on the globe. Its circumference, according to the French charts, is about fifteen hundred miles; but I believe, that if it was coafted round, and the utmoft extent of every bay taken, it would exceed fixteen hundred.

After I firft entered it from Goddard's River on the weft Bay, I coafted near twelve hundred miles of the north and eaft fhores of it, and obferved that the greateft part of that extenfive tract was bounded by rocks and uneven ground. The water in general appeared to lie on a bed of rocks. When it was calm, and the fun fhone bright, I could fit in my canoe, where the depth was upwards of fix fathoms, and plainly fee huge piles of ftone at the bottom, of different fhapes, fome of which appeared as if they were hewn. The water at this time was as pure and tranfparent as air; and my canoe feemed as if it hung fufpended ed in that element. It was impossible to look attentively through this limpid medium at the rocks below, without finding, before many minutes were elapsed, your head swim, and your eyes no longer able to behold the dazzling scene.

I discovered also by accident another extraordinary property in the waters of this lake. Though it was in the month of July that I passed over it, and the surface of the water, from the heat of the superambient air, impregnated with no small degree of warmth, yet on letting down a cup to the depth of about a fathom, the water drawn from thence was so excessively cold, that it had the same effect when received into the mouth as ice.

The situation of this Lake is variously laid down; but from the most exact observations I could make, it lies between forty-six and fifty degrees of north-latitude, and between eighty-four and ninety-three degrees of west longitude from the meridian of London.

There are many islands in this lake, two of which are very large; and if the land of them is proper for cultivation, there appears to be sufficient to form on each a considerable province; especially on Isle Royal, which cannot be less than an hundred miles long, and in many places forty broad. But there is no way at present of ascertaining the exact length or breadth of either. Even the French, who always kept a small schooner on this lake, whilst they were in possession of Canada, by which they could have made this discovery, have only acquired a slight knowledge of the external parts of these islands; at least they have never published any account of the internal parts of them, that I could get intelligence of.

Nor was I able to discover from any of the conversations which I held with the neighbouring Indians, that they had ever made any settlements on them, or even landed there in their hunting excursions. From what I could gather by their discourse, they suppose them to have been, from their first information, the residence of the Great Spirit; and relate many ridiculous stories of enchantment and magical tricks that had been experienced by such as were obliged through stress of weather to take shelter on them.

One of the Chipéway chiefs told me, that some of their people being once driven on the island of Mauropas, which lies towards the north-east part of the lake, found on it large quantities of a heavy shining yellow sand, that from their description must have been gold dust. Being struck with the beautiful appearance of it, in the morning, when they re-entered their canoe, they attempted to bring some away; but a spirit of an amazing size, according to their account sixty feet in height, strode in the water after them, and commanded them to deliver back what they had taken away. Terrified at his gigantic stature, and seeing that he had nearly overtaken them, they were glad to restore their shining treasure; on which they were suffered to depart without further molestation. Since this incident, no Indian that has ever heard of it, will venture near the same haunted coast. Besides this, they recounted to me many other stories of these islands, equally fabulous.

The country on the north and east parts of Lake Superior is very mountainous and barren. The weather being intensely cold in the winter, and the sun having but little power in the summer, vegetation there is very slow; and consequently but little fruit is to be found on its shore. It however produces some few species in great abundance. Whirtleberries of an uncommon size, and fine flavour, grow on the mountains near the lake in amazing quantities; as do black currants and goosberries in the same luxuriant manner.

But the fruit which exceeds all the others, is a berry resembling a rasberry in its manner of growth, but of a lighter red, and much larger; its taste is far more delicious than the fruit I have compared it too, notwithstanding that it is so highly esteemed in Europe: it grows on a shrub of the nature of a vine, with leaves similar to those of the grape; and I am persuaded that was it transplanted into a warmer and more kindly climate, it would prove a most rare and delicious fruit.

Two very large rivers empty themselves into this lake, on the north and north-east side; one is called the Nipegon River, or, as the French pronounce it, the Allanipegon, which leads to a band of the Chipeways, inhabiting a lake of the same name, and the other is termed the Michipicooton River, the source of which is situated towards James's Bay, from whence there is but a short carriage to another river, which empties itself into that bay, at a fort belonging to the company. It was by this passage that a party of French from Michillimackinac invaded the settlements of that society in the reign of Queen Anne. Having taken and destroyed their forts, they brought the cannon which they found in them to the fortress from whence they had issued; these were small brass pieces, and remain there to this present time; having, through the usual revolutions of fortune, returned to the possession of their former masters.

Not far from the Nipegon is a small river, that just before it enters the lake, has a perpendicular fall from the top of a mountain, of more than six hundred feet. Being very narrow, it appears at a distance like a white garter suspended in the air.

A few Indians inhabit round the eastern borders of this lake, supposed to be the remains of the Algonkins, who formerly possessed this country, but who have been nearly extirpated by the Iroquois of Canada. Lake Superior has near forty rivers that fall into it, some of which are of a considerable size. On the south-side of it is a remarkable point or cape, of about sixty miles in length, called Point Chegomegan. It might as properly be termed a peninsula, as it is nearly separated from the continent, on the east side, by a narrow bay that extends from east to west. Canoes have but a short portage across the isthmus,

mus, whereas if they coaſt it round, the voyage is more than an hundred miles.

About that diſtance to the weſt of the cape juſt deſcribed, a conſiderable river falls into the lake, the head of which is compoſed of a great aſſemblage of ſmall ſtreams. This river is remarkable for the abundance of virgin copper that is found on and near its banks. A metal which is met with alſo in ſeveral other places on this coaſt. I obſerved that many of the ſmall iſlands, particularly thoſe on the eaſtern ſhores, were covered with copper ore. They appeared like beds of copperas, of which many tuns lay in a ſmall ſpace.

A company of adventurers from England began, ſoon after the conqueſt of Canada, to bring away ſome of this metal, but the diſtracted ſituation of affairs in America has obliged them to relinquiſh their ſcheme. It might in future times be made a very advantageous trade, as the metal, which coſts nothing on the ſpot, and requires but little expence to get it on board, could be conveyed in boats or canoes through the Falls of St. Marie, to the Iſle of St. Joſeph, which lies at the bottom of the Straights near the entrance into Lake Huron; from thence it might be put on board larger veſſels, and in them tranſported acroſs that lake to the Falls of Niagara; there being carried by land acroſs the Portage, it might be conveyed without much more obſtruction to Quebec. The cheapneſs and eaſe with which any quantity of it may be procured, will make up for the length of way that is neceſſary to tranſport it before it reaches the ſea coaſt, and enable the proprietors to ſend it to foreign markets on as good terms as it can be exported from other countries.

Lake Superior abounds with a variety of fiſh, the principal and beſt are the trout and ſturgeon, which may be caught at almoſt any ſeaſon in the greateſt abundance. The trouts in general weigh about twelve pounds, but ſome are caught that exceed fifty. Beſides theſe, a ſpecies of white fiſh is taken in great quantities here, that reſemble a ſhad in their ſhape, but they are rather thicker, and leſs bony; they weigh about four pounds each, and are of a delicious taſte. The beſt way of catching theſe fiſh is with a net; but the trout might be taken at all times with the hook. There are likewiſe many ſorts of ſmaller fiſh in great plenty here, and which may be taken with eaſe; among theſe is a ſort reſembling a herring, that are generally made uſe of as a bait for the trout. Very ſmall crabs, not larger than half a crown piece, are found both in this and Lake Michegan.

This Lake is as much affected by ſtorms as the Atlantic Ocean; the waves run as high, and are equally as dangerous to ſhips. It diſcharges its waters from the ſouth-eaſt corner, through the Straights of St. Marie. At the upper end of theſe Straights ſtands a fort that receives its name from them, commanded by Monſ. Cadot, a French Canadian, who being proprietor of the ſoil, is ſtill permitted to keep poſſeſſion of it. Near this fort is a very strong rapid, against which, though it is impossible for canoes to afcend, yet when conducted by careful pilots, they might pafs down without danger.

Though Lake Superior, as I have before obferved, is fupplied by near forty rivers, many of which are confiderable ones, yet it does not appear that one tenth part of the waters which are conveyed into it by thefe rivers, are carried off at this evacuation. How fuch a fuperabundance of waters can be difpofed of, as it muft certainly be by fome means or other, without which the circumference of the lake would be continually enlarging, I know not: that it does not empty itfelf, as the Mediterranean fea is fuppofed to do, by an under current, which perpetually counteracts that near the furface, is certain; for the ftream which falls over the rock is not more than five or fix feet in depth, and the whole of it paffes on through the Straights into the adjacent lake; nor is it probable that fo great a quantity can be abforbed by exhalations; confequently they muft find a paffage through fome fubterranean cavities, deep, unfathomable, and never to be explored.

The Falls of St. Marie do not defcend perpendicularly as thofe of Niagara or St. Anthony do, but confift of a rapid which continues near three quarters of a mile, over which canoes well piloted might pafs.

At the bottom of thefe Falls, Nature has formed a moft commodious ftation for catching the fifh which are to be found there in immenfe quantities. Perfons ftanding on the rocks that lie adjacent to it, may take with dipping nets, about the months of September and October, the white fifh before mentioned; at that feafon, together with feveral other fpecies, they croud up to this fpot in fuch amazing fhoals, that enough may be taken to fupply, when properly cured, thoufands of inhabitants throughout the year.

The Straights of St. Marie are about forty miles long, bearing fouth-eaft, but varying much in their breadth. The current between the Falls and Lake Huron is not fo rapid as might be expected, nor do they prevent the navigation of fhips of burden as far up as the ifland of St. Jofeph.

It has been obferved by travellers that the entrance into Lake Superior, from thefe Straights, affords one of the moft pleafing profpects in the world. The place in which this might be viewed to the greateft advantage, is juft at the opening of the lake, from whence may be feen on the left, many beautiful little iflands that extend a confiderable way before you; and on the right, an agreeable fucceffion of fmall points of land, that project a little way into the water, and contribute, with the iflands, to render this delightful bafon (as it might be termed) calm and fecure from the ravages of thofe tempeftuous winds by which the adjoining lake is frequently troubled.

Lake Huron, into which you now enter from the Straights of St. Marie, is the next in magnitude to Lake Superior. It

lies

lies between forty-two and forty-fix degrees of north latitude, and feventy-nine and eighty-five degrees of weft longitude. Its fhape is nearly triangular, and its circumference about one thoufand miles.

On the north fide of it lies an ifland that is remarkable for being near an hundred miles in length, and no more than eight miles broad. This ifland is known by the name of Manataulin, which fignifies a Place of Spirits, and is confidered by the Indians as facred as thofe already mentioned in Lake Superior.

About the middle of the fouth-weft fide of this lake, is Saganaum Bay. The capes that feparate this bay from the lake, are about eighteen miles diftant from each other; near the middle of the intermediate fpace ftand two iflands, which greatly tend to facilitate the paffage of canoes and fmall veffels, by affording them fhelter, as without this fecurity it would not be prudent to venture acrofs fo wide a fea; and the coafting round the bay would make the voyage long and tedious. This bay is about eighty miles in length, and in general about eighteen or twenty miles broad.

Nearly half way between Saganaum Bay and the north-weft corner of the Lake, lies another, which is termed Thunder Bay. The Indians, who have frequented thefe parts from time immemorial, and every European traveller that has paffed through it, have unanimoufly agreed to call it by this name, on account of the continual thunder they have always obferved here. The bay is about nine miles broad, and the fame in length, and whilft I was paffing over it, which took me up near twenty-four hours, it thundered and lightened during the greateft part of the time to an exceffive degree.

There appeared to be no vifible reafon for this that I could difcover, nor is the country in general fubject to thunder; the hills that ftood around were not of a remarkable height, neither did the external parts of them feem to be covered with any fulphureous fubftance. But as this phænomenon muft originate from fome natural caufe, I conjecture that the fhores of the bay, or the adjacent mountains, are either impregnated with an uncommon quantity of fulphureous matter, or contain fome metal or mineral apt to attract in a great degree, the electrical particles that are hourly borne over them by the paffant clouds. But the folution of this, and thofe other philofophical remarks which cafually occur throughout thefe pages, I leave to the difcuffion of abler heads.

The fifh in Lake Huron are much the fame as thofe in Lake Superior. Some of the land on its banks is very fertile, and proper for cultivation, but in other parts it is fandy and barren. The promontory that feparates this lake from Lake Michegan, is compofed of a vaft plain, upwards of one hundred miles long, but varying in its breadth, being from ten to fifteen miles broad. This tract, as I have before obferved, is divided into almoft an equal portion between the Ottowaw and Chipeway Indians.

At

At the north-east corner this lake has a communication with Lake Michegan, by the Straits of Michillimackinac already described.

I had like to have omitted a very extraordinary circumstance, relative to these Straights. According to observations made by the French, whilst they were in possession of the fort: although there is no diurnal flood or ebb to be perceived in these waters, yet, from an exact attention to their state, a periodical alteration in them has been discovered. It was observed that they arose by gradual, but almost imperceptible degrees till they had reached the height of about three feet. This was accomplished in seven years and a half; and in the same space they as gently decreased, till they had reached their former situation; so that in fifteen years they had completed this inexplicable revolution.

At the time I was there, the truth of these observations could not be confirmed by the English, as they had then been only a few years in possession of the fort; but they all agreed that some alteration in the limits of the Straights was apparent. All these lakes are so affected by the winds, as sometimes to have the appearance of a tide, according as they happen to blow; but this is only temporary and partial.

A great number of the Chipéway Indians live scattered around this Lake, particularly near Saganaum Bay. On its banks are found an amazing quantity of the sand cherries, and in the adjacent country nearly the same fruits as those that grow about the other lakes.

From the Falls of St. Marie I leisurely proceeded back to Michillimackinac, and arrived there the beginning of November 1767, having been fourteen months on this extensive tour, travelled near four thousand miles, and visited twelve nations of Indians lying to the west and north of this place. The winter setting in soon after my arrival, I was obliged to tarry there till the June following, the navigation over Lake Huron for large vessels not being open, on account of the ice, till that time. Meeting here with sociable company, I passed these months very agreeably, and without finding the hours tedious.

One of my chief amusements was that of fishing for trouts. Though the Straights were covered with ice, we found means to make holes through it, and letting down strong lines of fifteen yards in length, to which were fixed three or four hooks baited with the small fish before described, we frequently caught two at a time of forty pounds weight each; but the common size is from ten to twenty pounds. These are most delicious food. The method of preserving them during the three months the winter generally lasts, is by hanging them up in the air; and in one night they will be frozen so hard that they will keep as well as if they were cured with salt.

I have

I have only pointed out in the plan of my travels the circuit I made from my leaving Michillimackinac till I arrived again at that fort. Those countries that lie nearer to the colonies have been so often and so minutely described, that any further account of them would be useless. I shall therefore only give my Readers in the remainder of my journal, as I at first proposed, a description of the other great lakes of Canada, many of which I have navigated over, and relate at the same time a few particular incidents that I trust will not be found inapplicable or unentertaining.

In June 1768 I left Michillimackinac, and returned in the Gladwyn Schooner, a vessel of about eighty tons burthen, over Lake Huron to Lake St. Claire, where we left the ship, and proceeded in boats to Detroit. This lake is about ninety miles in circumference, and by the way of Huron River, which runs from the south corner of Lake Huron, receives the waters of the three great lakes, Superior, Michegan, and Huron. Its form is rather round, and in some places it is deep enough for the navigation of large vessels, but towards the middle of it there is a bar of sand, which prevents those that are loaded from passing over it. Such as are in ballast only may find water sufficient to carry them quite through; the cargoes, however, of such as are freighted must be taken out, and after being transported across the bar in boats, re-shipped again.

The river that runs from Lake St. Claire to Lake Erie (or rather the Straight, for thus it might be termed from its name) is called Detroit, which is in French, the Straight. It runs nearly south, has a gentle current, and depth of water sufficient for ships of considerable burthen. The town of Detroit is situated on the western banks of this river, about nine miles below Lake St. Claire.

Almost opposite on the eastern shore, is the village of the ancient Hurons: a tribe of Indians which have been treated of by so many writers, that adhering to the restrictions I have laid myself under of only describing places and people little known, or incidents that have passed unnoticed by others, I shall omit giving a description of them. A missionary of the order of Carthusian Friars, by permission of the bishop of Canada, resides among them.

The banks of the River Detroit, both above and below these towns, are covered with settlements that extend more than twenty miles; the country being exceedingly fruitful, and proper for the cultivation of wheat, Indian corn, oats and peas. It has also many spots of fine pasturage; but as the inhabitants, who are chiefly French that submitted to the English government, after the conquest of these parts by General Amherst, are more attentive to the Indian trade than to farming, it is but badly cultivated.

The town of Detroit contains upwards of one hundred houses. The streets are somewhat regular, and have a range of very convenient

venient and handsome barracks, with a spacious parade at the south end. On the west side lies the King's garden, belonging to the governor, which is very well laid out and kept in good order. The fortifications of the town consist of a strong stockade, made of round piles, fixed firmly in the ground, and lined with palisades. These are defended by some small bastions, on which are mounted a few indifferent cannon of an inconsiderable size, just sufficient for its defence against the Indians, or an enemy not provided with artillery.

The garrison, in time of peace, consists of two hundred men, commanded by a field officer, who acts as chief magistrate under the governor of Canada. Mr. Turnbull, captain of the 60th regiment, or Royal Americans, was commandant when I happened to be there. This gentleman was deservedly esteemed and respected, both by the inhabitants and traders, for the propriety of his conduct; and I am happy to have an opportunity of thus publickly making my acknowledgments to him for the civilities I received from him during my stay.

In the year 1762, in the month of July, it rained on this town and the parts adjacent, a sulphureous water of the colour and consistence of ink; some of which being collected into bottles, and wrote with appeared perfectly intelligible on the paper, and answered every purpose of that useful liquid. Soon after, the Indian wars already spoken of, broke out in these parts. I mean not to say that this incident was ominous of them, notwithstanding it is well known that innumerable well attested instances of extraordinary phænomena happening before extraordinary events, have been recorded in almost every age by historians of veracity; I only relate the circumstances as a fact of which I was informed by many persons of undoubted probity, and leave my readers, as I have hitherto done, to draw their own conclusions from it.

Pontiac, under whom the party that surprized Fort Michillimackinac, as related in the former part of this work, acted, was an enterprizing chief or head-warrior of the Miames. During the late war between the English and the French, he had been a steady friend to the latter, and continued his inveteracy to the former, even after peace had been concluded between these two nations. Unwilling to put an end to the depredations he had been so long engaged in, he collected an army of confederate Indians, consisting of the nations before enumerated, with an intention to renew the war. However, instead of openly attacking the English settlements, he laid a scheme for taking by surprize those forts on the extremities which they had lately gained possession of.

How well the party he detached to take Fort Michillimackinac succeeded, the reader already knows. To get into his hands Detroit, a place of greater consequence, and much better guarded, required greater resolution, and more consummate art. He of course took the management of this expedition on himself,

himself, and drew near it with the principal body of his troops. He was however prevented from carrying his designs into execution by an apparently trivial and unforeseen circumstance. On such does the fate of mighty Empires frequently depend!

The town of Detroit, when Pontiac formed his plan, was garrisoned by about three hundred men, commanded by Major Gladwyn, a gallant officer. As at that time every appearance of war was at an end, and the Indians seemed to be on a friendly footing, Pontiac approached the Fort, without exciting any suspicions in the breast of the governor or the inhabitants. He encamped at a little distance from it, and sent to let the commandant know that he was come to trade; and being desirous of brightening the chain of peace between the English and his nation, desired that he and his chiefs might be admitted to hold a council with him. The governor still unsuspicious, and not in the least doubting the sincerity of the Indians, granted their general's request, and fixed on the next morning for their reception.

The evening of that day, an Indian woman who had been employed by Major Gladwyn, to make him a pair of Indian shoes, out of curious elk-skin, brought them home. The Major was so pleased with them, that, intending these as a present for a friend, he ordered her to take the remainder back, and make it into others for himself. He then directed his servant to pay her for those she had done, and dismissed her. The woman went to the door that led to the street, but no further; she there loitered about as if she had not finished the business on which she came. A servant at length observed her, and asked her why she staid there; she gave him, however, no answer.

Some short time after, the governor himself saw her; and enquired of his servant what occasioned her stay. Not being able to get a satisfactory answer, he ordered the woman to be called in. When she came into his presence he desired to know what was the reason of her loitering about, and not hastening home before the gates were shut, that she might complete in due time the work he had given her to do. She told him, after much hesitation, that as he had always behaved with great goodness towards her, she was unwilling to take away the remainder of the skin, because he put so great a value upon it; and yet had not been able to prevail upon herself to tell him so. He then asked her, why she was more reluctant to do so now, than she had been when she made the former pair. With increased reluctance she answered, that she never should be able to bring them back.

His curiosity being now excited, he insisted on her disclosing to him the secret that seemed to be struggling in her bosom for utterance. At last, on receiving a promise that the intelligence she was about to give him should not turn to her prejudice, and that if it appeared to be beneficial she should be rewarded for it, she informed him, that at the council to be held with the Indians

dians the following day, Pontiac and his chiefs intended to murder him; and, after having maſſacred the garriſon and inhabitants, to plunder the town. That for this purpoſe all the chiefs who were to be admitted into the council-room had cut their guns ſhort, ſo that they could conceal them under their blankets; with which, at a ſignal given by their general, on delivering the belt, they were all to riſe up, and inſtantly to fire on him and his attendants. Having effected this, they were immediately to ruſh into the town, where they would find themſelves ſupported by a great number of their warriors, that were to come into it during the ſitting of the council, under pretence of trading, but privately armed in the ſame manner. Having gained from the woman every neceſſary particular relative to the plot, and alſo the means by which ſhe acquired a knowledge of them, he diſmiſſed her with injunctions of ſecrecy, and a promiſe of fulfilling on his part with punctuality the engagements he had entered into.

The intelligence the governor had juſt received, gave him great uneaſineſs; and he immediately conſulted the officer who was next to him in command on the ſubject. But that gentleman conſidering the information as a ſtory invented for ſome artful purpoſes, adviſed him to pay no attention to it. This concluſion however had happily no weight with him. He thought it prudent to conclude it to be true, till he was convinced that it was not ſo; and therefore, without revealing his ſuſpicions to any other perſon, he took every needful precaution that the time would admit of. He walked round the fort during the whole night, and ſaw himſelf that every centinel was on duty, and every weapon of defence in proper order.

As he traverſed the ramparts which lay neareſt to the Indian camp, he heard them in high feſtivity, and, little imagining that their plot was diſcovered, probably pleaſing themſelves with the anticipation of their ſucceſs. As ſoon as the morning dawned, he ordered all the garriſon under arms; and then imparting his apprehenſions to a few of the principal officers, gave them ſuch directions as he thought neceſſary. At the ſame time he ſent round to all the traders, to inform them, that as it was expected a great number of Indians would enter the town that day, who might be inclined to plunder, he deſired they would have their arms ready, and repel every attempt of that kind.

About ten o'clock, Pontiac and his chiefs arrived; and were conducted to the council-chamber, where the governor and his principal officers, each with piſtols in their belts, awaited his arrival. As the Indians paſſed on, they could not help obſerving that a greater number of troops than uſual were drawn up on the parade, or marching about. No ſooner were they entered, and ſeated on the ſkins prepared for them, than Pontiac aſked the governor on what occaſion his young men, meaning the ſoldiers, were thus drawn up, and parading the ſtreets. He

received

received for answer, that it was only intended to keep them perfect in their exercise.

The Indian chief-warrior now began his speech, which contained the strongest professions of friendship and good-will towards the English; and when he came to the delivery of the belt of wampum, the particular mode of which, according to the woman's information, was to be the signal for his chiefs to fire, the governor and all his attendants drew their swords half-way out of their scabbards; and the soldiers at the same instant made a clattering with their arms before the doors, which had been purposely left open. Pontiac, though one of the boldest of men, immediately turned pale, and trembled; and instead of giving the belt in the manner proposed, delivered it according to the usual way. His chiefs, who had impatiently expected the signal, looked at each other with astonishment, but continued quiet, waiting the result.

The governor in his turn made a speech; but instead of thanking the great warrior for the professions of friendship he had just uttered, he accused him of being a traitor. He told him that the English, who knew every thing, were convinced of his treachery and villainous designs; and as a proof that they were well acquainted with his most secret thoughts and intentions, he stepped towards the Indian chief that sat nearest to him, and drawing aside his blanket discovered the shortened firelock. This entirely disconcerted the Indians, and frustrated their design.

He then continued to tell them, that as he had given his word at the time they desired an audience, that their persons should be safe, he would hold his promise inviolable, though they so little deserved it. However he advised them to make the best of their way out of the fort, lest his young men, on being acquainted with their treacherous purposes, should cut every one of them to pieces.

Pontiac endeavoured to contradict the accusation, and to make excuses for his suspicious conduct; but the governor, satisfied of the falsity of his protestations, would not listen to him. The Indians immediately left the fort, but instead of being sensible of the governor's generous behaviour, they threw off the mask, and the next day made a regular attack upon it.

Major Gladwyn has not escaped censure for this mistaken lenity; for probably had he kept a few of the principal chiefs prisoners, whilst he had them in his power, he might have been able to have brought the whole confederacy to terms, and have brought the whole confederacy to terms, and have prevented a war. But he atoned for this oversight, by the gallant defence he made for more than a year, amidst a variety of discouragements.

During that period some very smart skirmishes happened between the besiegers and the garrison, of which the following

was

was the principal and most bloody: Captain Delzel, a brave officer, prevailed on the governor to give him the command of about two hundred men, and to permit him to attack the enemy's camp. This being complied with, he sallied from the town before day-break; but Pontiac, receiving from some of his swift-footed warriors, who were constantly employed in watching the motions of the garrison, timely intelligence of their design, he collected together the choicest of his troops, and met the detachment at some distance from his camp, near a place since called Bloody-Bridge.

As the Indians were vastly superior in numbers to captain Delzel's party, he was soon over-powered and driven back. Being now nearly surrounded, he made a vigorous effort to regain the bridge he had just crossed, by which alone he could find a retreat; but in doing this he lost his life, and many of his men fell with him. However, Major Rogers, the second in command, assisted by Lieutenant Breham, found means to draw off the shattered remains of their little army, and conducted them into the fort.

Thus considerably reduced, it was with difficulty the Major could defend the town; notwithstanding which, he held out against the Indians till he was relieved, as after this they made but few attacks on the place, and only continued to blockade it.

The Gladwyn Schooner (that in which I afterwards took my passage from Michillimackinac to Detroit, and which I since learn was lost with all her crew on Lake Erie, through the obstinacy of the commander, who could not be prevailed upon to take in sufficient ballast) arrived about this time near the town with a reinforcement and necessary supplies. But before this vessel could reach the place of its destination, it was most vigorously attacked by a detachment from Pontiac's army. The Indians surrounded it in their canoes, and made great havock among the crew.

At length the captain of the schooner, with a considerable number of his men being killed, and the savages beginning to climb up the sides from every quarter, the Lieutenant (Mr. Jacobs, who afterwards commanded, and was lost in it) being determined that the stores should not fall into the enemy's hands, and seeing no other alternative, ordered the gunner to set fire to the powder-room, and blow the ship up. This order was on the point of being executed, when a chief of the Hurons, who understood the English language, gave out to his friends the intention of the commander. On receiving this intelligence, the Indians hurried down the sides of the ship with the greatest precipitation, and got as far from it as possible; whilst the commander immediately took advantage of their consternation, and arrived without any further obstruction at the town.

This seasonable supply gave the garrison fresh spirits; and Pontiac being now convinced that it would not be in his power to reduce the place, proposed an accommodation; the governor wishing as much to get rid of such troublesome enemies, who obstructed the intercourse of the traders with the neighbouring nations, listened to his proposals, and having procured advantageous terms, agreed to a peace. The Indians soon after separated, and returned to their different provinces; nor have they since thought proper to disturb, at least in any great degree, the tranquillity of these parts.

Pontiac henceforward seemed to have laid aside the animosity he had hitherto borne towards the English, and apparently became their zealous friend. To reward this new attachment, and to insure a continuance of it, government allowed him a handsome pension. But his restless and intriguing spirit would not suffer him to be grateful for this allowance, and his conduct at length grew suspicious; so that going, in the year 1767, to hold a council in the country of the Illinois, a faithful Indian, who was either commissioned by one of the English governors, or instigated by the love he bore the English nation, attended him as a spy; and being convinced from the speech Pontiac made in the council, that he still retained his former prejudices against those for whom he now professed a friendship, he plunged his knife into his heart, as soon as he had done speaking, and laid him dead on the spot. But to return from this digression.

Lake Erie receives the waters by which it is supplied from the three great lakes, through the Straights of Detroit, that lie at its north-west corner. This lake is situated between forty-one and forty-three degrees of north latitude, and between seventy-eight and eighty-three degrees of west longitude. It is near 300 miles long from east to west, and about forty in its broadest part: and a remarkable long narrow point lies on its north side, that projects for several miles into the lake towards the south-east.

There are several islands near the west end of it so infested with rattle-snakes, that it is very dangerous to land on them. It is impossible that any place can produce a greater number of all kinds of these reptiles than this does, particularly of the water-snake. The Lake is covered near the banks of the islands with the large pond-lily; the leaves of which lie on the surface of the water so thick, as to cover it entirely for many acres together; and on each of these lay, when I passed over it, wreaths of water-snakes basking in the sun, which amounted to myriads.

The most remarkable of the different species that infest this lake, is the hissing-snake, which is of the small speckled kind, and about eighteen inches long. When any thing approaches, it flattens itself in a moment, and its spots, which are of various dyes, become visibly brighter through rage; at the same time it blows from its mouth, with great force, a subtile wind, that is reported to be of a nauseous smell; and if drawn in with the breath of the unwary traveller, will infallibly bring on a decline, that in a few months must prove mortal, there being no remedy yet difcovered which can counteract its baneful influence.

The ftones and pebbles on the fhores of this lake are moft of them tinged, in a greater or lefs degree, with fpots that refemble brafs in their colour, but which are of a more fulphureous nature. Small pieces, about the fize of hazle-nuts, of the fame kinds of ore, are found on the fands that lie on its banks, and under the water.

The navigation of this lake is efteemed more dangerous than any of the others, on account of many high lands that lie on the borders of it, and project into the water, in a perpendicular direction for many miles together; fo that whenever fudden ftorms arife, canoes and boats are frequently loft, as there is no place for them to find a fhelter.

This Lake difcharges its waters at the north-eaft end, into the River Niagara, which runs north and fouth, and is about thirty-fix miles in length; from whence it falls into Lake Ontario. At the entrance of this river, on its eaftern fhore, lies Fort Niagara; and, about eighteen miles further up, thofe remarkable Falls which are efteemed one of the moft extraordinary productions of nature at prefent known.

As thefe have been vifited by fo many travellers, and fo frequently defcribed, I fhall omit giving a particular defcription of them, and only obferve, that the waters by which they are fupplied, after taking their rife near two thoufand miles to the north-weft, and paffing through the Lakes Superior, Michegan, Huron, and Erie, during which they have been receiving conftant accumulations, at length rufh down a ftupendous precipice of one hundred and forty feet perpendicular; and in a ftrong rapid, that extends to the diftance of eight or nine miles below, fall nearly as much more: this River foon after empties itfelf into Lake Ontario.

The noife of thefe Falls may be heard an amazing way. I could plainly diftinguifh them in a calm morning more than twenty miles. Others have faid that at particular times, and when the wind fits fair, the found of them reaches fifteen leagues.

The land about the Falls is exceedingly hilly and uneven, but the greateft part of that on the Niagara River is very good, efpecially for grafs and pafturage.

Fort Niagara ftands nearly at the entrance of the weft end of Lake Ontario, and on the eaft part of the Straights of Niagara. It was taken from the French in the year 1759, by the forces under the command of Sir William Johnfon, and at prefent is defended by a confiderable garrifon.

Lake Ontario is the next, and leaft of the five great Lakes of Canada. Its fituation is between forty-three and forty-five degrees of latitude, and between feventy-fix and feventy-nine degrees of weft longitude. The form of it is nearly oval, its greateft length being from north-eaft to fouth-weft, and in circumference,

cumference, about fix hundred miles. Near the fouth-eaft part it receives the waters of the Ofwego River, and on the north-eaft difcharges itfelf into the River Cataraqui. Not far from the place where it iffues, Fort Frontenac formerly ſtood, which was taken from the French during the laſt war, in the year 1758, by a fmall army of Provincials under Col. Bradftreet.

At the entrance of Ofwego river ſtands a fort of the fame name, garrifoned only at prefent by an inconfiderable party. This fort was taken in the year 1756, by the French, when a great part of the garrifon, which confifted of the late Shirley's and Pepperil's regiments, were maffacred in cold blood by the favages.

In Lake Ontario are taken many forts of fifh, among which is the Ofwego Bafs, of an excellent flavour, and weighing about three or four pounds. There is alfo a fort called the Cat-head or Pout, which are in general very large, fome of them weighing eight or ten pounds; and they are efteemed a rare difh when properly dreffed.

On the north-weft part of this Lake, and to the fouth-eaft of Lake Huron, is a tribe of Indians called Miffifauges, whofe town is denominated Toronto, from the lake on which it lies; but they are not very numerous. The country about Lake Ontario, efpecially the more north and eaftern parts, is compofed of good land, and in time may make very flourifhing fettlements.

The Oniada Lake, fituated near the head of the River Ofwego, receives the waters of Wood-Creek, which takes its rife not far from the Mohawks River. Thefe two lie fo adjacent to each other, that a junction is effected by fluices at Fort Stanwix, about twelve miles from the mouth of the former. This lake is about thirty miles long from eaft to weft, and near fifteen broad. The country around it belongs to the Oniada Indians.

Lake Champlain, the next in fize to Lake Ontario, and which lies nearly eaft from it, is about eighty miles in length, north and fouth, and in its broadeſt part fourteen. It is well ſtored with fifh, and the lands that lie on all the borders of it, or about its rivers, very good.

Lake George, formerly called by the French Lake St. Sacrament, lies to the fouth weft of the laft-mentioned lake, and is about thirty-five miles long from north-eaft to fouth-weft, but of no great breadth. The country around it is very mountainous, but in the vallies the land is tolerably good.

When thefe two lakes were firft difcovered, they were known by no other name than that of the Iroquois Lakes; and I believe in the firft plans taken of thofe parts were fo denominated. The Indians alfo that were then called the Iroquois, are fince known by the name of the Five Mohawk nations, and the Mohawks of Canada. In the late war, the former, which confift of the Onondagoes, the Oniadas, the Seneeas, the Tufcarories, and Iroondocks, fought on the fide of the Englifh: the latter,

which

which are called the Cohnawaghans, and St. Francis Indians, joined the French.

A vast tract of land that lies between the two last mentioned lakes, and Lake Ontario, was granted in the year 1629, by the Plymouth Company, under a patent they had received from King James I. to Sir Ferdinando Gorges, and to Captain John Mason, the head of that family, afterwards distinguished from others of the same name by the Masons of Connecticut. The countries specified in this grant are said to begin ten miles from the heads of the rivers that run from the east and south into Lake George and Lake Champlain; and continuing from these in a direct line westward, extend to the middle of Lake Ontario; from thence, being bounded by the Cataraqui, or river of the Iroquois, they take their course to Montreal, as far as Fort Sorrell, which lies at the junction of this river with the Richlieu; and from that point are inclosed by the last-mentioned river till it returns back to the two lakes.

This immense space was granted, by the name of the Province of Laconia, to the aforesaid gentlemen on specified conditions, and under certain penalties; but none of these amounted, in case of omission in the fulfillment of any part of them, to forfeiture, a fine only could be exacted.

On account of the continual wars to which these parts have been subject, from their situation between the settlements of the English, the French, and the Indians, this grant has been suffered to lie dormant by the real proprietors. Notwithstanding which, several towns have been settled since the late war, on the borders of Lake Champlain, and grants made to different people by the governor of New-York, of part of these territories, which are now become annexed to that province.

There are a great number of lakes on the north of Canada, between Labrador, Lake Superior; and Hudson's Bay, but these are comparatively small. As they lie out of the track that I pursued, I shall only give a summary account of them. The most westerly of these are the Lakes Nipising and Tamiscaming. The first lies at the head of the French River, and runs into Lake Huron; the other on the Ottowaw River, which empties itself into the Cataraqui, at Montreal. These Lakes are each about one hundred miles in circumference.

The next is Lake Mistassin, on the head of Rupert's River, that falls into James's Bay. This Lake is so irregular from the large points of land by which it is intersected on every side, that it is difficult either to describe its shape, or to ascertain its size. It however appears on the whole to be more than two hundred miles in circumference.

Lake St. John, which is about eighty miles round, and of a circular form, lies on the Saguenay River, directly north of Quebec, and falls into the St. Lawrence, somewhat north-east of that city. Lake Manikouagone lies near the head of the Black River, which empties itself into the St. Lawrence to the east-

ward

ward of the laſt-mentioned river, near the coaſt of Labrador, and is about ſixty miles in circumference. Lake Pertibi, Lake Wincktagan, Lake Etchelaugon, and Lake Papenouagane, with a number of other ſmall lakes, lie near the heads of the Buſtard River to the north of the St. Lawrence. Many others, which it is unneceſſary to particularize here, are alſo found between the Lakes Huron and Ontario.

The whole of thoſe I have enumerated, amounting to upwards of twenty, are within the limits of Canada; and from this account it might be deduced, that the northern parts of North-America, through theſe numerous inland ſeas, contain a greater quantity of water than any other quarter of the globe.

In October 1768 I arrived at Boſton, having been abſent from it on this expedition two years and five months, and during that time travelled near ſeven thouſand miles. From thence, as ſoon as I had properly digeſted my Journal and Charts, I ſet out for England, to communicate the diſcoveries I had made, and to render them beneficial to the kingdom. But the proſecution of my plans for reaping theſe advantages have hitherto been obſtructed by the unhappy diviſions that have been fomented between Great-Britain and the Colonies by their mutual enemies. Should peace once more be reſtored, I doubt not but that the countries I have deſcribed will prove a more abundant ſource of riches to this nation than either its Eaſt or Weſt Indian ſettlements; and I ſhall not only pride myſelf, but ſincerely rejoice in being the means of pointing out to it ſo valuable an acquiſition.

I cannot conclude the account of my extenſive travels, without expreſſing my gratitude to that beneficent Being who inviſibly protected me through thoſe perils which unavoidably attend ſo long a tour among fierce and untutored ſavages.

At the ſame time let me not be accuſed of vanity or preſumption, if I declare that the motives alledged in the introduction of this work, were not the only ones that induced me to engage in this arduous undertaking. My views were not ſolely confined to the advantages that might accrue either to myſelf, or the community to which I belonged; but nobler purpoſes contributed principally to urge me on.

The confined ſtate, both with regard to civil and religious improvements, in which ſo many of my fellow creatures remained, arouſed within my boſom an irreſiſtible inclination to explore the almoſt unknown regions which they inhabited; and as a preparatory ſtep towards the introduction of more poliſhed manners, and more humane ſentiments, to gain a knowledge of their language, cuſtoms, and principles.

I confeſs that the little benefit too many of the Indian nations have hitherto received from their intercourſe with thoſe who denominate themſelves Chriſtians, did not tend to encourage my charitable purpoſes; yet as many, though not the generality, might receive ſome benefit from the introduction among them

them of the polity and religion of the Europeans, without retaining only the errors or vices that from the depravity and perversion of their professors are unhappily attendant on these, I determined to persevere.

Nor could I flatter myself that I should be able to accomplish alone this great design; however, I was willing to contribute as much as lay in my power towards it. In all public undertakings would every one do this, and furnish with alacrity his particular share towards it, what stupendous works might not be completed.

It is true that the Indians are not without some sense of religion, and such as proves that they worship the Great Creator, with a degree of purity unknown to nations who have greater opportunities of improvement; but their religious principles are far from being so faultless as described by a learned writer, or unmixed with opinions and ceremonies that greatly lessen their excellency in this point. So that could the doctrines of genuine and vital Christianity be introduced among them, pure and untainted as it flowed from the lips of its Divine Institutor, it would certainly tend to clear away that superstitious or idolatrous dross by which the rationality of their religious tenets are obscured. Its mild and beneficent precepts would likewise conduce to soften their implacable dispositions, and to refine their savage manners; an event most desirable; and happy shall I esteem myself if this publication shall prove the means of pointing out the path by which salutary instructions may be conveyed to them, and the conversion, though but of a few, be the consequence.

Conclusion of the JOURNAL, &c.

OF THE

ORIGIN, MANNERS, CUSTOMS,

RELIGION AND LANGUAGE

OF THE

INDIANS.

CHAPTER I.

Of their ORIGIN.

THE means by which America received its first inhabitants, have, since the time of its discovery by the Europeans, been the subject of numberless difquisitions. Was I to endeavour to collect the different opinions and reasonings on the various writers that have taken up the pen in defence of their conjectures, the enumeration would much exceed the bounds I have prescribed myself, and oblige me to be less explicit on points of greater moment.

From the obscurity in which this debate is enveloped, thro' the total difuse of letters among every nation of Indians on this extensive continent, and the uncertainty of oral tradition at the distance of so many ages, I fear, that even after the most minute investigation we shall not be able to settle it with any great

degree

degree of certainty. And this apprehenfion will receive additional force, when it is confidered that the diverfity of language, which is apparently diftinct between moft of the Indians, tends to afcertain that this population was not effected from one particular country, but from feveral neighbouring ones, and completed at different periods.

Moft of the hiftorians or travellers that have treated on the American Aborigines difagree in their fentiments relative to them. Many of the ancients are fuppofed to have known that this quarter of the globe not only exifted, but alfo that it was inhabited. Plato in his Timæus has afferted, that beyond the ifland which he calls Atalantis, and which according to his defcription was fituated in the weftern Ocean, there were a great number of other iflands, and behind thofe a vaft continent.

Oviedo, a celebrated Spanifh author of a much later date, has made no fcruple to affirm that the Antilles are the famous Hefperides fo often mentioned by the poets; which are at length reftored to the kings of Spain, the defcendants of king Hefperus, who lived upwards of three thoufand years ago, and from whom thefe iflands received their name.

Two other Spaniards, the one, Father Gregorio Garcia, a Dominican, the other, Father Jofeph De Acofta, a Jefuit, have written on the origin of the Americans.

The former, who had been employed in the miffions of Mexico and Peru, endeavoured to prove from the traditions of the Mexicans, Peruvians, and others, which he received on the fpot, and from the variety of characters, cuftoms, languages, and religion obfervable in the different countries of the new world, that different nations had contributed to the peopling of it.

The latter, Father De Acofta, in his examination of the means by which the firft Indians of America might have found a paffage to that continent, difcredits the conclufions of thofe who have fuppofed it to be by fea, becaufe no ancient author has made mention of the compafs: and concludes, that it muft be either by the north of Afia and Europe, which adjoin to each other, or by thofe regions that lie to the fouthward of the Straights of Magellan. He alfo rejects the affertions of fuch as have advanced that it was peopled by the Hebrews.

John De Laët, a Flemifh writer, has controverted the opinions of thefe Spanifh fathers, and of many others who have written on the fame fubject. The hypothefis he endeavours to eftablifh, is, that America was certainly peopled by the Scythians or Tartars; and that the tranfmigration of thefe people happened foon after the difperfion of Noah's grandfons. He undertakes to fhow, that the moft northern Americans have a greater refemblance, not only in the features of their countenances, but alfo in their complexion and manner of living, to the Scythians, Tartars, and Samoeides, than to any other nations.

In

In anſwer to Grotius, who had aſſerted that ſome of the Norwegians paſſed into America by way of Greenland, and over a vaſt continent, he ſays, that it is well known that Greenland was not diſcovered till the year 964; and both Gomera and Herrera inform us that the Chichimeques were ſettled on the Lake of Mexico in 721. He adds, that theſe ſavages, according to the uniform tradition of the Mexicans who diſpoſſeſſed them, came from the country ſince called New Mexico, and from the neighbourhood of California; conſequently North America, muſt have been inhabited many ages before it could receive any inhabitants from Norway by way of Greenland.

It is no leſs certain, he obſerves, that the real Mexicans founded their empire in 902, after having ſubdued the Chichimeques, the Otomias, and other barbarous nations, who had taken poſſeſſion of the country round the Lake of Mexico, and each of whom ſpoke a language peculiar to themſelves. The real Mexicans are likewiſe ſuppoſed to come from ſome of the countries that lie near California, and that they performed their journey for the moſt part by land; of courſe they could not come from Norway.

De Laët further adds, that though ſome of the inhabitants of North America may have entered it from the north-weſt, yet, as it is related by Pliny, and ſome other writers, that on many of the iſlands near the weſtern coaſt of Africa, particularly on the Canaries, ſome ancient edifices were ſeen, it is highly probable from their being now deſerted, that the inhabitants may have paſſed over to America; the paſſage being neither long nor difficult. This migration, according to the calculation of thoſe authors, muſt have happened more than two thouſand years ago, at a time when the Spaniards were much troubled by the Carthaginians; from whom having obtained a knowledge of navigation, and the conſtruction of ſhips, they might have retired to the Antilles, by the way of the weſtern iſles, which were exactly half way on their voyage.

He thinks alſo that Great Britain, Ireland, and the Orcades were extremely proper to admit of a ſimilar conjecture. As a proof, he inſerts the following paſſage from the hiſtory of Wales, written by Dr. David Powel, in the year 1170.

This hiſtorian ſays, that Madoc, of the ſons of Prince Owen Gwynnith, being diſguſted at the civil wars which broke out between his brothers, after the death of their father, fitted out ſeveral veſſels, and having provided them with every thing neceſſary for a long voyage, went in queſt of new lands to the weſtward of Ireland; there he diſcovered very fertile countries, but deſtitute of inhabitants; when landing part of his people, he returned to Britain, where he raiſed new levies, and afterwards tranſported them to his colony.

The Flemiſh Author then returns to the Scythians, between whom and the Americans he draws a parallel. He obſerves that ſeveral nations of them to the north of the Caſpian Sea, led a wandering life; which, as well as many other of their customs, and way of living, agrees in many circumstances with the Indians of America. And though the resemblances are not absolutely perfect, yet the emigrants, even before they left their own country, differed from each other, and went not by the same name. Their change of abode effected what remained.

He further says, that a similar likeness exists between several American nations, and the Samœides who are settled, according to the Russian accounts, on the great River Oby. And it is more natural, continues he, to suppose that Colonies of these nations passed over to America by crossing the icy sea on their sledges, than for the Norwegians to travel all the way Grotius has marked out for them.

This writer makes many other remarks that are equally sensible, and which appear to be just; but he intermixes with these some that are not so well founded.

Emanuel de Moraez, a Portugueze, in his history of Brazil, asserts, that America has been wholly peopled by the Carthaginians and Israelites. He brings as a proof of this assertion, the discoveries the former are known to have made at a great distance beyond the coast of Africa. The progress of which being put a stop to by the senate of Carthage, those who happened to be then in the newly discovered countries, being cut off from all communication with their countrymen, and destitute of many necessaries of life, fell into a state of barbarism. As to the Israelites, this author thinks that nothing but circumcision is wanted in order to constitute a perfect resemblance between them and the Brazilians.

George De Hornn, a learned Dutchman, has likewise written on this subject. He sets out with declaring, that he does not believe it possible America could have been peopled before the flood, considering the short space of time which elapsed between the creation of the world and that memorable event. In the next place he lays it down as a principle, that after the deluge, men and other terrestrial animals penetrated into that country both by sea and by land; some through accident, and some from a formed design. That birds got thither by flight; which they were enabled to do by resting on the rocks and islands that are scattered about in the Ocean.

He further observes, that wild beasts may have found a free passage by land; and that if we do not meet with horses or cattle, (to which he might have added elephants, camels, rhinoceros, and beasts of many other kinds) it is because those nations that passed thither, were either not acquainted with their use, or had no convenience to support them.

Having totally excluded many nations that others have admitted as the probable first settlers of America, for which he gives substantial reasons, he supposes that it began to be peopled by the north; and maintains, that the primitive colonies spread
themselves

themselves by the means of the isthmus of Panama through the whole extent of the continent.

He believes that the first founders of the Indian Colonies were Scythians. That the Phœnicians and Carthaginians afterwards got footing in America acrofs the Atlantic Ocean, and the Chinese by way of the Pacific. And that other nations might from time to time have landed there by one or other of these ways, or might possibly have been thrown on the coast by tempests: since, through the whole extent of that Continent, both in its northern and southern parts, we meet with undoubted marks of a mixture of the northern nations with those who have come from other places. And lastly, that some Jews and Christians might have been carried there by such like events, but that this must have happened at a time when the whole of the New World was already peopled.

After all, he acknowledges that great difficulties attend the determination of the question. These, he fays, are occasioned in the first place by the imperfect knowledge we have of the extremities of the globe, towards the north and south pole; and in the next place to the havock which the Spaniards, the first discoverers of the new world, made among its most ancient monuments; as witnefs the great double road betwixt Quito and Cuzco, an undertaking fo stupendous, that even the most magnificent of those executed by the Romans, cannot be compared to it.

He fuppofes alfo another migration of the Phœnicians, than those already mentioned, to have taken place; and this was during a three years voyage made by the Tyrian fleet in the service of King Solomon. He afferts on the authority of Josephus, that the port at which this embarkation was made, lay in the Mediterranean. The fleet, he adds, went in quest of elephants teeth and peacocks to the western Coast of Africa, which is Tarfifh; then to Ophir for gold, which is Haité, or the island of Hispaniola; and in the latter opinion he is supported by Columbus, who, when he discovered that island, thought he could trace the furnaces in which the gold was refined.

To these migrations which preceded the Christian æra, he adds many others of a later date from different nations, but these I have not time to enumerate. For the fame reafon I am obliged to pafs over numberlefs writers on this fubject; and shall content myfelf with only giving the fentiments of two or three more.

The first of these is Pierre De Charlevoix, a Frenchman, who, in his journal of a voyage to North America, made so lately as the year 1720, has recapitulated the opinions of a variety of authors on this head, to which he has fubjoined his own conjectures. But the latter cannot without fome difficulty be extracted, as they are fo interwoven with the paffages he

has

has quoted, that it requires much attention to discriminate them.

He seems to allow that America might have received its first inhabitants from Tartary and Hyrcania. This he confirms, by observing that the lions and tigers which are found in the former, must have come from those countries, and whose passage serves for a proof that the two hemispheres join to the northward of Asia. He then draws a corroboration of this argument, from a story he says he has often heard related by Father Grollon, a French Jesuit, as an undoubted matter of fact.

This father, after having laboured some time in the missions of New France, passed over to those of China. One day as he was travelling in Tartary, he met a Huron woman whom he had formerly known in Canada. He asked her by what adventure she had been carried into a country so distant from her own. She made answer, that having been taken in war, she had been conducted from nation to nation, till she had reached the place at which she then was.

Monsieur Charlevoix says further, that he had been assured another Jesuit, passing through Nantz, in his return from China, had related much such another affair of a Spanish woman from Florida. She also had been taken by certain Indians, and given to those of a more distant country; and by these again to another nation, till having thus been successively passed from country to country, and travelled through regions extremely cold, she at last found herself in Tartary. Here she had married a Tartar, who had attended the conquerors in China, where she was then settled.

He acknowledges as an allay to the probability of these stories, that those who had sailed farthest to the eastward of Asia, by pursuing the Coast of Jesso or Kamtschatka, have pretended that they had perceived the extremity of this continent; and from thence have concluded that there could not possibly be any communication by land. But he adds that Francis Guella, a Spaniard, is said to have asserted, that this separation is no more than a straight, about one hundred miles over, and that some late voyages of the Japonese give grounds to think that this straight is only a bay, above which there is passage over land.

He goes on to observe, that though there are few wild beasts to be met with in North America, except a kind of tigers without spots, which are found in the country of the Iroquoise, yet towards the tropics there are lions and real tigers, which, notwithstanding, might have come from Hyrcania and Tartary; for as by advancing gradually southward they met with climates more agreeable to their natures, they have in time abandoned the northern countries.

He quotes both Solinus and Pliny to prove that the Scythian Anthropophagi once depopulated a great extent of country, as far as the promontory Tabin; and also an author of later date, Mark Pol, a Venetian, who, he says, tells us, that to the north-
east

east of China and Tartary there are vast uninhabited countries, which might be sufficient to confirm any conjectures concerning the retreat of a great number of Scythians into America.

To this he adds, that we find in the ancients the names of some of these nations. Pliny speaks of the Tabians; Solinus mentions the Apuleans, who had for neighbours the Massagetes, whom Pliny since assures us to have entirely disappeared. Ammianus Marcellinus expresly tells us, that the fear of the Anthropophagi obliged several of the inhabitants of those countries to take refuge elsewhere. From all these authorities Monsieur Charlevoix concludes, that there is at least room to conjecture that more than one nation in America had a Scythian or Tartarian original.

He finishes his remarks on the authors he has quoted, by the following observations. It appears to me that this controversy may be reduced to the two following articles; first, how the new world might have been peopled; and secondly, by whom, and by what means it has been peopled.

Nothing, he asserts, may be more easily answered than the first. America might have been peopled as the three other parts of the world have been. Many difficulties have been formed on this subject, which have been deemed insolvable, but which are far from being so. The inhabitants of both hemispheres are certainly the descendants of the same father; the common parent of mankind received an express command from Heaven to people the whole world, and accordingly it has been peopled.

To bring this about it was necessary to overcome all difficulties that lay in the way, and they have been got over. Were these difficulties greater with respect to peopling the extremities of Asia, Africa, and Europe, or the transporting men into the islands which lie at a considerable distance from those continents, than to pass over into America? certainly not.

Navigation, which has arrived at so great perfection within these three or four centuries, might possibly have been more perfect in those early ages than at this day. Who can believe that Noah and his immediate descendants knew less of this art than we do? That the builder and pilot of the largest ship that ever was, a ship that was formed to traverse an unbounded ocean, and had so many shoals and quick-sands to guard against, should be ignorant of, or should not have communicated to those of his descendants who survived him, and by whose means he was to execute the order of the Great Creator; I say, who can believe he should not have communicated to them the art of sailing upon an ocean, which was not only more calm and pacific, but at the same time confined within its ancient limits?

Admitting this, how easy is it to pass, exclusive of the passage already described, by land from the coast of Africa to Brazil, from the Canaries to the Western Islands, and from them to the Antilles? From the British Isles, or the coast of France, to Newfoundland, the passage is neither long nor difficult; I might say

say as much of that from China to Japan; from Japan, or the Phillipines, to the Isles Mariannes; and from thence to Mexico.

There are islands at a considerable distance from the continent of Asia, where we have not been surprized to find inhabitants, why then should we wonder to meet with people in America? Nor can it be imagined that the grandsons of Noah, when they were obliged to separate, and spread themselves in conformity to the designs of God, over the whole earth, should find it absolutely impossible to people almost one half of it.

I have been more copious in my extracts from this author than I intended, as his reasons appear to be solid, and many of his observations just. From this encomium, however, I must exclude the stories he has introduced of the Huron and Floridan women, which I think I might venture to pronounce fabulous.

I shall only add, to give my readers a more comprehensive view of Monsieur Charlevoix's dissertation, the method he proposes to come at the truth of what we are in search of.

The only means by which this can be done, he says, is by comparing the languages of the Americans with the different nations, from whence we might suppose they have peregrinated. If we compare the former with those words that are considered as primitives, it might possibly set us upon some happy discovery. And this way of ascending to the original of nations, which is by far the least equivocal, is not so difficult as might be imagined. We have had, and still have, travellers and missionaries who have attained the languages that are spoken in all the provinces of the new world; it would only be necessary to make a collection of their grammars and vocabularies, and to collate them with the dead and living languages of the old world, that pass for originals, and the similarity might easily be traced. Even the different dialects, in spite of the alterations they have undergone, still retain enough of the mother tongue to furnish considerable lights.

Any enquiry into the manners, customs, religion, or traditions of the Americans, in order to discover by that means their origin, he thinks would prove fallacious. A disquisition of that kind, he observes, is only capable of producing a false light, more likely to dazzle, and to make us wander from the right path, than to lead us with certainty to the point proposed.

Ancient traditions are effaced from the minds of such as either have not, or for several ages have been without those helps that are necessary to preserve them. And in this situation is full one half of the world. New events, and a new arrangement of things, give rise to new traditions, which efface the former, and are themselves effaced in turn. After one or two centuries have passed, there no longer remain any traces of the first traditions; and thus we are involved in a state of uncertainty.

He concludes with the following remarks, among many others. Unforeseen accidents, tempests, and shipwrecks, have certainly

contributed

contributed to people every habitable part of the world: and ought we to wonder after this, at perceiving certain resemblances, both of persons and manners between nations that are most remote from each other, when we find such a difference between those that border on one another? As we are destitute of historical monuments, there is nothing, I repeat it, but a knowledge of the primitive languages that is capable of throwing any light upon these clouds of impenetrable darkness.

By this enquiry we should at least be satisfied, among that prodigious number of various nations inhabiting America, and differing so much in languages from each other, which are those who make use of words totally and entirely different from those of the old world, and who consequently must be reckoned to have passed over to America in the earliest ages, and those who, from the analogy of their language with such as are at present used in the three other parts of the globe, leave room to judge that their migration has been more recent, and which ought to be attributed to shipwrecks, or to some accident similar to those which have been spoken of in the course of this treatise.

I shall only add the opinion of one author more, before I give my own sentiments on the subject, and that is of James Adair, Esq; who resided forty years among the Indians, and published the history of them in the year 1772. In his learned and systematical history of those nations, inhabiting the western parts of the most southern of the American colonies; this gentleman without hesitation pronounces that the American Aborigines are descended from the Israelites, either whilst they were a maritime power, or soon after their general captivity.

This descent he endeavours to prove from their religious rites, their civil and martial customs, their marriages, their funeral ceremonies, their manners, language, traditions, and from a variety of other particulars. And so complete is his conviction on this head, that he fancies he finds a perfect and indisputable similitude in each. Through all these I have not time to follow him, and shall therefore only give a few extracts to show on what foundation he builds his conjectures, and what degree of credit he is entitled to on this point.

He begins with observing, that though some have supposed the Americans to be descended from the Chinese, yet neither their religion, laws, or customs agree in the least with those of the Chinese; which sufficiently proves that they are not of this line. Besides, as our best ships are now almost half a year in sailing for China (our author does not here recollect that this is from a high northern latitude, across the Line, and then back again greatly to the northward of it, and not directly athwart the Pacific Ocean, for only one hundred and eleven degrees) or from thence to Europe, it is very unlikely they should attempt such dangerous discoveries, with their supposed small vessels, against rapid currents, and in dark and sickly Monsoons.

He

He further remarks, that this is more particularly improbable, as there is reason to believe that this nation was unacquainted with the use of the loadstone to direct their course.

China, he says, is about eight thousand miles distant from the American continent, which is twice as far as across the Atlantic Ocean. And we are not informed by any ancient writer of their maritime skill, or so much as any inclination that way, besides small coasting voyages. The winds blow likewise, with little variation from east to west within the latitudes thirty and odd, north and south, and therefore these could not drive them on the American coast, it lying directly contrary to such a course.

Neither could persons, according to this writer's account, sail to America from the north by the way of Tartary or Ancient Scythia; that, from its situation, never having been or can be a maritime power; and it is utterly impracticable, he says, for any to come to America by sea from that quarter. Besides, the remaining traces of their religious ceremonies, and civil and martial customs, are quite opposite to the like vestiges of the Old Scythians.

Even in the moderate northern climates there is not to be seen the least trace of any ancient stately buildings, or of any thick settlements, as are said to remain in the less healthy regions of Peru and Mexico. And several of the Indian nations assure us, that they crossed the Mississippi before they made their present northern settlements; which, connected with the former arguments, he concludes will sufficiently explode that weak opinion of the American Aborigines being lineally descended from the Tartars or ancient Scythians.

Mr Adair's reasons for supposing that the Americans derive their origin from the Jews are,

First, because they are divided into tribes, and have chiefs over them as the Israelites had.

Secondly, because, as by a strict permanent divine precept, the Hebrew nation were ordered to worship, at Jerusalem, Jehovah the true and living God, so do the Indians, stiling him Yohewah. The ancient Heathens, he adds, it is well known worshipped a plurality of gods, but the Indians pay their religious devoirs to the Great beneficent, supreme, holy Spirit of Fire, who resides, as they think, above the clouds, and on earth also with unpolluted people. They pay no adoration to images, or to dead persons, neither to the celestial luminaries, to evil spirits, nor to any created beings whatever.

Thirdly, because, agreeable to the theocracy or divine government of Israel, the Indians think the Deity to be the immediate head of their state.

Fourthly, because, as the Jews believe in the ministration of angels, the Indians also believe that the higher regions are inhabited by good spirits.

Fifthly,

Fifthly, because the Indian language and dialects appear to have the very idiom and genius of the Hebrew. Their words and sentences being expressive, concise, emphatical, sonorous, and bold; and often, both in letters, and signification, are synonimous with the Hebrew language.

Sixthly, because they count their time after the manner of the Hebrews.

Seventhly, because in conformity to, or after the manner of the Jews, they have their prophets, high-priests, and other religious orders.

Eighthly, because their festivals, fasts, and religious rites have a great resemblance to those of the Hebrews.

Ninthly, because the Indians, before they go to war, have many preparatory ceremonies of purification and fasting, like what is recorded of the Israelites.

Tenthly, because the same taste for ornaments, and the same kind, are made use of by the Indians, as by the Hebrews.

These and many other arguments of a similar nature, Mr. Adair brings in support of his favourite system; but I should imagine, that if the Indians are really derived from the Hebrews, among their religious ceremonies, on which he chiefly seems to build his hypothesis, the principal, that of circumcision, would never have been laid aside, and its very remembrance obliterated.

Thus numerous and diverse are the opinions of those who have hitherto written on this subject! I shall not, however, either endeavour to reconcile them, or to point out the errors of each, but proceed to give my own sentiments on the origin of the Americans; which are founded on conclusions drawn from the most rational arguments of the writers I have mentioned, and from my own observations; the consistency of these I shall leave to the judgment of my Readers.

The better to introduce my conjectures on this head, it is necessary first to ascertain the distances between America and those parts of the habitable globe that approach nearest to it.

The Continent of America, as far as we can judge from all the researches that have been made near the poles, appears to be entirely separated from the other quarters of the world. That part of Europe which approaches nearest to it, is the coast of Greenland, lying in about seventy degrees of north latitude; and which reaches within twelve degrees of the coast of Labrador, situated on the north-east borders of this continent. The coast of Guinea is the nearest part of Africa; which lies about eighteen hundred and sixty miles north-east from the Brazils. The most eastern coast of Asia, which extends to the Korean Sea on the north of China, projects north-east through eastern Tartary and Kamschatka to Siberia, in about sixty degrees of north latitude. Towards which the western coasts of America, from California to the Straights of Annian, extend near-

ly

ly north-weſt, and lie in about forty-ſix degrees of the ſame latitude.

Whether the Continent of America ſtretches any farther north than theſe ſtraights, and joins to the eaſtern parts of Aſia, agreeable to what has been aſſerted by ſome of the writers I have quoted, or whether the lands that have been diſcovered in the intermediate parts are only an archipelago of iſlands, verging towards the oppoſite continent, is not yet aſcertained.

It being, however, certain that there are many conſiderable iſlands which lie between the extremities of Aſia and America, viz. Japon, Jeſo or Jedſo, Gama's Land, Behring's Iſle, with many others diſcovered by Tſchirikow, and beſides theſe, from fifty degrees north there appearing to be a cluſter of iſlands that reach as far as Siberia, it is probable from their proximity to America, that it received its firſt inhabitants from them.

This concluſion is the moſt rational I am able to draw, ſuppoſing that ſince the Aborigines got footing on this continent, no extraordinary or ſudden change in the poſition or ſurface of it has taken place, from inundations, earthquakes, or any revolutions of the earth that we are at preſent unacquainted with.

To me it appears highly improbable that it ſhould have been peopled from different quarters, acroſs the Ocean, as others have aſſerted. From the ſize of the ſhips made uſe of in thoſe early ages, and the want of the compaſs, it cannot be ſuppoſed that any maritime nation would by choice venture over the unfathomable ocean, in ſearch of diſtant continents. Had this however been attempted, or had America been firſt accidentally peopled from ſhips freighted with paſſengers of both ſexes, which were driven by ſtrong eaſterly winds acroſs the Atlantic, theſe ſettlers muſt have retained ſome traces of the language of the country from whence they migrated; and this ſince the diſcovery of it by the Europeans muſt have been made out. It alſo appears extraordinary that ſeveral of theſe accidental migrations, as allowed by ſome, and theſe from different parts, ſhould have taken place.

Upon the whole, after the moſt critical enquiries, and the matureſt deliberation, I am of opinion, that America received its firſt inhabitants from the north-eaſt, by way of the great archipelago juſt mentioned, and from theſe alone. But this might have been effected at different times, and from various parts: from Tartary, China, Japon, or Kamſchatka, the inhabitants of theſe places reſembling each other in colour, features, and ſhape; and who, before ſome of them acquired a knowledge of the arts and ſciences, might have likewiſe reſembled each other in their manners, cuſtoms, religion, and language.

The only difference between the Chineſe nation and the Tartars lies in the cultivated ſtate of the one, and the unpoliſhed ſituation of the others. The former have become a commercial people, and dwell in houſes formed into regular towns and cities; the latter live chiefly in tents, and rove about in different

rent hords, without any fixed abode. Nor can the long and bloody wars thefe two nations have been engaged in, exterminate their hereditary fimilitude. The prefent family of the Chinife emperors is of Tartarian extraction; and if they were not fenfible of fome claim befide that of conqueft, fo numerous a people would fcarcely fit quiet under the dominion of ftrangers.

It it very evident that fome of the manners and cuftoms of the American Indians refemble thofe of the Tartars; and I make no doubt but that in fome future æra, and this is not a very diftant one, it will be reduced to a certainty, that during fome of the wars between the Tartars and the Chinefe, a part of the inhabitants of the northern provinces were driven from their native country, and took refuge in fome of the ifles before-mentioned, and from thence found their way into America. At different periods each nation might prove victorious, and the conquered by turns fly before their conquerors; and from hence might arife the fimilitude of the Indians to all thefe people, and that animofity which exifts between fo many of their tribes.

It appears plainly to me that a great fimilarity between the Indian and Chinefe is confpicuous in that particular cuftom of fhaving or plucking off the hair, and leaving only a fmall tuft on the crown of the head. This mode is faid to have been enjoined by the Tartarian emperors on their acceffion to the throne of China, and confequently is a further proof that this cuftom was in ufe among the Tartars; to whom as well as the Chinefe, the Americans might be indebted for it.

Many words alfo are ufed both by the Chinefe and Indians, which have a refemblance to each other, not only in their found, but their fignification. The Chinefe call a flave, fhungo; and the Naudoweffie Indians, whofe language from their little intercourfe with the Europeans is the leaft corrupted, term a dog, fhungufh. The former denominate one fpecies of their tea, fhoufong; the latter call their tobacco, fhoufaffau. Many other of the words ufed by the Indians contain the fyllables che, chaw, and chu, after the dialect of the Chinefe.

There probably might be found a fimilar connection between the language of the Tartars and the American Aborigines, were we as well acquainted with it as we are, from a commercial intercourfe, with that of the Chinefe.

I am confirmed in thefe conjectures, by the accounts of Kamfchatka, publifhed a few years ago by order of the Emprefs of Ruffia. The author of which fays, that the fea which divides that peninfula from America is full of iflands; and that the diftance between Tfchukotskoi-Nofs, a promontory which lies at the eaftern extremity of that country, and the coaft of America, is not more than two degrees and a half of a great circle. He further fays, that there is the greateft reafon to fuppofe that Afia and America once joined at this place, as the coafts of both continents appear to have been broken into capes and bays,

which

which answer each other; more especially as the inhabitants of this part of both resemble each other in their persons, habits, customs, and food. Their language, indeed, he observes, does not appear to be the same, but then the inhabitants of each district in Kamschatka speak a language as different from each other, as from that spoken on the opposite coast. These observations, to which he adds, the similarity of the boats of the inhabitants of each coast, and a remark that the natives of this part of America are wholly strangers to wine and tobacco, which he looks upon as a proof that they have as yet had no communication with the natives of Europe, he says, amount to little less than a demonstration that America was peopled from this part of Asia.

The limits of my present undertaking will not permit me to dwell any longer on this subject, or to enumerate any other proofs in favour of my hypothesis. I am however so thoroughly convinced of the certainty of it, and so desirous have I been to obtain every testimony which can be procured in its support, that I once made an offer to a private society of gentlemen, who were curious in such researches, and to whom I had communicated my sentiments on this point, that I would undertake a journey, on receiving such supplies as were needful, through the north-east parts of Europe and Asia to the interior parts of America, and from thence to England; making, as I proceeded, such observations both on the languages and manners of the people with whom I should be conversant, as might tend to illustrate the doctrine I have here laid down, and to satisfy the curiosity of the learned or inquisitive; but as this proposal was judged rather to require a national than a private support, it was not carried into execution.

I am happy to find, since I formed the foregoing conclusions, that they correspond with the sentiments of that great and learned historian Doctor Robertson; and though, with him, I acknowledge that the investigation, from its nature, is so obscure and intricate, that the conjectures I have made can only be considered as conjectures, and not indisputable conclusions, yet they carry with them a greater degree of probability than the suppositions of those who assert that this continent was peopled from another quarter.

One of the Doctor's quotations from the Journals of Behring and Tschirikow, who sailed from Kamschatka, about the year 1741, in quest of the New World, appears to carry great weight with it, and to afford our conclusions firm support: " These
" commanders having shaped their course towards the east, dis-
" covered land, which to them appeared to be part of the Ame-
" rican continent; and according to their observations, it seems
" to be situated within a few degrees of the north-west coast of
" California. They had there some intercourse with the inha-
" bitants, who seemed to them to resemble the North-Ameri-
" cans; as they presented to the Russians the Calumet or Pipe
" of

" of Peace, which is a symbol of friendship universal among
" the people of North America, and an usage of arbitrary in-
" stitution peculiar to them."

One of this incomparable writer's own arguments in support of his hypothesis, is also urged with great judgment, and appears to be nearly conclusive. He says, "We may lay it down
" as a certain principle in this enquiry, that America was not
" peopled by any nation of the ancient continent, which had
" made considerable progress in civilization. The inhabitants
" of the New World were in a state of society so extremely
" rude, as to be unacquainted with those arts which are the
" first essays of human ingenuity in its advance towards im-
" provement. Even the most cultivated nations of America
" were strangers to many of those simple inventions, which
" were almost coeval with society in other parts of the world,
" and were known in the earliest periods of civil life. From
" this it is manifest that the tribes which originally migrated to
" America, came off from nations which must have been no
" less barbarous than their posterity, at the time when they were
" first discovered by the Europeans. If ever the use of iron
" had been known to the savages of America, or to their pro-
" genitors, if ever they had employed a plough, a loom, or a
" forge, the utility of these inventions would have preserved
" them, and it is impossible that they should have been aban-
" doned or forgotten."

CHAPTER II.

Of their PERSONS, DRESS, &c.

FROM the first settlement of the French in Canada, to the conquest of it by the English in 1760, several of that nation, who had travelled into the interior parts of North America, either to trade with the Indians, or to endeavour to make converts of them have published accounts of their customs, manners, &c.

The principal of these are Father Louis Hennipin, Monf. Charlevoix, and the Baron Le Hontan. The first, many years ago, published some very judicious remarks, which he was the better enabled to do by the assistance he received from the maps and diaries of the unfortunate M. De la Salle, who was assassinated whilst he was on his travels, by some of his own party. That gentleman's journals falling into Father Hennipin's hands, he was enabled by them to publish many interesting particulars relative to the Indians. But in some respects he fell very short of that knowledge which it was in his power to have attained from his long residence among them. Nor was he always (as has been already observed) exact in his calculations, or just in the intelligence he has given us.

The accounts published by the other two, particularly those of Charlevoix, are very erroneous in the geographical parts, and many of the stories told by the Baron are mere delusions.

Some of the Jesuits, who heretofore travelled into these parts, have also written on this subject; but as few, if any, of their works have been translated into the English language, the generality of Readers are not benefited by them; and, indeed, had this been done, they would have reaped but few advantages from them, as they have chiefly confined their observations to the religious principles of the savages, and the steps taken for their conversion.

Since the conquest of Canada, some of our own countrymen, who have lived among the Indians, and learned their language, have published their observations; however as their travels have not extended to any of the interior parts I treat of, but have only been made among the nations that border on our settlements, a knowledge of the genuine and uncontaminated customs and manners of the Indians could not have been acquired by them.

The southern tribes, and those that have held a constant intercourse with the French or English, cannot have preserved their manners or their customs in their original purity. They could not avoid acquiring the vices with the language of those they conversed with; and the frequent intoxications they experienced through the baneful juices introduced among them by the Europeans, have completed a total alteration in their characters.

In such as these, a confused medley of principles or usages are only to be observed; their real and unpolluted customs could be seen among those nations alone that have held but little communications with the provinces. These I found in the north-west parts, and therefore flatter myself that I am able to give a more just account of the customs and manners of the Indians, in their ancient purity, than any that has been hitherto published. I have made observations on thirty nations, and though most of these have differed in their languages, there has appeared a great similarity in their manners, and from these have I endeavoured to extract the following remarks.

As I do not propose to give a regular and connected system of Indian concerns, but only to relate such particulars of their manners, customs, &c. as I thought most worthy of notice, and which interfere as little as possible with the accounts given by other writers, I must beg my Readers to excuse their not be-
arranged

arranged fyftematically, or treated of in a more copious manner.

The Indian nations do not appear to me to differ fo widely in their make, colour, or conftitution from each other, as reprefented by fome writers. They are in general flight made, rather tall and ftrait, and you feldom fee any among them deformed; their skin is of a reddifh or copper colour; their eyes are large and black, and their hair of the fame hue, but very rarely is it curled; they have good teeth, and their breath is as fweet as the air they draw in; their cheek-bones rather raifed, but more fo in the women than the men; the former are not quite fo tall as the European women, however you frequently meet with good faces and agreeable perfons among them, although they are more inclined to be fat than the other fex.

I fhall not enter into a particular enquiry whether the Indians are indebted to nature, art, or the temperature of the climate for the colour of their skin, nor fhall I quote any of the contradictory accounts I have read on this fubject; I fhall only fay, that it appears to me to be the tincture they received originally from the hands of their Creator; but at what period the variation which is at prefent vifible, both in the complexion and features of many nations took place, at what time the European whitenefs, the jetty hue of the African, or the copper caft of the American were given them; which was the original colour of the firft inhabitants of the earth, or which might be efteemed the moft perfect, I will not pretend to determine.

Many writers have afferted, that the Indians, even at the matureft period of their exiftence, are only furnifhed with hair on their heads; and that notwithftanding the profufion with which that part is covered, thofe parts which among the inhabitants of other climates are ufually the feat of this excrefcence, remain entirely free from it. Even Doctor Robertfon, through their mifreprefentations, has contributed to propagate the error; and fuppofing the remark juftly founded, has drawn feveral conclufions from it relative to the habit and temperature of their bodies, which are confequently invalid. But from minute enquiries, and a curious infpection, I am able to declare, (however refpectable I may hold the authority of thefe hiftorians in other points) that their affertions are erroneous, and proceeding from the want of a thorough knowledge of the cuftoms of the Indians.

After the age of puberty, their bodies, in their natural ftate, are covered in the fame manner as thofe of the Europeans. The men, indeed, efteem a beard very unbecoming, and take great pains to get rid of it, nor is there any ever to be perceived on their faces, except when they grow old, and become inattentive to their appearance. Every crinous efflorefcence on the other parts of the body is held unfeemly by them, and both fexes employ much time in their extirpation.

The

The Naudoweffies, and the remote nations, pluck them out with bent pieces of hard wood, formed into a kind of nippers; whilft thofe who have communication with Europeans procure from them wire, which they twift into a fcrew or worm; applying this to the part, they prefs the rings together, and with a fudden twitch draw out all the hairs that are inclofed between them.

The men of every nation differ in their drefs very little from each other, except thofe who trade with the Europeans; thefe exchange their furs for blankets, fhirts and other apparel, which they wear as much for ornament as neceffity. The latter faften by a girdle around their waifts about half a yard of broadcloth, which covers the middle parts of their bodies. Thofe who wear fhirts never make them faft either at the wrift or collar; this would be a moft infufferable confinement to them. They throw their blanket loofe upon their fhoulders, and holding the upper fide of it by the two corners, with a knife in one hand, and a tobacco pouch, pipe, &c. in the other; thus accoutred they walk about in their villages or camps: but in their dances they feldom wear this covering.

Thofe among the men who wifh to appear gayer than the reft, pluck from their heads all the hair, except from a fpot on the top of it, about the fize of a crown-piece, where it is permitted to grow to a confiderable length: on this are faftened plumes of feathers of various colours, with filver or ivory quills. The manner of cutting and ornamenting this part of the head diftinguifhes different nations from each other.

They paint their faces red and black, which they efteem as greatly ornamental. They alfo paint themfelves when they go to war; but the method they make ufe of on this occafion differs from that wherein they ufe it merely as a decoration.

The young Indians, who are defirous of excelling their companions in finery, flit the outward rim of both their ears; at the fame time they take care not to feparate them entirely, but leave the flefh thus cut, ftill untouched at both extremities: around this fpongy fubftance, from the upper to the lower part, they twift brafs wire, till the weight draws the amputated rim into a bow of five or fix inches diameter, and drags it almoft down to the fhoulder. This decoration is efteemed to be exceffively gay and becoming.

It is alfo a common cuftom among them to bore their nofes, and wear in them pendants of different forts. I obferved that fea fhells were much worn by thofe of the interior parts, and reckoned very ornamental; but how they procure them I could not learn; probably by their traffic with other nations nearer the fea.

They go without any covering for the thigh, except that before fpoken of, round the middle, which reaches down half way the thighs; but they make for their legs a fort of ftocking, either of fkins or cloth: thefe are fewed as near to the fhape

of

of the leg as poſſible, ſo as to admit of being drawn on and off. The edges of the ſtuff of which they are compoſed are left annexed to the ſeam, and hang looſe for about the breadth of a hand; and this part, which is placed on the outſide of the leg, is generally ornamented by thoſe who have any communication with Europeans, if of cloth, with ribands or lace, if of leather, with embroidery and porcupine quills curiouſly coloured. Strangers who hunt among the Indians, in the parts where there is a great deal of ſnow, find theſe ſtockings much more convenient than any others.

Their ſhoes are made of the skin of the deer, elk, or buffalo: theſe, after being ſometimes dreſſed according to the European manner, at others with the hair remaining on them, are cut into ſhoes, and faſhioned ſo as to be eaſy to the feet, and convenient for walking. The edges round the ancle are decorated with pieces of braſs or tin fixed around leather ſtrings, about an inch long, which being placed very thick, make a cheerful tinkling noiſe either when they walk or dance.

The women wear a covering of ſome kind or other from the neck to the knees. Thoſe who trade with the Europeans wear a linen garment, the ſame as that uſed by the men; the flaps of which hang over the petticoat. Such as dreſs after their ancient manner, make a kind of ſhift with leather, which covers the body but not the arms. Their petticoats are made either of leather or cloth, and reach from the waiſt to the knee. On their legs they wear ſtockings and ſhoes, made and ornamented as thoſe of the men.

They differ from each other in the mode of dreſſing their heads, each following the cuſtom of the nation or band to which they belong, and adhering to the form made uſe of by their anceſtors from time immemorial.

I remarked that moſt of the females, who dwell on the eaſt ſide of the Miſſiſſippi, decorate their heads by incloſing their hair either in ribands, or in plates of ſilver; the latter is only made uſe of by the higher ranks, as it is a coſtly ornament. The ſilver they uſe on this occaſion is formed into thin plates of about four inches broad, in ſeveral of which they confine their hair. That plate which is neareſt the head is of a conſiderable width; the next narrower, and made ſo as to paſs a little way under the other, and in this manner they faſten into each other, and gradually tapering, deſcend to the waiſt. The hair of the Indian women being in general very long, this proves an expenſive method.

But the women that live to the weſt of the Miſſiſſippi, viz. the Naudoweſſies, the Aſſinipoils, &c. divide their hair in the middle of the head, and form it into two rolls, one againſt each ear. Theſe rolls are about three inches long, and as large as their wriſts. They hang in a perpendicular attitude at the front of each ear, and deſcend as far as the lower part of it,

The women of every nation generally place a spot of paint, about the size of a crown-piece, against each ear; some of them put paint on their hair, and sometimes a small spot in the middle of the forehead.

The Indians, in general, pay a greater attention to their dress, and to the ornaments with which they decorate their persons, than to the accommodation of their huts or tents. They construct the latter in the following simple and expeditious manner.

Being provided with poles of a proper length, they fasten two of them across, near their ends, with bands made of bark. Having done this, they raise them up, and extend the bottom of each as wide as they purpose to make the area of the tent: they then erect others of an equal height, and fix them so as to support the two principal ones. On the whole they lay skins of the elk or deer, sewed together, in quantity sufficient to cover the poles, and by lapping over to form the door. A great number of skins are sometimes required for this purpose, as some of their tents are very capacious. That of the chief warrior of the Naudowessies was at least forty feet in circumference, and very commodious.

They observe no regularity in fixing their tents when they encamp, but place them just as it suits their conveniency.

The huts also, which those who use not tents, erect when they travel, for very few tribes have fixed abodes, or regular towns, or villages, are equally simple, and almost as soon constructed.

They fix small pliable poles in the ground, and bending them till they meet at the top and form a semi-circle, then lash them together. These they cover with mats made of rushes platted, or with birch bark, which they carry with them in their canoes for this purpose.

These cabins have neither chimnies nor windows; there is only a small aperture left in the middle of the roofs through which the smoke is discharged, but as this is obliged to be stopped up when it rains or snows violently, the smoke then proves exceedingly troublesome.

They lie on skins, generally those of the bear, which are placed in rows on the ground; and if the floor is not large enough to contain beds sufficient for the accommodation of the whole family, a frame is erected about four or five feet from the ground, in which the younger part of it sleep.

As the habitations of the Indians are thus rude, their domestic utensils are few in number, and plain in their formation. The tools wherewith they fashion them are so aukward and defective, that it is not only impossible to form them with any degree of neatness or elegance, but the time required in the execution is so considerable, as to deter them from engaging in the manufacture of such as are not absolutely necessary.

The Naudowessies make the pots in which they boil their victuals of the black clay or stone mentioned in my Journal; which resists the effects of the fire, nearly as well as iron. When they roast, if it is a large joint, or a whole animal, such as a beaver, they fix it as Europeans do, on a spit made of a hard wood, and placing the ends on two forked props, now and then turn it. If the piece is smaller they spit it as before, and fixing the spit in an erect but flanting position, with the meat inclining towards the fire, frequently change the sides, till every part is sufficiently roasted.

They make their dishes in which they serve up their meat, and their bowls and pans, out of the knotty excrescences of the maple tree, or any other wood. They fashion their spoons with a tolerable degree of neatness (as these require much less trouble than large utensils) from a wood that is termed in America Spoon Wood, and which greatly resembles box wood.

Every tribe are now possessed of knives, and steels to strike fire with. These being so essentially needful for the common uses of life, those who have not an immediate communication with the European traders, purchase them of such their neighbours as are situated nearer the settlements, and generally give in exchange for them slaves.

CHAPTER III.

Of their MANNERS, QUALIFICATIONS, *&c.*

WHEN the Indian women sit down, they place themselves in a decent attitude, with their knees close together; but from being accustomed to this posture, they walk badly, and appear to be lame.

They have no midwives amongst them, their climate, or some peculiar happiness in their constitutions, rendering any assistance at that time unnecessary. On these occasions they are confined but a few hours from their usual employments, which are commonly very laborious, as the men, who are remarkably indolent, leave to them every kind of drudgery; even in their hunting parties the former will not deign to bring home the game, but send their wives for it, though it lies at a very considerable distance.

The women place their children soon after they are born on boards stuffed with soft moss, such as is found in morasses or meadows. The child is laid on its back in one of these kind of cradles, and, being wrapped in skins or cloth to keep it warm, is secured in it by small bent pieces of timber.

To

To thefe machines they faften ftrings, by which they hang them to branches of trees; or if they find not trees at hand, faften them to a ftump or ftone, whilft they tranfact any needful bufinefs. In this pofition are the children kept for fome months, When they are taken out, the boys are fuffered to go naked, and the girls are covered from the neck to the knees with a fhift and a fhort petticoat.

The Indian women are remarkably decent during their menftrual illnefs. Thofe nations that are moft remote from the European fettlements, as the Naudoweffies, &c. are more particularly attentive to this point; though they all without exception adhere in fome degree to the fame cuftom.

In every camp or town there is an appartment appropriated for their retirement at this time, to which both fingle and married retreat, and feclude themfelves with the utmoft ftrictnefs during this period from all fociety. Afterwards they purify themfelves in running ftreams, and return to their different employments.

The men on thefe occafions moft carefully avoid holding any communication with them; and the Naudoweffies are fo rigid in this obfervance, that they will not fuffer any belonging to them to fetch fuch things as are neceffary, even fire, from thefe female lunar retreats, though the want of them is attended with the greateft inconvenience. They are alfo fo fuperftitious as to think, if a pipe ftem cracks, which among them is made of wood, that the poffeffor has either lighted it at one of thefe polluted fires, or held fome converfe with a woman during her retirement, which is efteemed by them moft difgraceful and wicked.

The Indians are extremely circumfpect and deliberate in every word and action; there is nothing that hurries them into any intemperate warmth, but that inveteracy to their enemies, which is rooted in every Indian heart, and never can be eradicated. In all other inftances they are cool, and remarkably cautious, taking care not to betray on any account whatever their emotions. If an Indian has difcovered that a friend is in danger of being intercepted and cut of by one to whom he has rendered himfelf obnoxious; he does not inform him in plain and explicit terms of the danger he runs by purfuing the track near which his enemy lies in wait for him, but he firft cooly asks him which way he is going that day; and having received his anfwer, with the fame indifference tells him that he has been informed that a dog lies near the fpot, which might probably do him a mifchief. This hint proves fufficient; and his friend avoids the danger with as much caution as if every defign and motion of his enemy had been pointed out to him.

This apathy often fhews itfelf on occafions that would call forth all the fervour of a fufceptible heart. If an Indian has been abfent from his family and friends many months, either on a war or hunting party, when his wife and children meet him at fome diftance from his habitation, inftead of the affectionate fen-
sations

sations that would naturally arise in the breast of more refined beings, and be productive of mutual congratulations, he continues his course without paying the least attention to those who surrounded him, till he arrives at his home.

He there sits down, and with the same unconcern as if he had not been absent a day, smokes his pipe; those of his acquaintance who have followed him, do the same; and perhaps it is several hours before he relates to them the incidents which have befallen him during his absence, though perhaps he has left a father, brother, or son on the field, whose loss he ought to have lamented, or has been unsuccessful in the undertaking that called him from his home.

Has an Indian been engaged for several days in the chace, or on any other laborious expedition, and by accident continued thus long without food, when he arrives at the hut or tent of a friend where he knows his wants may be immediately supplied, he takes care not to show the least symptoms of impatience, or to betray the extreme hunger by which he is tortured; but on being invited in, sits contentedly down, and smokes his pipe with as much composure as if every appetite was allayed, and he was perfectly at ease; he does the same if among strangers. This custom is strictly adhered to by every tribe, as they esteem it a proof of fortitude, and think the reverse would intitle them to the appellation of old women.

If you tell an Indian that his children have greatly signalized themselves against an enemy, have taken many scalps, and brought home many prisoners, he does not appear to feel any extraordinary pleasure on the occasion; his answer generally is, " It " is well," and he makes very little further enquiry about it. On the contrary, if you inform him that his children are slain or taken prisoners, he makes no complaints, he only replies, " It " does not signify;" and probably, for some time at least, asks not how it happened.

This seeming indifference, however, does not proceed from an entire suppression of the natural affections; for notwithstanding they are esteemed savages, I never saw among any other people greater proofs of parental or filial tenderness; and although they meet their wives after a long absence with the stoical indifference just mentioned, they are not, in general, void of conjugal affection.

Another peculiarity is observable in their manner of paying their visits. If an Indian goes to visit a particular person in a family, he mentions to whom his visit is intended, and the rest of the family immediately retiring to the other end of the hut or tent, are careful not to come near enough to interrupt them during the whole of the conversation. The same method is pursued if a man goes to pay his respects to one of the other sex; but then he must be careful not to let love be the subject of his discourse, whilst the day light remains.

The Indians discover an amazing sagacity, and acquire with the greatest readiness any thing that depends upon the attention of the mind. By experience and an acute observation, they attain many perfections to which Europeans are strangers. For instance, they will cross a forest or a plain which is two hundred miles in breadth, and reach with great exactness the point at which they intended to arrive, keeping during the whole of that space in a direct line, without any material deviations; and this they will do with the same ease, whether the weather be fair or cloudy.

With equal acuteness will they point to that part of the heavens the sun is in, though it be intercepted by clouds or fogs. Besides this, they are able to pursue with incredible facility the traces of man or beast, either on leaves or grass; and on this account it is with great difficulty a flying enemy escapes discovery.

They are indebted for these talents not only to nature, but to an extraordinary command of the intellectual faculties, which can only be acquired by an unremitted attention, and by long experience.

They are in general very happy in a retentive memory; they can recapitulate every particular that has been treated of in council, and remember the exact time when these were held. Their belts of wampum preserve the substance of the treaties they have concluded with the neighbouring tribes for ages back, to which they will appeal, and refer with as much perspicuity and readiness as Europeans can to their written records.

Every nation pays great respect to old age. The advice of a father will seldom meet with any extraordinary attention from the young Indians, probably they receive it with only a bare assent; but they will tremble before a grandfather, and submit to his injunction with the utmost alacrity. The words of the ancient part of their community are esteemed by the young as oracles. If they take during their hunting parties any game that is reckoned by them uncommonly delicious, it is immediately presented to the oldest of their relations.

They never suffer themselves to be overburdened with care, but live in a state of perfect tranquillity and contentment. Being naturally indolent, if provision just sufficient for their subsistence can be procured with little trouble, and near at hand, they will not go far, or take any extraordinary pains for it, though by so doing they might acquire greater plenty, and of a more estimable kind.

Having much leisure time they indulge this indolence to which they are so prone, by eating, drinking, or sleeping, and rambling about in their towns or camps. But when necessity obliges them to take the field, either to oppose an enemy, or to procure themselves food, they are alert and indefatigable. Many instances of their activity, on these occasions, will be given when I treat of their wars.

The infatuating spirit of gaming is not confined to Europe; the Indians also feel the bewitching impulse, and often lose their arms, their apparel, and every thing they are possessed of. In this case, however, they do not follow the example of more refined gamesters, for they neither murmur nor repine; not a fretful word escapes them, but they bear the frowns of fortune with a philosophic composure.

The greatest blemish in their character is that savage disposition which impels them to treat their enemies with a severity every other nation shudders at. But if they are thus barbarous to those with whom they are at war, they are friendly, hospitable, and humane in peace. It may with truth be said of them, that they are the worst enemies, and the best friends, of any people in the whole world.

The Indians in general are strangers to the passion of jealousy; and brand a man with folly that is distrustful of his wife. Among some bands the very Idea is not known; as the most abandoned of their young men very rarely attempt the virtue of married women, nor do these often put themselves in the way of solicitation. Yet the Indian women in general are of an amorous temperature, and before they are married are not the less esteemed for the indulgence of their passions.

The Indians in their common state are strangers to all distinction of property, except in the articles of domestic use, which every one considers as his own, and increases as circumstances admit. They are extremely liberal to each other, and supply the deficiency of their friends with any superfluity of their own.

In dangers they readily give assistance to those of their band, who stand in need of it, without any expectation of return, except of those just rewards that are always conferred by the Indians on merit. Governed by the plain and equitable laws of nature, every one is rewarded solely according to his deserts; and their equality of condition, manners, and privileges, with that constant and sociable familiarity which prevails throughout every Indian nation, animates them with a pure and truly patriotic spirit, that tends to the general good of the society to which they belong.

If any of their neighbours are bereaved by death, or by an enemy of their children, those who are possessed of the greatest number of slaves, supply the deficiency; and these are adopted by them, and treated in every respect as if they really were the children of the person to whom they are presented.

The Indians, except those who live adjoining to the European colonies, can form to themselves no idea of the value of money; they consider it, when they are made acquainted with the uses to which it is applied by other nations, as the source of innumerable evils. To it they attribute all the mischiefs that are prevalent among Europeans, such as treachery, plundering, devastations, and murder.

They

They esteem it irrational that one man should be possessed of a greater quantity than another, and are amazed that any honour should be annexed to the possession of it. But that the want of this useless metal should be the cause of depriving persons of their liberty, and that on account of this partial distribution of it, great numbers should be immured within the dreary walls of a prison, cut off from that society of which they constitute a part, exceeds their belief. Nor do they fail, on hearing this part of the European system of government related, to charge the institutors of it with a total want of humanity, and to brand them with the names of savages and brutes.

They shew almost an equal degree of indifference for the productions of art. When any of these are shewn them, they say, "It is pretty, I like to look at it," but are not inquisitive about the construction of it, neither can they form proper conceptions of its use. But if you tell them of a person who is able to run with great agility, that is well skilled in hunting, can direct with unerring aim a gun, or bend with ease a bow, that can dextrously work a canoe, understands the art of war, is acquainted with the situation of a country, and can make his way without a guide, through an immense forest, subsisting during this on a small quantity of provisions, they are in raptures; they listen with great attention to the pleasing tale, and bestow the highest commendations on the hero of it.

CHAPTER IV.

Their Method of reckoning TIME, *&c.*

CONSIDERING their ignorance of astronomy, time is very rationally divided by the Indians. Those in the interior parts (and of those I would generally be understood to speak) count their years by winters; or, as they express themselves, by snows.

Some nations among them reckon their years by moons, and make them consist of twelve synodical or lunar months, observing, when thirty moons have waned, to add a supernumerary one, which they term the lost moon; and then begin to count as before. They pay a great regard to the first appearance of every moon, and on the occasion always repeat some joyful sounds, stretching at the same time their hands towards it.

Every month has with them a name expressive of its season; for instance, they call the month of March (in which their year generally

generally begins at the first New Moon after the vernal Equinox) the Worm Month or Moon; becaufe at this time the worms quit their retreats in the bark of the trees, wood, &c. where they have fheltered themfelves during the winter.

The month of April is termed by them the month of Plants. May, the Month of Flowers. June, the Hot Moon. July, the Buck Moon. Their reafon for thus denominating thefe is obvious.

Auguft, the Sturgeon Moon; becaufe in this month they catch great numbers of that fifh.

September, the Corn Moon; becaufe in that month they gather in their Indian corn.

October, the Travelling Moon; as they leave at this time their villages, and travel towards the places where they intend to hunt during the winter.

November, the Beaver Moon; for in this month the beavers begin to take fhelter in their houfes, having laid up a fufficient ftore of provifions for the winter feafon.

December, the Hunting Moon, becaufe they employ this month in purfuit of their game.

January, the Cold Moon, as it generally freezes harder, and the cold is more intenfe in this than in any other month.

February they call the Snow Moon, becaufe more fnow commonly falls during this month, than any other in the winter.

When the moon does not fhine they fay the moon is dead; and fome call the three laft days of it the naked days. The moon's firft appearance they term its coming to life again.

They make no divifion of weeks; but days they count by fleeps; half days by pointing to the fun at noon; and quarters by the rifing and the fetting of the fun: to exprefs which in their traditions they make ufe of very fignificant hieroglyphicks.

The Indians are totally unfkilled in geography as well as all the other fciences, and yet, as I have before hinted, they draw on their birch bark very exact charts or maps of the countries with which they are acquainted. The latitude and longitude is only wanting to make them tolerably complete.

Their fole knowledge in aftronomy confifts in being able to point out the pole-ftar; by which they regulate their courfe when they travel in the night.

They reckon the diftance of places, not by miles or leagues, but by a day's journey, which, according to the beft calculations I could make, appears to be about twenty Englifh miles. Thefe they alfo divide into halves and quarters, and will demonftrate them in their maps with great exactnefs, by the hieroglyphicks juft mentioned, when they regulate in council their war parties, or their moft diftant hunting excurfions.

They have no idea of arithmetic; and though they are able to count to any number, figures as well as letters appear myfterious to them, and above their comprehenfion.

During

During my abode with the Naudoweffies, fome of the chiefs obferving one day a draft of an eclipfe of the moon, in a book of aftronomy which I held in my hand, they defired I would permit them to look at it. Happening to give them the book fhut, they began to count the leaves till they came to the place in which the plate was. After they had viewed it, and asked many queftions relative to it, I told them they needed not to have taken fo much pains to find the leaf on which it was drawn, for I could not only tell in an inftant the place, without counting the leaves, but alfo how many preceded it.

They feemed greatly amazed at my affertion, and begged that I would demonftrate to them the poffibility of doing it. To this purpofe I defired the chief that held the book, to open it at any particular place, and juft fhewing me the page carefully to conceal the edges of the leaves, fo that I might not be able to count them.

This he did with the greateft caution; notwithftanding which, by looking at the folio, I told him, to his great furprize, the number of leaves. He counted them regularly over, and difcovered that I was exact. And when, after repeated trials, the Indians found I could do it with great readinefs, and without ever erring in my calculation, they all feemed as much aftonifhed as if I had raifed the dead. The only way they could account for my knowledge, was by concluding that the book was a fpirit, and whifpered me anfwers to whatever I demanded of it.

This circumftance, trifling as it might appear to thofe who are lefs illiterate, contributed to increafe my confequence, and to augment the favourable opinion they already entertained of me.

CHAPTER V.

Of their GOVERNMENT, *&c.*

EVERY feparate body of Indians is divided into bands or tribes; which band or tribe forms a little community with the nation to which it belongs. As the nation has fome particular fymbol by which it is diftinguifhed from others, fo each tribe has a badge from which it is denominated: as that of the Eagle, the Panther, the Tiger, the Buffalo, &c. &c. One band of the Naudoweffie is reprefented by a Snake, another a Tortoife, a third a Squirrel, a fourth a Wolf, and a fifth a Buffalo. Throughout every nation they particularize themfelves in the fame manner, and the meaneft perfon among them will remember his lineal defcent, and diftinguifh himfelf by his refpective family.

Dif

Did not many circumstances tend to confute the supposition, I should be almost induced to conclude from this distinction of tribes, and the particular attachment of the Indians to them, that they derive their origin, as some have asserted, from the Israelites.

Besides this, every nation distinguish themselves by the manner of constructing their tents or huts. And so well versed are all the Indians in this distinction, that though there appears to be no difference on the nicest observation made by an European, yet they will immediately discover, from the position of a pole left in the ground, what nation has encamped on the spot many months before.

Every band has a chief who is termed the Great Chief or the chief Warrior; and who is chosen in consideration of his experience in war, and of his approved valour, to direct their military operations, and to regulate all concerns belonging to that department. But this chief is not considered as the head of the state; besides the great warrior who is elected for his war-like qualifications, there is another who enjoys a pre-eminence as his hereditary right, and has the more immediate management of their civil affairs. This chief might with greater propriety be denominated the Sachem; whose assent is necessary in all conveyances and treaties, to which he affixes the mark of the tribe or nation.

Though these two are considerd as the heads of the band, and the latter is usually denominated their king, yet the Indians are sensible of neither civil or military subordination. As every one of them entertains a high opinion of his consequence, and is extremely tenacious of his liberty, all injunctions that carry with them the appearance of a positive command, are instantly rejected with scorn.

On this account, it is seldom that their leaders are so indiscreet as to give out any of their orders in a peremptory stile; a bare hint from a chief that he thinks such a thing necessary to be done, instantly arouses an emulation among the inferior ranks, and it is immediately executed with great alacrity. By this method the disgustful part of the command is evaded, and an authority that falls little short of absolute sway instituted in its room.

Among the Indians no visible form of government is established; they allow of no such distinction as magistrate and subject, every one appearing to enjoy an independence that cannot be controuled. The object of government among them is rather foreign than domestic, for their attention seems more to be employed in preserving such an union among the members of their tribe as will enable them to watch the motions of their enemies, and to act against them with concert and vigour, than to maintain interior order by any public regulations. If a scheme that appears to be of service to the community is proposed by the chief, every one is at liberty to chuse whether he will assist in

carrying

carrying it on; for they have no compulsory laws that lay them under any restrictions. If violence is committed, or blood is shed, the right of revenging these misdemeanours are left to the family of the injured; the chiefs assume neither the power of inflicting or moderating the punishment.

Some nations, where the dignity is hereditary, limit the succession to the female line. On the death of a chief, his sister's son sometimes succeeds him in preference to his own son; and if he happens to have no sister, the nearest female relation assumes the dignity. This accounts for a woman being at the head of the Winnebagoe nation, which, before I was acquainted with their laws, appeared strange to me.

Each family has a right to appoint one of its chiefs to be an assistant to the principal chief, who watches over the interest of his family, and without whose consent nothing of a public nature can be carried into execution. These are generally chosen for their ability in speaking; and such only are permitted to make orations in their councils and general assemblies.

In this body, with the hereditary chief at its head, the supreme authority appears to be lodged; as by its determination every transaction relative to their hunting, to their making war or peace, and to all their public concerns are regulated. Next to these, the body of warriors, which comprehends all that are able bear arms, hold their rank. This division has sometimes at its head the chief of the nation, if he has signalized himself by any renowned action, if not, some chief that has rendered himself famous.

In their councils, which are held by the foregoing members, every affair of consequence is debated; and no enterprize of the least moment undertaken, unless it there meets with the general approbation of the chiefs. They commonly assemble in a hut or tent appropriated to this purpose, and being seated in a circle on the ground, the eldest chief rises and makes a speech; when he has concluded, another gets up; and thus they all speak, if necessary by turns.

On this occasion their language is nervous, and their manner of expression emphatical. Their style is adorned with images, comparisons, and strong metaphors, and is equal in allegories to that of any of the eastern nations. In all their set speeches they express themselves with much vehemence, but in common discourse according to our usual method of speech.

The young men are suffered to be present at the councils, though they are not allowed to make a speech till they are regularly admitted: they however listen with great attention, and to shew that they both understand, and approve of the resolutions taken by the assembled chiefs, they frequently exclaim, " That is right." " That is good."

The customary mode among all the ranks of expressing their assent, and which they repeat at the end of almost every period, is by uttering a kind of forcible aspiration, which sounds like an union of the letters OAH. CHAP.

CHAPTER VI.

Of their FEASTS.

MANY of the Indian nations neither make use of bread, salt, or spices; and some of them have never seen or tasted of either. The Naudowessies in particular have no bread, nor any substitute for it. They eat the wild rice which grows in great quantities in different parts of their territories; but they boil it and eat it alone. They also eat the flesh of the beasts they kill, without having recourse to any farinaceous substance to absorb the grosser particles of it. And even when they consume the sugar which they have extracted from the maple tree, they use it not to render some other food palatable, but generally eat it by itself.

Neither have they any idea of the use of milk, although they might collect great quantities from the buffalo or the elk; they only consider it as proper for the nutriment of the young of these beasts during their tender state. I could not perceive that any inconveniency attended the total disuse of articles esteemed so necessary and nutricious by other nations, on the contrary, they are in general healthy and vigorous.

One dish however, which answers nearly the same purpose as bread, is in use among the Ottagaumies, the Saukies, and the more eastern nations, where Indian corn grows, which is not only much esteemed by them, but it is reckoned extremely palatable by all the Europeans who enter their dominions. This is composed of their unripe corn as before described, and beans in the same state, boiled together with bear's flesh, the fat of which moistens the pulse, and renders it beyond comparison delicious. They call this food Succatosh.

The Indians are far from being canibals, as they are said to be. All their victuals are either roasted or boiled; and this in the extreme. Their drink is generally the broth in which it has been boiled.

Their food consists of the flesh of the bear, the buffalo, the elk, the deer, the beaver, and the racoon; which they prepare in the manner just mentioned. They usually eat the flesh of the deer which is naturally dry, with that of the bear which is fat and juicy; and though the latter is extremely rich and luscious, it is never known to cloy.

In the spring of the year the Naudowessies eat the inside bark of a shrub, that they gather in some part of their country; but I could neither learn the name of it, or discover from whence they got it. It was of a brittle nature and easily masticated. The taste of it was very agreeable, and they said it was extremely nourishing. In flavour it was not unlike the turnip, and when received into the mouth resembled that root both in its pulpous and frangible nature.

The lower ranks of the Indians are exceedingly nasty in dressing their victuals, but some of the chiefs are very neat and cleanly in their apparel, tents, and food.

They commonly eat in large parties, so that their meals may properly be termed feasts; and this they do without being restricted to any fixed or regular hours, but just as their appetites require, and convenience suits.

They usually dance either before or after every meal; and by this cheerfulness probably render the Great Spirit, to whom they consider themselves as indebted for every good, a more acceptable sacrifice than a formal and unanimated thanksgiving. The men and women feast apart: and each sex invite by turns their companions, to partake with them of the food they happen to have; but in their domestic way of living the men and women eat together.

No people are more hospitable, kind, and free than the Indians. They will readily share with any of their own tribe the last part of their provisions, and even with those of a different nation, if they chance to come in when they are eating. Though they do not keep one common stock, yet that community of goods which is so prevalent among them, and their generous disposition, render it nearly of the same effect.

When the chiefs are convened on any public business, they always conclude with a feast, at which their festivity and cheerfulness knows no limits.

CHAPTER VII.

Of their DANCES.

DANCING is a favourite exercise among the Indians; they never meet on any public occasion, but this makes a part of the entertainment. And when they are not engaged in war or hunting, the youth of both sexes amuse themselves in this manner every evening.

They always dance, as I have just observed, at their feast.

In thefe as well as all their other dances, every man rifes in his turn, and moves about with great freedom and boldnefs; finging as he does fo, the exploits of his anceftors. During this the company, who are feated on the ground in a circle, around the dancer, join with him in marking the cadence, by an odd tone, which they utter all together, and which founds, "Heh, heh, heh." Thefe notes, if they might be fo termed, are articulated with a harfh accent, and ftrained out with the utmoft force of their lungs; fo that one would imagine their ftrength muft be foon exhaufted by it; inftead of which, they repeat it with the fame violence during the whole of their entertainment.

The women, particularly thofe of the weftern nations, dance very gracefully. They carry themfelves erect, and with their arms hanging down clofe to their fides, move firft a few yards to the right, and then back again to the left. This movement they perform without taking any fteps as an European would do, but with their feet conjoined, moving by turns their toes and heels. In this manner they glide with great agility to a certain diftance, and then return; and let thofe who join in the dance be ever fo numerous, they keep time fo exactly with each other that no interruption enfues. During this, at ftated periods, they mingle their fhrill voices, with the hoarfer ones of the men, who fit around (for it is to be obferved that the fexes never intermix in the fame dance) which, with the mufic of the drums and chichicoes, make an agreeable harmony.

The Indians have feveral kinds of dances, which they ufe on different occafions, as the Pipe or Calumate Dance, the War Dance, the Marriage Dance, and the Dance of the Sacrifice. The movements in every one of thefe are diffimilar; but it is almoft impoffible to convey any idea of the points in which they are unlike.

Different nations likewife vary in their manner of dancing. The Chipéways throw themfelves into a greater variety of attitudes than any other people; fometimes they hold their heads erect, at others they bend them almoft to the ground; then recline on one fide, and immediately after on the other. The Naudoweffies carry themfelves more upright, ftep firmer, and move more gracefully. But they all accompany their dances with the difagreeable noife juft mentioned.

The Pipe Dance is the principal, and the moft pleafing to a fpectator of any of them, being the leaft frantic, and the movement of it moft graceful. It is but on particular occafions that it is ufed; as when ambaffadors from an enemy arrive to treat of peace, or when ftrangers of eminence pafs through their territories.

The War Dance, which they ufe both before they fet out on their war parties, and on their return from them, ftrikes terror into ftrangers. It is performed, as the others, amidft a circle of the warriors; a chief generally begins it, who moves
from

from the right to the left, singing at the same time both his own exploits, and those of his ancestors. When he has concluded his account of any memorable action, he gives a violent blow with his war-club, against a post that is fixed in the ground, near the center of the assembly, for this purpose.

Every one dances in his turn, and recapitulates the wondrous deeds of his family, till they all at last join in the dance. Then it becomes truly alarming to any stranger that happens to be among them, as they throw themselves into every horrible and terrifying posture that can be imagined, rehearsing at the same time the parts they expect to act against their enemies in the field. During this they hold their sharp knives in their hands, with which, as they whirl about, they are every moment in danger of cutting each others throats; and did they not shun the threatened mischief with inconceivable dexterity, it could not be avoided. By these motions they intend to represent the manner in which they kill, scalp, and take their prisoners. To heighten the scene, they set up the same hideous yells, cries, and war-hoops they use in time of action: so that it is impossible to consider them in any other light than as an assembly of demons.

I have frequently joined in this dance with them, but it soon ceased to be an amusement to me, as I could not lay aside my apprehensions of receiving some dreadful wound, that from the violence of their gestures must have proved mortal.

I found that the nations to the westward of the Missisippi, and on the borders of Lake Superior, still continue to make use of the Pawwaw or Black Dance. The people of the colonies tell a thousand ridiculous stories of the Devil being raised in this dance by the Indians. But they allow that this was in former times, and is now nearly extinct among those who live adjacent to the European settlements. However I discovered that it was still used in the interior parts; and though I did not actually see the Devil raised by it, I was witness to some scenes that could only be performed by such as dealt with him, or were very expert and dextrous jugglers.

Whilst I was among the Naudowessies, a dance, which they thus termed, was performed. Before the dance began, one of the Indians was admitted into a society which they denominated Wakon-Kitchewah, that is, the Friendly Society of the Spirit. This society is composed of persons of both sexes, but such only can be admitted into it as are of unexceptionable character, and who receive the approbation of the whole body. To this admission succeeded the Pawwaw Dance (in which I saw nothing that could give rise to the reports I had heard) and the whole, according to their usual custom, concluded with a grand feast.

The initiation being attended with some very singular circumstances, which, as I have before observed, must be either the effect of magic, or of amazing dexterity, I shall give a particular account of the whole procedure. It was performed at the time of
the

the new moon, in a place appropriated to the purpose, near the centre of their camp, that would contain about two hundred people. Being a stranger, and on all occasions treated by them with great civility, I was invited to see the ceremony, and placed close to the rails of the inclosure.

About twelve o'clock they began to assemble; when the sun shone bright, which they considered as a good omen, for they never by choice hold any of their public meetings unless the sky be clear and unclouded. A great number of chiefs first appeared, who were dressed in their best apparel; and after them came the head-warrior, clad in a long robe of rich furs, that trailed on the ground, attended by a retinue of fifteen or twenty persons, painted and dressed in the gayest manner. Next followed the wives of such as had been already admitted into the society; and in the rear a confused heap of the lower ranks, all contributing as much as lay in their power to make the appearance grand and showy.

When the assembly was seated, and silence proclaimed, one of the principal chiefs arose, and in a short but masterly speech informed his audience of the occasion of their meeting. He acquainted them that one of their young men wished to be admitted into their society; and taking him by the hand presented him to their view, asking them, at the same time, whether they had any objection to his becoming one of their community.

No objection being made, the young candidate was placed in the centre, and four of the chiefs took their stations close to him; after exhorting him, by turns, not to faint under the operation he was about to go through, but to behave like an Indian and a man, two of them took hold of his arms, and caused him to kneel; another placed himself behind him, so as to receive him when he fell, and the last of the four retired to the distance of about twelve feet from him exactly in front.

This disposition being completed, the chief that stood before the kneeling candidate, began to speak to him with an audible voice. He told him that he himself was now agitated by the same spirit which he should in a few moments communicate to him; that it would strike him dead, but that he would instantly be restored again to life; to this he added, that the communication, however terrifying, was a necessary introduction to the advantages enjoyed by the community into which he was on the point of being admitted.

As he spoke this, he appeared to be greatly agitated; till at last his emotions became so violent, that his countenance was distorted, and his whole frame convulsed. At this juncture he threw something that appeared both in shape and colour like a small bean, at the young man, which seemed to enter his mouth, and he instantly fell as motionless as if he had been shot. The chief that was placed behind him received him in his arms, and, by the assistance of the other two, laid him on the ground to all appearance bereft of life.

Having

Having done this, they immediately began to rub his limbs, and to strike him on the back, giving him such blows, as seemed more calculated to still the quick, than to raise the dead. During these extraordinary applications, the speaker continued his harangue, desiring the spectators not to be surprized, or to despair of the young man's recovery, as his present inanimate situation proceeded only from the forcible operation of the spirit, on faculties that had hitherto been unused to inspirations of this kind.

The candidate lay several minutes without sense or motion; but at length, after receiving many violent blows, he began to discover some symptoms of returning life. These, however, were attended with strong convulsions, and an apparent obstruction in his throat. But they were soon at an end; for having discharged from his mouth the bean, or whatever it was that the chief had thrown at him, but which on the closest inspection I had not perceived to enter it, he soon after appeared to be tolerably recovered.

This part of the ceremony being happily effected, the officiating chiefs disrobed him of the cloaths he had usually worn, and put on him a set of apparel entirely new. When he was dressed, the speaker once more took him by the hand, and presented him to the society as a regular and thoroughly initiated member, exhorting them, at the same time, to give him such necessary assistance, as being a young member, he might stand in need of. He then also charged the newly elected brother to receive with humility, and to follow with punctuality the advice of his elder brethren.

All those who had been admitted within the rails, now formed a circle around their new brother, and the music striking up, the great chief sung a song, celebrating as usual their martial exploits.

The only music they make use of is a drum, which is composed of a piece of a hollow tree curiously wrought, and over one end of which is strained a skin, this they beat with a single stick, and it gives a sound that is far from harmonious, but it just serves to beat time with. To this they sometimes add the chichicoe, and in their war dances they likewise use a kind of fife, formed of a reed, which makes a shrill harsh noise.

The whole assembly were by this time united, and the dance began; several singers assisted the music with their voices, and the women joining in the chorus at certain intervals, they produced together a not unpleasing but savage harmony. This was one of the most agreeable entertainments I saw whilst I was among them.

I could not help laughing at a singular childish custom I observed they introduced into this dance, and which was the only one that had the least appearance of conjuration. Most of the members carried in their hands an otter or martin's skin, which being taken whole from the body, and filled with wind, on being

compressed

compressed made a squeaking noise through a small piece of wood organically formed and fixed in its mouth. When this instrument was presented to the face of any of the company, and the sound emitted, the person receiving it instantly fell down to appearance dead. Sometimes two or three, both men and women, were on the ground together; but immediately recovering, they rose up and joined again in the dance. This seemed to afford, even the chiefs themselves, infinite diversion. I afterwards learned that these were their Dii Penates or Houshold Gods.

After some hours spent in this manner the feast began; the dishes being brought near me, I perceived that they consisted of dog's flesh; and I was informed that at all their public grand feasts they never made use of any other kind of food. For this purpose, at the feast I am now speaking of, the new candidate provides fat dogs, if they can be procured at any price.

In this custom of eating dog's flesh on particular occasions, they resemble the inhabitants of some of the countries that lie on the north-east borders of Asia. The author of the account of Kamschatka, published by order of the Empress of Russia (before referred to) informs us, that the people inhabiting Koreka, a country north of Kamschatka, who wander about in hords like the Arabs, when they pay their worship to the evil beings, kill a rein-deer or a dog, the flesh of which they eat, and leave the head and tongue sticking on a pole with the front towards the east. Also that when they are afraid of any infectious distemper, they kill a dog, and winding the guts about two poles, pass between them. These customs, in which they are nearly imitated by the Indians, seem to add strength to my supposition, that America was first peopled from this quarter.

I know not under what class of dances to rank that performed by the Indians who came to my tent when I landed near Lake Pepin, on the banks of the Mississippi, as related in my Journals. When I looked out, as I there mentioned, I saw about twenty naked young Indians, the most perfect in their shape, and by far the handsomest of any I had ever seen, coming towards me, and dancing as they approached, to the music of their drums. At every ten or twelve yards they halted, and set up their yells and cries.

When they reached my tent, I asked them to come in; which, without deigning to make me any answer, they did. As I observed that they were painted red and black, as they usually are when they go against an enemy, and perceived that some parts of the war-dance were intermixed with their other movements, I doubted not but they were set on by the inimical chief who had refused my salutation: I therefore determined to sell my life as dear as possible. To this purpose, I received them sitting on my chest, with my gun and pistols beside me, and ordered my men to keep a watchful eye on them, and to be also upon their guard.

The

The Indians being entered, they continued their dance alternately, singing at the same time of their heroic exploits, and the superiority of their race over every other people. To enforce their language, though it was uncommonly nervous and expressive, and such as would of itself have carried terror to the firmest heart, at the end of every period they struck their war-clubs against the poles of my tent, with such violence, that I expected every moment it would have tumbled upon us. As each of them, in dancing round, passed by me, they placed their right hands over their eyes, and coming close to me, looked me steadily in the face, which I could not construe into a token of friendship. My men gave themselves up for lost, and I acknowledge, for my own part, that I never found my apprehensions more tumultuous on any occasion.

When they had nearly ended their dance, I presented to them the pipe of peace, but they would not receive it. I then, as my last resource, thought I would try what presents would do; accordingly I took from my chest some ribands and trinkets, which I laid before them. These seemed to stagger their resolutions, and to avert in some degree their anger; for after holding a consultation together, they sat down on the ground, which I considered as a favourable omen.

Thus it proved, as in a short time they received the pipe of peace, and lighting it, first presented it to me, and then smoaked with it themselves. Soon after they took up the presents, which had hitherto lain neglected, and appearing to be greatly pleased with them, departed in a friendly manner. And never did I receive greater pleasure than at getting rid of such formidable guests.

It was not ever in my power to gain a thorough knowledge of the designs of my visitors. I had sufficient reason to conclude that they were hostile, and that their visit, at so late an hour, was made through the instigation of the Grand Sautor; but I was afterwards informed that it might be intended as a compliment which they usually pay to the chiefs of every other nation who happen to fall in with them, and that the circumstances in their conduct, which had appeared so suspicious to me, were merely the effects of their vanity, and designed to impress on the minds of those whom they thus visited an elevated opinion of their valour and prowess. In the morning before I continued my route, several of their wives brought me a present of some sugar, for whom I found a few more ribands.

The Dance of the sacrifice is not so denominated from their offering up at the same time a sacrifice to any good or evil spirit, but is a dance to which the Naudowessies give that title from being used when any public fortunate circumstance befals them. Whilst I resided among them, a fine large deer accidentally strayed into the middle of their encampment, which they soon destroyed. As this happened just at the new moon, they
esteemed

esteemed it a lucky omen; and having roasted it whole, every one in the camp partook of it. After their feast, they all joined in a dance, which they termed, from its being somewhat of a religious nature, a Dance of the sacrifice.

CHAPTER VIII.

Of their HUNTING.

HUNTING, is the principal occupation of the Indians; they are trained to it from their earliest youth, and it is an exercise which is esteemed no less honourable than necessary towards their subsistence. A dextrous and resolute hunter is held nearly in as great estimation by them as a distinguished warrior. Scarcely any device which the ingenuity of man has discovered for ensnaring or destroying those animals that supply them with food, or whose skins are valuable to Europeans, is unknown to them.

Whilst they are engaged in this exercise, they shake off the indolence peculiar to their nature, and become active, persevering, and indefatigable. They are equally sagacious in finding their prey, and in the means they use to destroy it. They discern the footsteps of the beasts they are in pursuit of, although they are imperceptible to every other eye, and can follow them with certainty through the pathless forest.

The beasts that the Indians hunt, both for their flesh on which they subsist, and for their skins, of which they either make their apparel, or barter with the Europeans for necessaries, are the buffalo, the elk, the deer, the moose, carribboo, the bear, the beaver, the otter, the martin, &c. I defer giving a description of these creatures here, and shall only at present treat of their manner of hunting them.

The route they shall take for this purpose, and the parties that shall go on the different expeditions are fixed in their general councils which are held some time in the summer, when all the operations for the ensuing winter are concluded on. The chief-warrior, whose province it is to regulate their proceedings on this occasion, with great solemnity issues out an invitation to those who choose to attend him; for the Indians, as before observed, acknowledge no superiority, nor have they any idea of compulsion; and every one that accepts it prepares himself by fasting during several days.

The Indians do not fast as some other nations do, on the richest and most luxurious food, but they totally abstain from every kind either of victuals or drink; and such is their patience and resolution, that the most extreme thirst could not oblige them to taste a drop of water; yet amidst this severe abstinence they appear cheerful and happy.

The reasons they give for thus fasting, are, that it enables them freely to dream, in which dreams they are informed where they shall find the greatest plenty of game; and also that it averts the displeasure of the evil spirits, and induces them to be propitious. They also on these occasions blacken those parts of their bodies that are uncovered.

The fast being ended, and the place of hunting made known, the chief who is to conduct them, gives a grand feast to those who are to form the different parties; of which none of them dare to partake till they have bathed themselves. At this feast, notwithstanding they have fasted so long, they eat with great moderation; and the chief that presides employs himself in rehearsing the feats of those who have been most successful in the business they are about to enter upon. They soon after set out on the march towards the place appointed, painted or rather bedawbed with black, amidst the acclamations of all the people.

It is impossible to describe their agility or perseverance, whilst they are in pursuit of their prey; neither thickets, ditches, torrents, pools, or rivers stop them; they always go strait forward in the most direct line they possibly can, and there are few of the savage inhabitants of the woods that they cannot overtake.

When they hunt for bears, they endeavour to find out their retreats; for, during the winter, these animals conceal themselves in the hollow trunks of trees, or make themselves holes in the ground, where they continue without food, whilst the severe weather lasts.

When the Indians think they have arrived at a place where these creatures usually haunt, they form themselves into a circle according to their number, and moving onward, endeavour, as they advance towards the centre, to discover the retreats of their prey. By this means, if any lie in the intermediate space, they are sure of arousing them, and bringing them down either with their bows or their guns. The bears will take to flight at sight of a man or a dog, and will only make resistance when they are extremely hungry, or after they are wounded.

The Indian method of hunting the buffalo is by forming a circle or a square, nearly in the same manner as when they search for the bear. Having taken their different stations, they set the grass, which at this time is rank and dry, on fire, and these animals, who are extremely fearful of that element, flying with precipitation before it, great numbers are hemmed in a small compass, and scarcely a single one escapes.

They

They have different ways of hunting the elk, the deer, and the carribboo. Sometimes they seek them out in the woods, to which they retire during the severity of the cold, where they are easily shot from behind the trees. In the more northern climates they take the advantage of the weather to destroy the elk; when the sun has just strength enough to melt the snow and the frost in the night forms a kind of crust on the surface, this creature being heavy, breaks it with his forked hoofs, and with difficulty extricates himself from it: at this time therefore he is soon overtaken and destroyed.

Some nations have a method of hunting these animals which is more easily executed, and free from danger. The hunting party divide themselves into two bands, and choosing a spot near the borders of some river, one party embarks on board their canoes, whilst the other forming themselves into a semi-circle on the land, the flanks of which reach the shore, let loose their dogs, and by this means rouse all the game that lies within these bounds; they then drive them towards the river, into which they no sooner enter, than the greatest part of them are immediately dispatched by those who remain in the canoes.

Both the elk and the buffalo are very furious when they are wounded, and will return fiercely on their pursuers, and trample them under their feet, if the hunter finds no means to complete their destruction, or seeks for security in flight to some adjacent tree; by this method they are frequently avoided, and so tired with the pursuit, that they voluntarily give it over.

But the hunting in which the Indians, particularly those who inhabit the northern parts, chiefly employ themselves, and from which they reap the greatest advantage, is the beaver hunting. The season for this is throughout the whole of the winter, from November to April; during which time the fur of these creatures is in the greatest perfection. A description of this extraordinary animal, the construction of their huts, and the regulations of their almost rational community, I shall give in another place.

The hunters make use of several methods to destroy them. Those generally practised, are either that of taking them in snares, cutting through the ice, or opening their causeways.

As the eyes of these animals are very quick, and their hearing exceedingly accute, great precaution is necessary in approaching their abodes; for as they seldom go far from the water, and their houses are always built close to the side of some large river or lake, or dams of their own constructing, upon the least alarm they hasten to the deepest part of the water, and dive immediately to the bottom; as they do this they make a great noise by beating the water with their tails, on purpose to put the whole fraternity on their guard.

They take them with snares in the following manner: though the beavers usually lay up a sufficient store of provision to serve for their subsistence during the winter, they make from time to time excursions to the neighbouring woods to procure further

supplies

supplies of food. The hunters having found out their haunts, place a trap in their way, baited with small pieces of bark, or young shoots of trees, which the beaver has no sooner laid hold of, than a large log of wood falls upon him, and breaks his back; his enemies, who are upon the watch, soon appear, and instantly dispatch the helpless animal.

At other times, when the ice on the rivers and lakes is about half a foot thick, they make an opening through it with their hatchets, to which the beavers will soon hasten, on being disturbed at their houses, for a supply of fresh air. As their breath occasions a considerable motion in the waters, the hunter has sufficient notice of their approach, and methods are easily taken for knocking them on the head the moment they appear above the surface.

When the houses of the beavers happen to be near a rivulet, they are more easily destroyed: the hunters then cut the ice, and spreading a net under it, break down the cabins of the beavers, who never fail to make towards the deepest part, where they are entangled and taken. But they must not be suffered to remain there long, as they would soon extricate themselves with their teeth, which are well known to be excessively sharp and strong.

The Indians take great care to hinder their dogs from touching the bones of the beavers. The reasons they give for these precautions, are, first, that the bones are so excessively hard, that they spoil the teeth of the dogs; and, secondly, that they are apprehensive they shall so exasperate the spirits of the beavers by this permission, as to render the next hunting season unsuccessful.

The skins of these animals the hunters exchange with the Europeans for necessaries, and as they are more valued by the latter than any other kind of furs, they pay the greatest attention to this species of hunting.

When the Indians destroy buffalos, elks, deer, &c. they generally divide the flesh of such as they have taken among the tribe to which they belong. But in hunting the beaver a few families usually unite and divide the spoil between them. Indeed, in the first instance they generally pay some attention in the division to their own families; but no jealousies or murmurings are ever known to arise on account of any apparent partiality.

Among the Naudowessies, if a person shoots a deer, buffalo, &c. and it runs to a considerable distance before it drops, where a person belonging to another tribe, being nearer, first sticks a knife into it, the game is considered as the property of the latter, notwithstanding it had been mortally wounded by the former. Though this custom appears to be arbitrary and unjust, yet that people cheerfully submit to it. This decision is, however, very different from that practised by the Indians on the back of the colonies, where the first person that hits it is entitled to the best share.

CHAPTER IX.

Of their Manner of making WAR, *&c.*

THE Indians begin to bear arms at the age of fifteen, and lay them aside when they arrive at the age of sixty. Some nations to the southward, I have been informed, do not continue their military exercises after they are fifty.

In every band or nation there is a select number who are stiled the warriors, and who are always ready to act either offensively or defensively, as occasion requires. These are well armed, bearing the weapons commonly in use among them, which vary according to the situation of their countries. Such as have an intercourse with the Europeans make use of tomahawks, knives, and fire-arms; but those whose dwellings are situated to the westward of the Mississippi, and who have not an opportunity of purchasing these kinds of weapons, use bows and arrows, and also the Casse Tête or War-club.

The Indians that inhabit still farther to the westward, a country which extends to the South Sea, use in fight a warlike instrument that is very uncommon. Having great plenty of horses, they always attack their enemies on horseback, and encumber themselves with no other weapon, than a stone of a middling size, curiously wrought, which they fasten by a string, about a yard and a half long, to their right arms, a little above the elbow. These stones they conveniently carry in their hands, till they reach their enemies, and then swinging them with great dexterity, as they ride full speed, never fail of doing execution. The country which these tribes possess, abounding with large extensive plains, those who attack them seldom return; as the swiftness of the horses, on which they are mounted, enables them to overtake even the fleetest of their invaders.

The Naudowessies, who had been at war with this people, informed me, that unless they found morasses or thickets to which they could retire, they were sure of being cut off: to prevent this they always took care whenever they made an onset, to do it near such retreats as were impassable for cavalry, they then having a great advantage over their enemies, whose weapons would not there reach them.

Some nations make use of a javelin, pointed with bone, worked into different forms; but their Indian weapons in general are bows and arrows, and the short club already mentioned. The latter is made of a very hard wood, and the head of it fashioned

fashioned round like a ball, about three inches and a half diameter; in this rotund part is fixed an edge resembling that of a tomahawk, either of steel or flint, whichever they can procure.

The dagger is peculiar to the Naudoweffie nation, and of ancient construction, but they can give no account how long it has been in use among them. It was originally made of flint or bone, but since they have had communication with the European traders, they have formed it of steel. The length of it is about ten inches, and that part close to the handle nearly three inches broad. Its edges are keen, and it gradually tapers towards a point. They wear it in a sheath made of deer's leather, neatly ornamented with porcupine quills; and it is usually hung by a string, decorated in the same manner, which reaches as low only as the breast. This curious weapon is worn by a few of the principal chiefs alone, and considered both as an useful instrument, and an ornamental badge of superiority.

I observed among the Naudoweffies a few targets or shields made of raw buffalo hides, and in the form of those used by the ancients. But as the number of these was small, and I could gain no intelligence of the æra in which they first were introduced among them, I suppose those I saw had descended from father to son for many generations.

The reasons the Indians give for making war against one another, are much the same as those urged by more civilized nations for disturbing the tranquillity of their neighbours. The pleas of the former are however in general more rational and just, than such as are brought by Europeans in vindication of their proceedings.

The extension of empire is seldom a motive with these people to invade, and to commit depredations on the territories of those who happen to dwell near them. To secure the rights of hunting within particular limits, to maintain the liberty of passing through their accustomed tracks, and to guard those lands which they consider from a long tenure as their own, against any infringement, are the general causes of those dissensions that so often break out between the Indian nations, and which are carried on with so much animosity.

Though strangers to the idea of separate property, yet the most uncultivated among them are well acquainted with the rights of their community to the domains they possess, and oppose with vigour every encroachment on them.

Notwithstanding it is generally supposed that from their territories being so extensive, the boundaries of them cannot be ascertained, yet I am well assured that the limits of each nation in the interior parts are laid down in their rude plans with great precision. By theirs, as I have before observed, was I enabled to regulate my own; and after the most exact observations and enquiries found very few instances in which they erred.

But

But interest is not either the most frequent or most powerful incentive to their making war on each other. The passion of revenge, which is the distinguishing characteristic of these people, is the most general motive. Injuries are felt by them with exquisite sensibility, and vengeance pursued with unremitted ardour. To this may be added, that natural excitation which every Indian becomes sensible of as soon as he approaches the age of manhood to give proofs of his valour and prowess.

As they are early possessed with a notion that war ought to be the chief business of their lives, that there is nothing more desirous than the reputation of being a great warrior, and that the scalps of their enemies, or a number of prisoners are alone to be esteemed valuable, it is not to be wondered at that the younger Indians are continually restless and uneasy if their ardour is repressed, and they are kept in a state of inactivity. Either of these propensities, the desire of revenge, or the gratification of an impulse, that by degrees becomes habitual to them, is sufficient, frequently, to induce them to commit hostilities on some of the neighbouring nations.

When the chiefs find any occasion for making war, they endeavour to arouse these habitudes, and by that means soon excite their warriors to take arms. To this purpose they make use of their martial eloquence, nearly in the following words, which never fails of proving effectual; " The bones of our deceased " countrymen lie uncovered, they call out to us to revenge " their wrongs, and we must satisfy their request. Their spi-" rits cry out against us. They must be appeased. The genii, " who are the guardians of our honour, inspire us with a reso-" lution to seek the enemies of our murdered brothers. Let " us go and devour those by whom they were slain. Sit there-" fore no longer inactive, give way to the impulse of your na-" tural valour, anoint your hair, paint your faces, fill your " quivers, cause the forests to resound with your songs, con-" sole the spirits of the dead, and tell them they shall be re-" venged."

Animated by these exhortations the warriors snatch their arms in a transport of fury, sing the song of war, and burn with impatience to imbrue their hands in the blood of their enemies.

Sometimes private chiefs assemble small parties, and make excursions against those with whom they are at war, or such as have injured them. A single warrior, prompted by revenge or a desire to show his prowess, will march unattended for several hundred miles, to surprize and cut off a straggling party.

These irregular sallies, however, are not always approved of by the elder chiefs, though they are often obliged to connive at them; as in the instance before given of the Naudowessie and Chipeway nations.

But when a war is national, and undertaken by the community, their deliberations are formal and slow. The elders assemble

semble in council, to which all the head warriors and young men are admitted, where they deliver their opinions in solemn speeches, weighing with maturity the nature of the enterprize they are about to engage in, and balancing with great sagacity the advantages or inconveniences that will arise from it.

Their priests are also consulted on the subject, and even, sometimes, the advice of the most intelligent of their women is asked.

If the determination be for war, they prepare for it with much ceremony.

The chief warrior of a nation does not on all occasions head the war party himself, he frequently deputes a warrior of whose valour and prudence he has a good opinion. The person thus fixed on being first bedawbed with black, observes a fast of several days, during which he invokes the Great Spirit, or deprecates the anger of the evil ones, holding whilst it lasts no converse with any of his tribe.

He is particularly careful at the same time to observe his dreams, for on these do they suppose their success will in a great measure depend; and from the firm persuasion every Indian actuated by his own presumptuous thoughts is impressed with, that he shall march forth to certain victory, these are generally favourable to his wishes.

After he has fasted as long as custom prescribes, he assembles the warriors, and holding a belt of wampum in his hand, thus addresses them:

"Brothers! by the inspiration of the Great Spirit I now
"speak unto you, and by him am I prompted to carry into exe-
"cution the intentions which I am about to disclose to you.
"The blood of our deceased brothers is not yet wiped away;
"their bodies are not yet covered, and I am going to per-
"form this duty to them."

Having then made known to them all the motives that induce him to take up arms against the nation with whom they are to engage, he thus proceeds: "I have therefore resolved to "march through the war-path to surprize them. We will eat "their flesh, and drink their blood; we will take scalps, and "make prisoners; and should we perish in this glorious enter- "prize, we shall not be forever hid in the dust, for this belt "shall be a recompence to him who buries the dead." Having said this, he lays the belt on the ground, and he who takes it up declares himself his lieutenant, and is considered as the second in command; this, however, is only done by some distinguished warrior who has a right, by the number of his scalps, to the post.

Though the Indians thus assert that they will eat the flesh and drink the blood of their enemies, the threat is only to be considered as a figurative expression. Notwithstanding they sometimes devour the hearts of those they slay, and drink their blood, by way of bravado, or to gratify in a more complete

manner

manner their revenge, yet they are not naturally anthropophagi, nor ever feed on the flesh of men.

The chief is now washed from his fable covering, anointed with bear's fat, and painted with their red paint, in such figures as will make him appear most terrible to his enemies. He then sings the war song, and enumerates his warlike actions. Having done this he fixes his eyes on the sun, and pays his adorations to the Great Spirit, in which he is accompanied by all the warriors.

This ceremony is followed with dances, such as I have before described; and the whole concludes with a feast, which usually consists of dogs flesh.

This feast is held in the hut or tent of the chief warrior, to which all those who intend to accompany him in his expedition send their dishes to be filled; and during the feast, notwithstanding he has fasted so long, he sits composedly with his pipe in his mouth, and recounts the valorous deeds of his family.

As the hopes of having their wounds, should they receive any, properly treated, and expeditiously cured, must be some additional inducement to the warriors to expose themselves more freely to danger, the priests, who are also their doctors, prepare such medecines as will prove efficacious. With great ceremony they carry various roots and plants, and pretend that they impart to them the power of healing.

Notwithstanding this superstitious method of proceeding, it is very certain that they have acquired a knowledge of many plants and herbs that are of a medicinal quality, and which they know how to use with great skill.

From the time the resolution of engaging in a war is taken, to the departure of the warriors, the nights are spent in festivity, and their days in making the needful preparations.

If it is thought necessary by the nation going to war, to solicit the alliance of any neighbouring tribe, they fix upon one of their chiefs who speaks the language of that people well, and who is a good orator, and send to them by him a belt of wampum, on which is specified the purport of the embassy in figures that every nation is well acquainted with. At the same time he carries with him a hatchet painted red.

As soon as he reaches the camp or village to which he is destined, he acquaints the chief of the tribe with the general tenor of his commission, who immediately assembles a council, to which the ambassador is invited. There having laid the hatchet on the ground he holds the belt in his hand, and enters more minutely into the occasion of his embassy. In his speech he invites them to take up the hatchet, and as soon as he has finished speaking delivers the belt.

If his hearers are inclined to become auxiliaries to his nation, a chief steps forward and takes up the hatchet, and they immediately espouse with spirit the cause they have thus engaged to support. But if on this application neither the belt or hatchet

R   are

are accepted, the emissary concludes that the people whose assistance he solicits have already entered into an alliance with the foes of his nation, and returns with speed to inform his countrymen of his ill success.

The manner in which the Indians declare war against each other, is by sending a slave with a hatchet, the handle of which is painted red, to the nation which they intend to break with; and the messenger, notwithstanding the danger to which he is exposed from the sudden fury of those whom he thus sets at defiance, executes his commission with great fidelity.

Sometimes this token of defiance has such an instantaneous effect on those to whom it is presented, that in the first transports of their fury a small party will issue forth, without waiting for the permission of the elder chiefs, and slaying the first of the offending nation they meet, cut open the body and stick a hatchet of the same kind as that they have just received, into the heart of their slaughtered foe. Among the more remote tribes this is done with an arrow or spear, the end of which is painted red. And the more to exasperate, they dismember the body, to show that they esteem them not as men but as old women.

The Indians seldom take the field in large bodies, as such numbers would require a greater degree of industry to provide for their subsistence, during their tedious marches through dreary forests, or long voyages over lakes and rivers, than they would care to bestow.

Their armies are never encumbered with baggage or military stores. Each warrior, besides his weapons, carries with him only a mat, and whilst at a distance from the frontiers of the enemy supports himself with the game he kills or the fish he catches.

When they pass through a country where they have no apprehensions of meeting with an enemy, they use very little precaution: sometimes there are scarcely a dozen warriors left together, the rest being dispersed in pursuit of their game; but though they should have roved to a very considerable distance from the war-path, they are sure to arrive at the place of rendezvous by the hour appointed.

They always pitch their tents long before sun-set; and being naturally presumptuous, take very little care to guard against a surprize. They place great confidence in their Manitous, or houshold gods, which they always carry with them; and being persuaded that they take upon them the office of centinels, they sleep very securely under their protection.

These Manitous, as they are called by some nations, but which are termed Wakons, that is, spirits, by the the Naudowessies, are nothing more than the otter and martins skins I have already described, for which, however, they have a great veneration.

After they have entered the enemies country, no people can be more cautious and circumspect; fires are no longer lighted, no more shouting is heard, nor the game any longer pursued. They are not even permitted to speak; but must convey whatever they have to impart to each other by signs and motions.

They now proceed wholly by stratagem and ambuscade. Having discovered their enemies, they send to reconnoitre them; and a council is immediately held, during which they speak only in whispers, to consider of the intelligence imparted by those who were sent out.

The attack is generally made just before day-break, at which period they suppose the foes to be in their soundest sleep. Throughout the whole of the preceding night they will lie flat upon their faces, without stirring; and make their approaches in the same posture, creeping upon their hands and feet till they are got within bow-shot of those they have destined to destruction. On a signal given by the chief warrior, to which the whole body makes answer by the most hideous yells, they all start up, and discharging their arrows in the same instant, without giving their adversaries time to recover from the confusion into which they are thrown, pour in upon them with their war-clubs or tomahawks.

The Indians think there is little glory to be acquired from attacking their enemies openly in the field; their greatest pride is to surprise and destroy. They seldom engage without a manifest appearance of advantage. If they find the enemy on their guard, too strongly entrenched, or superior in numbers, they retire, provided there is an opportunity of doing so. And they esteem it the greatest qualification of a chief warrior, to be able to manage an attack, so as to destroy as many of the enemy as possible, at the expence of a few men.

Sometimes they secure themselves behind trees, hillocks, or stones, and having given one or two rounds retire before they are discovered. Europeans, who are unacquainted with this method of fighting too often find to their cost the destructive efficacy of it.

General Braddock was one of this unhappy number. Marching in the year 1755, to attack Fort Du Quesne, he was intercepted by a party of French and confederate Indians in their interest, who by this insidious method of engaging found means to defeat his army, which consisted of about two thousand brave and well-disciplined troops. So securely were the Indians posted, that the English scarcely knew from whence or by whom they were thus annoyed. During the whole of the engagement the latter had scarcely a sight of an enemy; and were obliged to retreat without the satisfaction of being able to take the least degree of revenge for the havock made among them. The General paid for his temerity with his life, and was accompanied in his fall by a great number of brave fellows; whilst his invisible enemies had only two or three of their number wounded.

When the Indians succeed in their silent approaches, and are able to force the camp which they attack, a scene of horror that

that exceeds description, ensues. The savage fierceness of the conquerors, and the desperation of the conquered, who well know what they have to expect should they fall alive into the hands of their assailants, occasion the most extraordinary exertions on both sides. The figure of the combatants all besmeared with black and red paint, and covered with the blood of the slain, their horrid yells, and ungovernable fury, are not to be conceived by those who have never crossed the Atlantic.

I have frequently been a spectator of them, and once bore a part in a similar scene. But what added to the horror of it was, that I had not the consolation of being able to oppose their savage attacks. Every circumstance of the adventure still dwells on my remembrance, and enables me to describe with greater perspicuity the brutal fierceness of the Indians when they have surprized or overpowered an enemy.

As a detail of the massacre at Fort William Henry in the year 1757, the scene to which I refer, cannot appear foreign to the design of this publication, but will serve to give my readers a just idea of the ferocity of this people, I shall take the liberty to insert it, apologizing at the same time for the length of the digression, and those egotisms which the relation renders unavoidable.

General Webb, who commanded the English army in North America, which was then encamped at Fort Edward, having intelligence that the French troops under Monsf. Montcalm were making some movements towards Fort William Henry, he detached a corps of about fifteen hundred men, consisting of English and Provincials, to strengthen the garrison. In this party I went as a volunteer among the latter.

The apprehensions of the English General were not without foundation; for the day after our arrival we saw Lake George (formerly Lake Sacrament) to which it lies contiguous, covered with an immense number of boats; and in a few hours we found our lines attacked by the French General, who had just landed with eleven thousand Regulars and Canadians, and two thousand Indians. Colonel Monro, a brave officer, commanded in the Fort, and had no more than two thousand three hundred men with him, our detachment included.

With these he made a gallant defence, and probably would have been able at last to preserve the Fort, had he been properly supported, and permitted to continue his efforts. On every summons to surrender sent by the French General, who offered the most honourable terms, his answer repeatedly was, That he yet found himself in a condition to repel the most vigorous attacks his besiegers were able to make; and if he thought his present force insufficient, he could soon be supplied with a greater number from the adjacent army.

But the Colonel having acquainted General Webb with his situation, and desired he would send him some fresh troops, the general dispatched a messenger to him with a letter, wherein he informed

informed him that it was not in his power to assist him, and therefore gave him orders to surrender up the Fort on the best terms he could procure. This packet fell into the hands of the French General, who immediately sent a flag of truce, desiring a conference with the governor.

They accordingly met, attended only by a small guard, in the centre between the lines; when Monf. Montcalm told the Colonel, that he was come in person to demand possession of the Fort, as it belonged to the King his master. The Colonel replied, that he knew not how that could be, nor should he surrender it up whilst it was in his power to defend it.

The French General rejoined, at the same time delivering the packet into the Colonel's hand, " By this authority do I make " the requisition." The brave Governor had no sooner read the contents of it, and was convinced that such were the orders of the commander in chief, and not to be disobeyed, than he hung his head in silence, and reluctantly entered into a negociation.

In consideration of the gallant defence the garrison had made, they were to be permitted to march out with all the honours of war, to be allowed covered waggons to transport their baggage to Fort Edward, and a guard to protect them from the fury of the savages.

The morning after the capitulation was signed, as soon as day broke, the whole garrison, now consisting of about two thousand men, besides women and children, were drawn up within the lines, and on the point of marching off, when great numbers of the Indians gathered about, and began to plunder. We were at first in hopes that this was their only view, and suffered them to proceed without opposition. Indeed it was not in our power to make any, had we been so inclined; for though we were permitted to carry off our arms, yet we were not allowed a single round of ammunition. In these hopes however we were disappointed: for presently some of them began to attack the sick and wounded, when such as were not able to crawl into the ranks, notwithstanding they endeavoured to avert the fury of their enemies by their shrieks or groans, were soon dispatched.

Here we were fully in expectation that the disturbance would have concluded; and our little army began to move; but in a short time we saw the front division driven back, and discovered that we were entirely encircled by the savages. We expected every moment that the guard, which the French, by the articles of capitulation, had agreed to allow us, would have arrived, and put an end to our apprehensions; but none appeared. The Indians now began to strip every one without exception of their arms and cloaths, and those who made the least resistance felt the weight of their tomahawks.

I happened to be in the rear division, but it was not long before I shared the fate of my companions. Three or four of the savages laid hold of me, and whilst some held their weapons

over

over my head, the others soon disrobed me of my coat, waistcoat, hat, and buckles, omitting not to take from me what money I had in my pocket. As this was transacted close by the passage that led from the lines on to the plain, near which a French centinel was posted, I ran to him and claimed his protection; but he only called me an English dog, and thrust me with violence back again into the midst of the Indians.

I now endeavoured to join a body of our troops that were crowded together at some distance; but innumerable were the blows that were made at me with different weapons as I passed on; luckily however the savages were so close together, that they could not strike at me without endangering each other. Notwithstanding which one of them found means to make a thrust at me with a spear, which grazed my side, and from another I received a wound, with the same kind of weapon, in my ankle. At length I gained the spot where my countrymen stood, and forced myself into the midst of them. But before I got thus far out of the hands of the Indians, the collar and wristbands of my shirt were all that remained of it, and my flesh was scratched and torn in many places by their savage gripes.

By this time the war-hoop was given, and the Indians began to murder those that were nearest to them without distinction. It is not in the power of words to give any tolerable idea of the horrid scene that now ensued; men, women, and children were dispatched in the most wanton and cruel manner, and immediately scalped. Many of these savages drank the blood of their victims, as it flowed warm from the fatal wound.

We now perceived, though too late to avail us, that we were to expect no relief from the French; and that, contrary to the agreement they had so lately signed to allow us a sufficient force to protect us from these insults, they tacitly permitted them; for I could plainly perceive the French officers walking about at some distance, discoursing together with apparent unconcern. For the honour of human nature I would hope that this flagrant breach of every sacred law, proceeded rather from the savage disposition of the Indians, which I acknowledge it is sometimes almost impossible to controul, and which might now unexpectedly have arrived to a pitch not easily to be restrained, than to any premeditated design in the French commander. An unprejudiced observer would, however, be apt to conclude, that a body of ten thousand christian troops, most christian troops, had it in their power to prevent the massacre from becoming so general. But whatever was the cause from which it arose, the consequences of it were dreadful, and not to be paralleled in modern history.

As the circle in which I stood inclosed by this time was much thinned, and death seemed to be approaching with hasty strides, it was proposed by some of the most resolute to make one vigorous effort, and endeavour to force our way through the savages, the only probable method of preserving our lives that now

now remained. This, however desperate, was resolved on, and about twenty of us sprung at once into the midst of them.

In a moment we were all separated, and what was the fate of my companions I could not learn till some months after, when I found that only six or seven of them effected their design. Intent only on my own hazardous situation, I endeavoured to make my way through my savage enemies in the best manner possible. And I have often been astonished since, when I have recollected with what composure I took, as I did, every necessary step for my preservation. Some I overturned, being at that time young and athletic, and others I passed by, dextrously avoiding their weapons; till at last two very stout chiefs, of the most savage tribes, as I could distinguish by their dress, whose strength I could not resist, laid hold of me by each arm, and began to force me through the crowd.

I now resigned myself to my fate, not doubting but that they intended to dispatch me, and then to satiate their vengeance with my blood, as I found they were hurrying me towards a retired swamp that lay at some distance. But before we had got many yards, an English gentleman of some distinction, as I could discover by his breeches, the only covering he had on, which were of fine scarlet velvet, rushed close by us. One of the the Indians instantly relinquished his hold, and springing on this new object, endeavoured to seize him as his prey; but the gentleman being strong, threw him on the ground, and would probably have got away, had not he who held my other arm, quitted me to assist his brother. I seized the opportunity, and hastened away to join another party of English troops that were yet unbroken, and stood in a body at some distance. But before I had taken many steps, I hastily cast my eye towards the gentleman, and saw the Indian's tomahawk gash into his back, and heard him utter his last groan; this added both to my speed and desperation.

I had left this shocking scene but a few yards, when a fine boy about twelve years of age, that had hitherto escaped, came up to me, and begged that I would let him lay hold of me, so that he might stand some chance of getting out of the hands of the savages. I told him that I would give him every assistance in my power, and to this purpose bid him lay hold; but in a few moments he was torn from my side, and by his shrieks I judge was soon demolished. I could not help forgetting my own cares for a minute, to lament the fate of so young a sufferer; but it was utterly impossible for me to take any methods to prevent it.

I now got once more into the midst of friends, but we were unable to afford each other any succour. As this was the division that had advanced the furthest from the fort, I thought there might be a possibility (though but a very bare one) of my forcing my way through the outer ranks of the Indians, and getting to a neighbouring wood, which I perceived at some distance.

tance. I was still encouraged to hope by the almost miraculous preservation I had already experienced.

Nor were my hopes in vain, or the efforts I made ineffectual. Suffice it to say, that I reached the wood; but by the time I had penetrated a little way into it, my breath was so exhausted that I threw myself into a brake, and lay for some minutes apparently at the last gasp. At length I recovered the power of respiration; but my apprehensions returned with all their former force, when I saw several savages pass by, probably in pursuit of me, at no very great distance. In this situation I knew not whether it was better to proceed, or endeavour to conceal myself where I lay, till night came on; fearing, however, that they would return the same way, I thought it most prudent to get farther from the dreadful scene of my past distresses. Accordingly, striking into another part of the wood, I hastened on as fast as the briars and the loss of one of my shoes would permit me; and after a slow progress of some hours, gained a hill that overlooked the plain which I had just left, from whence I could discern that the bloody storm still raged with unabated fury.

But not to tire my readers, I shall only add, that after passing three days without subsistence, and enduring the severity of the cold dews for three nights, I at length reached Fort Edward; where with proper care my body soon recovered its wonted strength, and my mind, as far as the recollection of the late melancholy events would permit, its usual composure.

It was computed that fifteen hundred persons were killed or made prisoners by these savages during this fatal day. Many of the latter were carried off by them and never returned. A few, through favourable accidents, found their way back to their native country, after having experienced a long and severe captivity.

The brave Colonel Monro had hastened away, soon after the confusion began, to the French camp to endeavour to procure the guard agreed by the stipulation; but his application proving ineffectual, he remained there till General Webb sent a party of troops to demand and protect him back to Fort Edward. But these unhappy occurrences, which wou'd probably have been prevented, had he been left to pursue his own plans, together with the loss of so many brave fellows, murdered in cold blood, to whose valour he had been so lately a witness, made such an impression on his mind, that he did not long survive. He died in about three months of a broken heart, and with truth might it be said, that he was an honour to his country.

I mean not to point out the following circumstance as the immediate judgment of heaven, and intended as an atonement for this slaughter; but I cannot omit that very few of those different tribes of Indians that shared in it ever lived to return home. The small-pox, by means of their communication with the Europeans, found its way among them, and made an equal havock to what they themselves had done. The methods they pursued on the first attack of that malignant disorder, to abate the fever attending it, rendered it fatal. Whilst their blood was in a state of fermentation, and nature was striving to throw out the peccant matter, they checked her operations by plunging into the water: the consequence was that they died by hundreds. The few that survived were transformed by it into hideous objects, and bore with them to the grave deep indented marks of this much-dreaded disease.

Monsieur Montcalm fell soon after on the plains of Quebec.

That the unprovoked cruelty of this commander was not approved of by the generality of his countrymen, I have since been convinced of by many proofs. One only however, which I received from a person who was witness to it, shall I at present give. A Canadian merchant, of some consideration, having heard of the surrender of the English fort, celebrated the fortunate event with great rejoicings and hospitality, according to the custom of that county; but no sooner did the news of the massacre which ensued reach his ears, than he put an immediate stop to the festivity, and exclaimed in the severest terms against the inhuman permission; declaring at the same time that those who had connived at it, had thereby drawn down, on that part of their king's dominions the vengeance of Heaven. To this he added, that he much feared the total loss of them would deservedly be the consequence. How truly this prediction has been verified we all know.

But to return—Though the Indians are negligent in guarding against surprizes, they are alert and dextrous in surprizing their enemies. To their caution and perseverance and stealing on the party they design to attack, they add that admirable talent, or rather instinctive qualification, I have already described, of tracing out those they are in pursuit of. On the smoothest grass, on the hardest earth, and even on the very stones, will they discover the traces of an enemy, and by the shape of the foot steps, and the distance between the prints, distinguish not only whether it is a man or woman who has passed that way, but even the nation to which they belong. However incredible this might appear, yet, from the many proofs I received whilst among them of their amazing sagacity in this point, I see no reason to discredit even these extraordinary exertions of it.

When they have overcome an enemy, and victory is no longer doubtful, the conquerors first dispatch all such as they think they shall not be able to carry off without great trouble, and then endeavour to take as many prisoners as possible; after this they return to scalp those who are either dead, or too much wounded to be taken with them.

At this business they are exceedingly expert. They seize the head of the disabled or dead enemy, and placing one of their feet on the neck, twist their left hand in the hair; by this means, having extended the skin that covers the top of the head, they draw

draw out their scalping knives, which are always kept in good order for this cruel purpose, and with a few dextrous strokes take off the part that is termed the scalp. They are so expeditious in doing this, that the whole time required scarcely exceeds a minute. These they preserve as monuments of their prowess, and at the same time as proofs of the vengeance they have inflicted on their enemies.

If two Indians seize in the same instant a prisoner, and seem to have an equal claim, the contest between them is soon decided; for to put a speedy end to any dispute that might arise, the person that is apprehensive he shall lose his expected reward, immediately has recourse to his tomahawk or war-club, and knocks on the head the unhappy cause of their contention.

Having compleated their purposes, and made as much havock as possible, they immediately retire towards their own country, with the spoil they have acquired, for fear of being pursued.

Should this be the case, they make use of many stratagems to elude the searches of their pursuers. They sometimes scatter leaves, sand, or dust over the prints of their feet; sometimes tread in each others footsteps; and sometimes lift their feet so high, and tread so lightly, as not to make any impression on the ground. But if they find all these precautions unavailing, and that they are near being overtaken, they first dispatch and scalp their prisoners, and then dividing, each endeavours to regain his native country by a different route. This prevents all farther pursuit; for their pursuers now despairing, either of gratifying their revenge, or of releasing those of their friends who were made captives, return home.

If the successful party is so lucky as to make good their retreat unmolested, they hasten with the greatest expedition to reach a country where they may be perfectly secure; and that their wounded companions may not retard their flight, they carry them by turns in litters, or if it is in the winter season draw them on sledges.

Their litters are made in a rude manner of the branches of trees. Their sledges consist of two small thin boards, about a foot wide when joined, and near six feet long. The fore-part is turned up, and the sides are bordered with small bands. The Indians draw these carriages with great ease, be they ever so much loaded, by means of a string which passes round the breast. This collar is called a Metump, and is in use throughout America, both in the settlements and the internal parts. Those used in the latter are made of leather, and very curiously wrought.

The prisoners during their march are guarded with the greatest care. During the day, if the journey is over land, they are always held by some of the victorious party; if by water, they are fastened to the canoe. In the night-time they are stretched along the ground quite naked, with their legs, arms, and neck fastened to hooks fixed in the ground. Besides this, cords are
tied

tied to their arms or legs, which are held by an Indian, who instantly awakes at the least motion of them.

Notwithstanding such precautions are usually taken by the Indians, it is recorded in the annals of New England, that one of the weaker sex, almost alone, and unassisted, found means to elude the vigilance of a party of warriors, and not only to make her escape from them, but to revenge the cause of her countrymen.

Some years ago, a small band of Canadian Indians, consisting of ten warriors attended by two of their wives, made an irruption into the back settlements of New England. They lurked for some time in the vicinity of one of the most exterior towns, and at length, after having killed and scalped several people, found means to take prisoner a woman who had with her a son of about twelve years of age. Being satisfied with the execution they had done, they retreated towards their native country, which lay at three hundred miles distance, and carried off with them their two captives.

The second night of their retreat, the woman, whose name, if I mistake not, was Rowe, formed a resolution worthy of the most intrepid heroe. She thought she should be able to get from her hands the manacles by which they were confined, and determined if she did so to make a desperate effort for the recovery of her freedom. To this purpose, when she concluded that her conquerors were in their soundest sleep, she strove to slip the cords from her hands. In this she succeeded; and cautioning her son, whom they had suffered to go unbound, in a whisper, against being surprized at what she was about to do, she removed to a distance with great wariness the defensive weapons of the Indians, which lay by their sides.

Having done this, she put one of the tomahawks into the hands of the boy, bidding him to follow her example; and taking another herself, fell upon the sleeping Indians, several of whom she instantly dispatched. But her attempt was nearly frustrated by the imbecility of her son, who wanting both strength and resolution, made a feeble stroke at one of them, which only served to awaken him; she however sprung at the rising warrior, and before he could recover his arms, made him sink under the weight of her tomahawk; and this she alternately did to all the rest, except one of the women, who awoke in time, and made her escape.

The heroine then took off the scalps of her vanquished enemies, and seizing also those they were carrying away with them as proofs of their success, she returned in triumph to the town from whence she had so lately been dragged, to the great astonishment of her neighbours, who could scarcely credit their senses, or the testimonies she bore of her amazonian intrepidity.

During their march they oblige their prisoners to sing their death-song, which generally consists of these or similar sentences:

tences: "I am going to die, I am about to suffer; but I will bear the severest tortures my enemies can inflict, with becoming fortitude. I will die like a brave man, and I shall then go to join the chiefs that have suffered on the same account." These songs are continued with necessary intervals, until they reach the village or camp to which they are going.

When the warriors are arrived within hearing, they set up different cries, which communicates to their friends a general history of the success of the expedition. The number of the death-cries they give, declares how many of their own party are lost; the number of war-hoops, the number of prisoners they have taken.

It is difficult to describe these cries, but the best idea I can convey of them is, that the former consists of the sound Whoo, Whoo, Whoop, which is continued in a long shrill tone, nearly till the breath is exhausted, and then broken off with a sudden elevation of the voice. The latter of a loud cry, of much the same kind, which is modulated into notes by the hand being placed before the mouth. Both of them might be heard to a very considerable distance.

Whilst these are uttering, the persons to whom they are designed to convey the intellegence, continue motionless and all attention. When this ceremony is performed, the whole village issue out to learn the particulars of the relation they have just heard in general terms, and according as the news prove mournful or the contrary, they answer by so many acclamations or cries of lamentation.

Being by this time arrived at the village or camp, the women and children arm themselves with sticks and bludgeons, and form themselves into two ranks, through which the prisoners are obliged to pass. The treatment they undergo before they reach the extremity of the line, is very severe. Sometimes they are so beaten over the head and face, as to have scarcely any remains of life; and happy would it be for them if by this usage an end was put to their wretched beings. But their tormentors take care that none of the blows they give prove mortal, as they wish to reserve the miserable sufferers for more severe inflictions.

After having undergone this introductory discipline, they are bound hand and foot, whilst the chiefs hold a council, in which their fate is determined. Those who are decreed to be put to death by the usual torments, are delivered to the chief of the warriors; such as are to be spared, are given into the hands of the chief of the nation: so that in a short time all the prisoners may be assured of their fate, as the sentence now pronounced is irrevocable. The former they term being consigned to the house of death, the latter to the house of grace.

Such captives as are pretty far advanced in life, and have acquired great honour by their war-like deeds, always atone for the blood they have spilt, by the tortures of fire. Their
success

success in war is readily known by the blue marks upon their breasts and arms, which are as legible to the Indians as letters are to Europeans.

The manner in which these hieroglyphicks are made, is by breaking the skin with the teeth of fish, or sharpened flints, dipped in a kind of ink made of the soot of pitch pine. Like those of the ancient Picts of Britain these are esteemed ornamental; and at the same time they serve as registers of the heroic actions of the warrior, who thus bears about him indelible marks of his valour.

The prisoners destined to death are soon led to the place of execution, which is generally in the centre of the camp or village; where, being stript, and every part of their bodies blackened, the skin of a crow or raven is fixed on their heads. They are then bound to a stake, with faggots heaped around them, and obliged, for the last time, to sing their death-song.

The warriors, for such it is only who commonly suffer this punishment, now perform in a more prolix manner this sad solemnity. They recount with an audible voice all the brave actions they have performed, and pride themselves in the number of enemies they have killed. In this rehearsal they spare not even their tormentors, but strive by every provoking tale they can invent, to irritate and insult them. Sometimes this has the desired effect, and the sufferers are dispatched sooner than they otherwise would have been.

There are many other methods which the Indians make use of to put their prisoners to death, but these are only occasional; that of burning is most generally used.

Whilst I was at the chief town of the Ottagaumies, an Illinois Indian was brought in, who had been made prisoner by one of their war parties. I had then an opportunity of seeing the customary cruelties inflicted by these people on their captives, through the minutest part of their process. After the previous steps necessary to his condemnation, he was carried, early in the morning, to a little distance from the town, where he was bound to a tree.

This being done, all the boys, who amounted to a great number, as the place was populous, were permitted to amuse themselves with shooting their arrows at the unhappy victim. As they were none of them more than twelve years old, and were placed at a considerable distance, they had not strength to penetrate to the vital parts, so that the poor wretch stood pierced with arrows, and suffering the consequent agonies, for more than two days.

During this time he sung his warlike exploits. He recapitulated every stratagem he had made use of to surprize his enemies: he boasted of the quantity of scalps he possessed, and enumerated the prisoners he had taken. He then described the different barbarous methods by which he had put the latter to

death,

death, and seemed even then to receive inconceivable pleasure from the recital of the horrid tale.

But he dwelt more particularly on the cruelties he had practised on such of the kindred of his present tormentors, as had fallen into his hands; endeavouring by these aggravated insults to induce them to increase his tortures, that he might be able to give greater proofs of fortitude. Even in the last struggles of life, when he was no longer able to vent in words the indignant provocation his tongue would have uttered, a smile of mingled scorn and triumph sat on his countenance.

This method of tormenting their enemies is considered by the Indians as productive of more than one beneficial consequence. It satiates, in a greater degree, that diabolical lust of revenge, which is the predominant passion in the breast of every individual of every tribe, and it gives the growing warriors an early propensity to that cruelty and thirst for blood, which is so necessary a qualification for such as would be thoroughly skilled in their savage art of war.

I have been informed, that an Indian who was under the hands of his tormentors, had the audacity to tell them, that they were ignorant old women, and did not know how to put brave prisoners to death. He acquainted them that he had heretofore taken some of their warriors, and instead of the trivial punishments they inflicted on him, he had devised for them the most excruciating torments; that having bound them to a stake, he had stuck their bodies full of sharp splinters of turpentine wood, to which he then set fire, and dancing around them enjoyed the agonizing pangs of the flaming victims.

This bravado, which carried with it a degree of insult, that even the accustomed ear of an Indian could not listen to unmoved, threw his tormentors off their guard, and shortened the duration of his torments; for one of the chiefs ran to him, and ripping out his heart, stopped with it the mouth from which had issued such provoking language.

Innumerable are the stories that may be told of the courage and resolution of the Indians, who happen to be made prisoners by their adversaries. Many that I have heard are so astonishing, that they seem to exceed the utmost limits of credibility; it is, however, certain that these savages are possessed with many heroic qualities, and bear every species of misfortune with a degree of fortitude which has not been outdone by any of the ancient heroes of either of Greece or Rome.

Notwithstanding these acts of severity exercised by the Indians towards those of their own species, who fall into their hands, some tribes of them have been remarked for their moderation to such female prisoners, belonging to the English colonies as have happened to be taken by them. Women of great beauty have frequently been carried off by them, and during a march of three or four hundred miles, through their retired forests, have lain by their sides without receiving any insult, and

their

their chastity has remained inviolate. Instances have happened where female captives, who have been pregnant at the time of their being taken, have found the pangs of child-birth come upon them in the midst of solitary woods, and savages their only companions; yet from these, savages as they were, have they received every assistance their situation would admit of, and been treated with a degree of delicacy and humanity they little expected.

This forbearance, it must be acknowledged does not proceed altogether from their dispositions, but is only inherent in those who have held some communication with the French missionaries. Without intending that their natural enemies, the English, should enjoy the benefit of their labours, these fathers have taken great pains to inculcate on the minds of the Indians the general principles of humanity, which has diffused itself through their manners, and has proved of public utility.

Those prisoners that are consigned to the house of grace, and these are commonly the young men, women and children, await the disposal of the chiefs, who, after the execution of such as are condemned to die, hold a council for this purpose.

A herald is sent round the village or camp, to give notice that such as have lost any relation in the late expedition, are desired to attend the distribution which is about to take place. Those women who have lost their sons or husbands, are generally satisfied in the first place; after these, such as have been deprived of friends of a more remote degree of consanguinity, or who choose to adopt some of the youth.

The division being made, which is done, as in other cases, without the least dispute, those who have received any share lead them to their tents or huts; and having unbound them, wash and dress their wounds if they happen to have received any; they then cloath them, and give them the most comfortable and refreshing food their store will afford.

Whilst their new domesticks are feeding, they endeavour to administer consolation to them; they tell them that as they are redeemed from death, they must now be cheerful and happy; and if they serve them well, without murmuring or repining, nothing shall be wanting to make them such atonement for the loss of their country and friends as circumstances will allow of.

If any men are spared, they are commonly given to the widows that have lost their husbands by the hand of the enemy, should there be any such, to whom, if they happen to prove agreeable, they are soon married. But should the dame be otherwise engaged, the life of him who falls to her lot is in great danger; especially if she fancies that her late husband wants a slave in the country of spirits, to which he is gone.

When this is the case, a number of young men take the devoted captive to some distance, and dispatch him without any ceremony: after he has been spared by the council, they con-

sider

sider him of too little consequence to be entitled to the torments allotted to those who have been judged worthy of them.

The women are usually distributed to the men, from whom they do not fail of meeting with a favourable reception. The boys and girls are taken into the families of such as have need of them, and are considered as slaves; and it is not uncommon that they are sold in the same capacity to the European traders, who come among them.

The Indians have no idea of moderating the ravages of war, by sparing their prisoners, and entering into a negotiation with the band from whom they have been taken, for an exchange. All that are captivated by both parties, are either put to death, adopted, or made slaves of. And so particular are every nation in this respect, that if any of their tribe, even a warrior, should be taken prisoner, and by chance be received into the house of grace, either as an adopted person or a slave, and should afterwards make his escape, they will by no means receive him, or acknowledge him as one of their band.

The condition of such as are adopted differs not in any one instance from the children of the nation to which they now belong. They assume all the rights of those whose places they supply, and frequently make no difficulty of going in the war-parties against their own countrymen. Should, however, any of these by chance make their escape, and be afterwards retaken, they are esteemed as unnatural children and ungrateful persons, who have deserted and made war upon their parents and benefactors, and are treated with uncommon severity.

That part of the prisoners which are considered as slaves, are generally distributed among the chiefs; who frequently make presents of some of them to the European governors of the out-posts, or to the superintendants or commissaries of Indian affairs. I have been informed that it was the Jesuits and French missionaries that first occasioned the introduction of these unhappy captives into the settlements, and who by so doing taught the Indians that they were valuable.

Their views indeed were laudable, as they imagined that by this method they should not only prevent much barbarity and bloodshed, but find the opportunities of spreading their religion among them increased. To this purpose they encouraged the traders to purchase such slaves as they met with.

The good effects of this mode of proceeding was not however equal to the expectations of these pious fathers. Instead of being the means of preventing cruelty and bloodshead, it only caused the dissensions between the Indian nations to be carried on with a greater degree of violence, and with unremitted ardour. The prize they fought for being no longer revenge or fame, but the acquirement of spirituous liquors, for which their captives were to be exchanged, and of which almost every nation is immoderately fond, they fought for their

enemies

enemies with unwonted alacrity, and were conſtantly on the watch to ſurprize and carry them off.

It might ſtill be ſaid that fewer of the captives are tormented and put to death, ſince theſe expectations of receiving ſo valuable a conſideration for them have been excited than there uſually had been; but it does not appear that their accuſtomed cruelty to the warriors they take, is in the leaſt abated; their natural deſire of vengeance muſt be gratified; they now only become more aſſiduous in ſecuring a greater number of young priſoners, whilſt thoſe who are made captive in their defence are tormented and put to death as before.

The miſſionaries finding that contrary to their wiſhes their zeal had only ſerved to increaſe the ſale of the noxious juices, applied to the Governor of Canada, in the year 1693, for a prohibition of this baneful trade. An order was iſſued accordingly, but it could not put a total ſtop to it; the French Couriers de Bois were hardy enough to carry it on clandeſtinely, notwithſtanding the penalty annexed to a breach of the prohibition was a conſiderable fine and impriſonment.

Some who were detected in the proſecution of it withdrew into the Indian countries, where they intermarried with the natives, and underwent a voluntary baniſhment. Theſe, however, being an abandoned and debauched ſet, their conduct contributed very little either towards reforming the manners of their new relations, or engaging them to entertain a favourable opinion of the religion they profeſſed. Thus did theſe inceſatigable religious men ſee their deſigns in ſome meaſure once more fruſtrated.

However, the emigration was productive of an effect which turned out to be beneficial to their nation. By the connection of theſe refugees with the Iroquois, Miſſiſſuages, Hurons, Miamies, Powtowottomies, Puants, Menomonies, Algonkins. &c. and the conſtant repreſentations theſe various nations received from them of the power and grandeur of the French, to the aggrandizement of whoſe monarch, notwithſtanding their baniſhment, they ſtill retained their habitual inclination, the Indians became inſenſibly prejudiced in favour of that people, and I am perſuaded will take every opportunity of ſhewing their attachment to them.

And this, even in deſpite of the diſgraceful eſtimation they muſt be held by them, ſince they have been driven out of Canada; for the Indians conſider every conquered people as in a ſtate of vaſſalage to their conquerors. After one nation has finally ſubdued another, and a conditional ſubmiſſion is agreed on, it is cuſtomary for the chiefs of the conquered, when they ſit in council with their ſubducrs, to wear petticoats, as an acknowledgement that they are in a ſtate of ſubjection, and ought to be ranked among the women. Their partiality to the French has however taken too deep root for time itſelf to eradicate it.

T

CHAP.

CHAPTER X.

Of their Manner of making PEACE, *&c.*

THE wars that are carried on between the Indian nations are in general hereditary, and continue from age to age with a few interruptions. If a peace becomes necessary, the principal care of both parties is to avoid the appearance of making the first advances.

When they treat with an enemy, relative to a suspension of hostilities, the chief who is commissioned to undertake the negociation, if it is not brought about by the mediation of some neighbouring band, abates nothing of his natural haughtiness: even when the affairs of his country are in the worst situation, he makes no concessions, but endeavours to persuade his adversaries that it is their interest to put an end to the war.

Accidents sometimes contribute to bring about a peace between nations that otherwise could not be prevailed on to listen to terms of accommodation. An instance of this, which I heard of in almost every nation I passed through, I shall relate.

About eighty years ago, the Iroquois and Chipéways, two powerful nations, were at war with the Ottagaumies and Saukies, who were much inferior to their adversaries both in numbers and strength. One winter near a thousand of the former made an excursion from Lake Ontario, by way of Toronto, towards the territories of their enemies. They coasted Lake Huron on its east and northern borders, till they arrived at the island of St. Joseph, which is situated in the Straights of St. Marie. There they crossed these Straights upon the ice about fifteen miles below the falls, and continued their route still westward. As the ground was covered with snow, to prevent a discovery of their numbers, they marched in a single file, treading in each others footsteps.

Four Chipéway Indians, passing that way, observed this army, and readily guessed from the direction of their march, and the precautions they took, both the country to which they were hastening, and their designs.

Notwithstanding the nation to which they belonged was at war with the Ottagaumies, and in alliance with their invaders, yet from a principle which cannot be accounted for, they took an instant resolution to apprize the former of their danger.

To

To this purpose they hastened away with their usual celerity, and, taking a circuit to avoid discovery, arrived at the hunting grounds of the Ottagaumies, before so large a body, moving in so cautious a manner, could do. There they found a party of about four hundred warriors, some of which were Saukies, whom they informed of the approach of their enemies.

The chiefs immediately collected their whole force, and held a council on the steps that were to be taken for their defence. As they were encumbered with their families, it was impossible that they could retreat in time; they therefore determined to choose the most advantageous spot, and to give the Iroquois the best reception in their power.

Not far from the place where they then happened to be, stood two small lakes, between which ran a narrow neck of land about a mile in length, and only from twenty to forty yards in breadth. Concluding that the Iroquois intended to pass through this defile, the united bands divided their little party into two bodies of two hundred each. One of these took post at the extremity of the pass that lay nearest to their hunting grounds, which they immediately fortified with a breast-work formed of palisades; whilst the other body took a compass round one of the lakes, with a design to hem their enemies in when they had entered the defile.

Their stratagem succeeded; for no sooner had the whole of the Iroquois entered the pass, than, being provided with wood for the purpose, they formed a similar breast-work on the other extremity, and thus enclosed their enemies.

The Iroquois soon perceived their situation, and immediately held a council on the measures that were necessary to be pursued to extricate themselves. Unluckily for them a thaw had just taken place, which had so far dissolved the ice as to render it impassible, and yet there still remained sufficient to prevent them from either passing over the lakes on rafts, or from swimming across. In this dilemma it was agreed that they should endeavour to force one of the breast-works; but they soon found them too well defended to effect their purpose.

Notwithstanding this disappointment, with the usual composure and unapprehensiveness of Indians, they amused themselves three or four days in fishing. By this time the ice being quite dissolved, they made themselves rafts, which they were enabled to do by some trees that fortunately grew on the spot, and attempted to cross one of the lakes.

They accordingly set off before day-break; but the Ottagaumies, who had been watchful of their motions, perceiving their design, detached one hundred and fifty men from each of their parties, to oppose their landing. These three hundred marched so expeditiously to the other side of the lake, that they reached it before their opponents had gained the shore, they being retarded by their poles sticking in the mud.

As soon as the confederates arrived, they poured in a very heavy fire, both from their bows and musquetry, on the Iroquois, which greatly disconcerted them; till the latter finding their situation desperate, leaped into the water, and fought their way through their enemies. This however they could not do without losing more than half their men.

After the Iroquois had landed, they made good their retreat, but were obliged to leave their enemies masters of the field, and in possession of all the furs they had taken during their winter's hunt. Thus dearly did they pay for an unprovoked excursion to such distance from the route they ought to have pursued, and to which they were only impelled by a sudden desire of cutting off some of their ancient enemies.

But had they known their strength they might have destroyed every man of the party that opposed them; which even at the first onset was only inconsiderable, and, when diminished by the action, totally unable to make any stand against them.

The victorious bands rewarded the Chipéways, who had been the means of their success, with a share of the spoils. They pressed them to take any quantity they chose of the richest of the furs, and sent them under an escort of fifty men, to their own country. The disinterested Chipéways, as the Indians in general are seldom actuated by mercenary motives, for a considerable time refused these presents, but were at length persuaded to accept of them.

The brave and well-concerted resistance here made by the Ottagaumies and Saukies, aided by the mediation of the Chipéways, who laying aside on this occasion the animosity they had so long born, those people approved of the generous conduct of their four chiefs, were together the means of effecting a reconciliation between these nations; and in process of time united them all in the bands of amity.

And I believe that all the Indians inhabiting that extensive country, which lies between Quebec, the banks of the Mississippi north of the Ouisconsin, and the settlements belonging to the Hudson's Bay Company, are at present in a state of profound peace. When their restless dispositions will not suffer them to remain inactive, these northern Indians seldom commit hostilities on each other, but make excursions to the southward, against the Cherokees, Choctahs, Chickfaws or Illinois..

Sometimes the Indians grow tired of a war which they have carried on against some neighbouring nation for many years without much success, and in this case they seek for mediators to begin a negotiation. These being obtained, the treaty is thus conducted.

A number of their own chiefs, joined by those who have accepted the friendly office, set out together for the country of their enemies; such as are chosen for this purpose, are chiefs of the most extensive abilities, and of the greatest integrity. They bear before them the Pipe of Peace, which I need not inform

inform my readers is of the same nature as a Flag of Truce among the Europeans, and is treated with the greatest respect and veneration, even by the most barbarous nations. I never heard of an instance wherein the bearers of this sacred badge of friendship were ever treated disrespectfully, or its rights violated. The Indians believe that the Great Spirit never suffers an infraction of this kind to go unpunished.

The Pipe of Peace, which is termed by the French the Calumet, for what reason I could never learn, is about four feet long. The bowl of it is made of red marble, and the stem of it of a light wood, curiously painted with hieroglyphicks in various colours, and adorned with feathers of the most beautiful birds; but it is not in my power to convey an idea of the various tints and pleasing ornaments of this much esteemed Indian implement.

Every nation has a different method of decorating these pipes, and they can tell at first sight to what band it belongs. It is used as an introduction to all treaties, and great ceremony attends the use of it on these occasions.

The assistant or aid-du-camp of the great warrior, when the chiefs are assembled and seated, fills it with tobacco mixed with the herbs before-mentioned, taking care at the same time that no part of it touches the ground. When it is filled, he takes a coal that is thoroughly kindled, from a fire which is generally kept burning in the midst of the assembly, and places it on the the tobacco.

As soon as it is sufficiently lighted, he throws off the coal. He then turns the stem of it towards the heavens, after this towards the earth, and now holding it horizontally, moves himself round till he has compleated a circle: by the first action he is supposed to present it to the Great Spirit, whose aid is thereby supplicated; by the second, to avert any malicious interposition of the evil spirits; and by the third to gain the protection of the spirits inhabiting the air, the earth, and the waters. Having thus secured the favour of those invisible agents, in whose power they suppose it is either to forward or obstruct the issue of their present deliberations, he presents it to the hereditary chief, who having taken two or three whiffs, blows the smoak from his mouth first towards heaven, and then around him upon the ground.

It is afterwards put in the same manner into the mouths of the ambassadors or strangers, who observe the same ceremony; then to the chief of the warriors, and to all the other chiefs in turn, according to their gradation. During this time the person who executes this honourable office holds the pipe slightly in his hand, as if he feared to press the sacred instrument; nor does any one presume to touch it but with his lips.

When the chiefs who are intrusted with the commission for making peace, approach the town or camp to which they are going, they begin to sing and dance the songs and dances appropriated

to

to this occasion. By this time the adverse party are apprized of their arrival, and divesting themselves of their wonted enmity at the sight of the Pipe of Peace, invite them to the habitation of the Great Chief, and furnish them with every conveniency during the negociation.

A council is then held; and when the speeches and debates are ended, if no obstructions arise to put a stop to the treaty, the painted hatchet is buried in the ground, as a memorial that all animosities between the contending nations have ceased, and a peace taken place. Among the ruder bands, such as have no communication with the Europeans, a war club, painted red, is buried, instead of the hatchet.

A belt of wampum is also given on this occasion, which serves as a ratification of the peace, and records to the latest posterity, by the hieroglyphicks into which the beads are formed, every stipulated article in the treaty.

These belts are made of shells found on the coasts of New England and Virginia, which are sawed out into beads of an oblong form, about a quarter of an inch long, and round like other beads. Being strung on leather strings, and several of them sewed neatly together with fine sinewy threads, they then compose what is termed a belt of Wampum.

The shells are generally of two colours, some white and others violet; but the latter are more highly esteemed than the former. They are held in as much estimation by the Indians, as gold, silver, or precious stones are by the Europeans.

The belts are composed of ten, twelve, or a greater number of strings, according to the importance of the affair in agitation, or the dignity of the person to whom it is presented. On more trifling occasions, strings of these beads are presented by the chiefs to each other, and frequently worn by them about their necks, as a valuable ornament,

CHAPTER XI.

Of their GAMES.

AS I have before observed, the Indians are greatly addicted to gaming, and will even stake, and lose with composure, all the valuables they are possessed of. They amuse themselves at several sorts of games, but the principal and most esteemed among them is that of the ball, which is not unlike the European game of tennis.

The

[151]

The balls they use are rather larger than those made use of at tennis, and are formed of a piece of deer-skin; which being moistened to render it supple, is stuffed hard with the hair of the same creature, and sewed with its sinews. The ball-sticks are about three feet long, at the end of which there is fixed a kind of racket, resembling the palm of the hand, and fashioned of thongs cut from a deer-skin. In these they catch the ball, and throw it to a great distance, if they are not prevented by some of the opposite party, who fly to intercept it.

This game is generally played by large companies, that sometimes consist of more than three hundred; and it is not uncommon for different bands to play against each other.

They begin by fixing two poles in the ground at about six hundred yards apart, and one of these goals belong to each party of the combatants. The ball is thrown up high in the centre of the ground, and in a direct line between the goals; towards which each party endeavours to strike it, and which-ever side first causes it to reach their own goal, reckons towards the game.

They are so exceeding dextrous in this manly exercise, that the ball is usually kept flying in different directions by the force of the rackets, without touching the ground during the whole contention; for they are not allowed to catch it with their hands. They run with amazing velocity in pursuit of each other, and when one is on the point of hurling it to a great distance, an antagonist overtakes him, and by a sudden stroke dashes down the ball.

The play with so much vehemence that they frequently wound each other, and sometimes a bone is broken; but notwithstanding these accidents there never appears to be any spite or wanton exertions of strength to effect them, nor do any disputes ever happen between the parties.

There is another game also in use among them worthy of remark, and this is the game of the Bowl or Platter. This game is played between two persons only. Each person has six or eight little bones not unlike a peach-stone either in size or shape, except that they are quadrangular; two of the sides of which are couloured black, and the others white. These they throw up into the air, from whence they fall into a bowl or platter placed underneath, and made to spin round.

According as these bones present the white or black side upwards they reckon the game: he that happens to have the greatest number turn up of a similar colour, counts five points; and forty is the game.

The winning party keeps his place, and the loser yields his to another who is appointed by one of the umpires; for a whole village is sometimes concerned in the party, and at times one band plays against another.

During

During this play the Indians appear to be greatly agitated, and at every decisive throw set up a hideous shout. They make a thousand contortions, addressing themselves at the same time to the bones, and loading with imprecations the evil spirits that assist their succefsful antagonists.

At this game some will lose their apparel, all the moveables of their cabins, and sometimes even their liberty, notwithstanding there are no people in the universe more jealous of the latter than the Indians are.

CHAPTER XII.

Of their MARRIAGE CEREMONIES, *&c.*

THE Indians allow of polygamy, and persons of every rank indulge themselves in this point. The chiefs in particular have a seraglio, which consists of an uncertain number, usually from six to twelve or fourteen. The lower ranks are permitted to take as many as there is a probability of their being able, with the children they may bear, to maintain. It is not uncommon for an Indian to marry two sisters; sometimes, if there happen to be more, the whole number; and notwithstanding this (as it appears to civilized nations) unnatural union, they all live in the greatest harmony.

The younger wives are submissive to the elder; and those who have no children, do such menial offices for those who are fertile, as causes their situation to differ but little from a state of servitude. However they perform every injunction with the greatest cheerfulness, in hopes of gaining thereby the affection of their husband, that they in their turns may have the happiness of becoming mothers, and be entitled to the respect attendant on that state.

It is not uncommon for an Indian, although he takes to himself so many wives, to live in a state of continence with many of them for several years. Such as are not so fortunate as to gain the favour of their husband, by their submissive and prudent behaviour, and by that means to share in his embraces, continue in their virgin state during the whole of their lives, except they happen to be presented by him to some stranger chief, whose abode among them will not admit of his entering into a more lasting connection. In this case they submit to the injunction of their husband without murmuring, and are not displeased at the temporary union. But if at any time it is known that they take this liberty without first receiving his consent,

they

they are punished in the same manner as if they had been guilty of adultery.

This custom is more prevalent among the nations which lie in the interior parts, than among those that are nearer the settlements, as the manners of the latter are rendered more conformable in some points to those of the Europeans, by the intercourse they hold with them.

The Indian nations differ but little from each other in their marriage ceremonies, and less in the manner of their divorces. The tribes that inhabit the borders of Canada, make use of the following custom.

When a young Indian has fixed his inclinations on one of the other sex, he endeavours to gain her consent, and if he succeeds, it is never known that her parents ever obstruct their union. When every preliminary is agreed on, and the day appointed, the friends and acquaintance of both parties assemble at the house or tent of the oldest relation of the bridegroom, where a feast is prepared on the occasion.

The company who meet to assist at the festival are sometimes very numerous; they dance, they sing, and enter into every other diversion usually made use of on any of their public rejoicings.

When these are finished, all those who attended merely out of ceremony depart, and the bridegroom and bride are left alone with three or four of the nearest and oldest relations of either side; those of the bridegroom being men, those of the bride, women.

Presently the bride, attended by these few friends, having withdrawn herself for the purpose, appears at one of the doors of the house, and is led to the bridegroom, who stands ready to receive her. Having now taken their station, on a mat placed in the centre of the room, they lay hold of the extremities of a wand, about four feet long, by which they continue separated, whilst the old men pronounce some short harangues suitable to the occasion.

The married couple after this make a public declaration of the love and regard they entertain for each other, and still holding the rod between them, dance and sing. When they have finished this part of the ceremony, they break the rod into as many pieces as there are witnesses present, who each take a piece, and preserve it with great care.

The bride is then reconducted out of the door at which she entered, where her young companions wait to attend her to her father's house; there the bridegroom is obliged to seek her, and the marriage is consummated. Very often the wife remains at her father's house till she has a child, when she packs up her apparel, which is all the fortune she is generally possessed of, and accompanies her husband to his habitation.

When from any dislike a separation takes place, for they are seldom known to quarrel, they generally give their friends a few days notice of their intentions, and sometimes offer reasons to juftify their conduct. The witneffes who were prefent at the marriage, meet on the day requefted, at the houfe of the couple that are about to feparate, and bringing with them the pieces of rod which they had received at their nuptials, throw them into the fire, in the prefence of all the parties.

This is the whole of the ceremony required, and the feparation is carried on without any murmurings or ill-will between the couple or their relations; and after a few months they are at liberty to marry again.

When a marriage is thus diffolved, the children which have been produced from it, are equally divided between them; and as children are efteemed a treafure by the Indians, if the number happens to be odd, the woman is allowed to take the better half.

Though this cuftom feems to encourage ficklenefs and frequent feparations, yet there are many of the Indians who have but one wife, and enjoy with her a ftate of connubial happinefs not to be exceeded in more refined focieties. There are alfo not a few inftances of women preferving an inviolable attachment to their hufbands, except in the cafes beforementioned, which are not confidered as either a violation of their chaftity or fidelity.

Although I have faid that the Indian nations differ very little from each other in their marriage ceremonies, there are fome exceptions. The Naudoweffies have a fingular method of celebrating their marriages, which feems to bear no refemblance to thofe made ufe of by any other nation I paffed through. When one of their young men has fixed on a young woman he approves of, he difcovers his paffion to her parents, who give him an invitation to come and live with them in their tent.

He accordingly accepts the offer, and by fo doing engages to refide in it for a whole year, in the character of a menial fervant. During this time he hunts, and brings all the game he kills to the family; by which means the father has an opportunity of feeing whether he is able to provide for the fupport of his daughter and the children that might be the confequence of their union. This however is only done whilft they are young men, and for their firft wife, and not repeated like Jacob's fervitudes.

When this period is expired, the marriage is folemnized after the cuftom of the country, in the following manner: Three or four of the oldeft male relations of the bridegroom, and as many of the bride's, accompany the young couple from their refpective tents, to an open part in the centre of the camp.

The chiefs and warriors being here affembled to receive them, a party of the latter are drawn up in two ranks on each fide of the bride and bridegroom immediately on their arrival. Their principal chief then acquaints the whole affembly with the defign of their meeting, and tells them that the couple before them, mentioning at the fame time their names, are come to avow publickly their intentions of living together as man and wife.

He

He then asks the two young people alternately, whether they defire that the union might take place. Having declared with an audible voice that they do fo, the warriors fix their arrows, and difcharge them over the heads of the married pair; this done, the chief pronounces them man and wife.

The bridegroom then turns round, and bending his body, takes his wife on his back, in which manner he carries her amidft the acclamations of the fpectators to his tent. This ceremony is fucceeded by the moft plentiful feaft the new married man can afford, and fongs and dances, according to the ufual cuftom, conclude the feftival.

Divorces happen fo feldom among the Naudoweffies, that I had not an opportunity of learning how they are accomplifhed.

Adultery is efteemed by them a heinous crime, and punifhed with the greateft rigour. The hufband in thefe cafes bites off the wife's nofe, and a feparation inftantly enfues. I faw an inftance wherein this mode of punifhment was inflicted, whilft I remained among them. The children, when this happens, are diftributed according to the ufual cuftom obferved by other nations, that is, they are equally divided.

Among the Indian as well as European nations, there are many that devote themfelves to pleafure, and notwithftanding the accounts given by fome modern writers of the frigidity of an Indian conftitution, become the zealous votaries of Venus. The young warriors that are thus difpofed, feldom want opportunities for gratifying their paffion; and as the mode ufually followed on thefe occafions is rather fingular, I shall defcribe it.

When one of thefe young debauchees imagines from the behaviour of the perfon he has chofen for his miftrefs, that he fhall not meet with any great obftruction to his fuit from her, he purfues the following plan.

It has been already obferved, that the Indians acknowledge no fuperiority, nor have they any ideas of fubordination, except in the neceffary regulations of their war or hunting parties; they confequently live nearly in a ftate of equality, purfuant to the firft principles of nature. The lover therefore is not apprehenfive of any check or countroul in the accomplifhment of his purpofes, if he can find a convenient opportunity for completing them.

As the Indians are alfo under no apprehenfion of robbers, or fecret enemies, they leave the doors of their tents or huts unfaftened during the night, as well as in the day. Two or three hours after funfet, the flaves or old people cover over the fire, that is generally burning in the midfts of their apartment, with afhes, and retire to their repofe.

Whilft darknefs thus prevails, and all is quiet, one of thefe fons of pleafure, wrapped up clofely in his blanket, to prevent his being known, will fometimes enter the apartment of his intended miftrefs. Having firft lighted at the fmothered fire a fmall fplinter of wood, which anfwers the purpofe of a match,

he

he approaches the place where she repofes, and gently pulling away the covering from the head, jogs her till she awakes. If she then rifes up, and blows out the light, he needs no further confirmation that his company is not difagreeable; but if, after he has difcovered himfelf, fhe hides her head, and takes no notice of him, he might reft affured that any further folicitations will prove vain, and that it is neceffary immediately for him to retire.

During his ftay he conceals the light as much as poffible in the hollow of his hands, and as the tents or rooms of the Indians are ufually large and capacious, he efcapes without detection. It is faid that the young women who aomit their lovers on thefe occafions, take great care, by an immediate application to herbs, with the potent efficacy of which they are well acquainted, to prevent the effects of thefe illicit amours from becoming vifible; for fhould the natural confequences enfue, they muft forever remain unmarried.

The children of the Indians are always diftinguifhed by the name of the mother; and if a woman marries feveral hufbands, and has iffue by each of them, they are all called after her. The reafon they give for this is, that as their offspring are indebted to the father for their fouls, the invifible part of their effence, and to the mother for their corporeal and apparent part, it is more rational that they fhould be diftinguifhed by the name of the latter, from whom they indubitably derive their being, than by that of the father, to which a doubt might fometimes arife whether they are juftly intitled.

There are fome ceremonies made ufe of by the Indians at the impofition of the name, and it is confidered by them as a matter of great importance; but what thefe are I could never learn, through the fecrecy obferved on the occafion. I only know that it is ufually given when the children have paffed the ftate of infancy.

Nothing can exceed the tendernefs fhown by them to their offspring; and a perfon cannot recommend himfelf to their favour by any method more certain, than by paying fome attention to the younger branches of their families. I can impute, in fome meafure, to the prefents I made to the children of the chiefs of the Naudoweffies, the hofpitable reception I met with when among them.

There is fome difficulty attends an explanation of the manner in which the Indians diftinguifh themfelves from each other. Befides the name of the animal by which every nation and tribe is denominated, there are others that are perfonal, and which the children receive from their mother.

The chiefs are alfo diftinguifhed by a name that has either fome reference to their abilities, or to the hieroglyphick of their families; and thefe are acquired after they arrive at the age of manhood. Such as have fignalized themfelves either in their war or hunting parties, or are poffeffed of fome eminent qualification,

fication, receive a name that serves to perpetuate the fame of these actions, or to make their abilities conspicuous.

Thus the great warrior of the Naudowessies was named Ottahtongoomlishcah, that is, the Great Father of Snakes; ottah being in English father, tongoom great, and lishcah a snake. Another chief was called Honahpawjatin, which means a swift runner over the mountains. And when they adopted me a chief among them, they named me Shebaygo, which signifies a writer, or a person that is curious in making hieroglyphicks, as they saw me often writing.

CHAPTER XIII.

Of their RELIGION.

IT is very difficult to attain a perfect knowledge of the religious principles of the Indians. Their ceremonies and doctrines have been so often ridiculed by the Europeans, that they endeavour to conceal them; and if, after the greatest intimacy, you desire any of them to explain to you their system of religion, to prevent your ridicule, they intermix with it many of the tenets they have received from the French missionaries, so that it is at last rendered an unintelligible jargon, and not to be depended upon.

Such as I could discover among the Naudowessies (for they also were very reserved in this point) I shall give my readers, without paying any attention to the accounts of others. As the religion of that people from their situation appears to be totally unadulterated with the superstitions of the church of Rome, we shall be able to gain from their religious customs a more perfect Idea of the original tenets and ceremonies of the Indians in general, than from those of any nations that approach nearer to the settlements.

It is certain they acknowledge one Supreme Being, or Giver of Life, who presides over all things. The Chipéways call this Being Manitou, or Kitchi-Manitou; the Naudowessies, Wakon or Tongo-Wakon, that is, the Great Spirit; and they look up to him as the source of good, from whom no evil can proceed. They also believe in a bad spirit, to whom they ascribe great power, and suppose that through his means all the evils which befall mankind are inflicted. To him therefore do they pray in their distresses, begging that he would either avert their troubles, or moderate them when they are no longer avoidable.

They say that the Great Spirit, who is infinitely good, neither wishes or is able to do any mischief to mankind; but on
the

the contrary, that he showers down on them all the blessings they deserve; whereas the evil spirit is continually employed in contriving how he may punish the human race; and to do which he is not only possessed of the will, but of the power.

They hold also that there are good spirits of a lesser degree, who have their particular departments, in which they are constantly contributing to the happiness of mortals. These they suppose to preside over all the extraordinary productions of nature, such as those lakes, rivers, or mountains that are of an uncommon magnitude; and likewise the beasts, birds, fishes, and even vegetables, or stones that exceed the rest of their species in size or singularity. To all of these they pay some kind of adoration. Thus when they arrive on the borders of Lake Superior, on the banks of the Mississippi, or any other great body of water, they present to the Spirit who resides there some kind of offering, as the prince of the Winnebagoes did when he attended me to the Falls of St. Anthony.

But at the same time I fancy that the ideas they annex to the word spirit, are very different from the conceptions more enlightened nations entertain of it. They appear to fashion to themselves corporeal representations of their gods, and believe them to be of a human form, though of a nature more excellent than man.

Of the same kind are their sentiments relative to a futurity. They doubt not but they shall exist in some future state; they however fancy that their employments there will be similar to those they are engaged in here, without the labour and difficulty annexed to them in this period of their existence.

They consequently expect to be translated to a delightful country, where they shall always have a clear unclouded sky, and enjoy a perpetual spring; where the forests will abound with game, and the lakes with fish, which might be taken without requiring a painful exertion of skill, or a laborious pursuit; in short, that they shall live for ever in regions of plenty, and enjoy every gratification they delight in here, in a greater degree.

To intellectual pleasures they are strangers; nor are these included in their scheme of happiness. But they expect that even these animal pleasures will be proportioned and distributed according to their merit; the skilful hunter, the bold and successful warrior, will be entitled to a greater share than those who through indolence or want of skill cannot boast of any superiority over the common herd.

The priests of the Indians are at the same time their physicians, and their conjurors; whilst they heal their wounds, or cure their diseases, they interpret their dreams, give them protective charms, and satisfy that desire which is so prevalent among them, of searching into futurity.

How well they execute the latter part of their professional engagements, and the methods they make use of on some of these occasions, I have already shewn in the exertions of the priest of
the

the Killistinoes, who was fortunate enough to succeed in extraordinary attempt near Lake Superior. They frequently are successful likewise in administering the salubrious herbs they have acquired a knowledge of; but that the ceremonies they make use of during the administration of them contributes to their success, I shall not take upon me to assert.

When any of the people are ill, the person who is invested with this triple character of doctor, priest, and magician, sits by the patient day and night, rattling in his ears a goad-shell filled with dry beans, called a Chichicoué, and making a disagreeable noise that cannot be well described.

This uncouth harmony one would imagine should disturb the sick person, and prevent the good effects of the doctor's prescription; but on the contrary they believe that the method made use of contributes to his recovery, by diverting from his malignant purposes the evil spirit who has inflicted the disorder; or at least that it will take off his attention, so that he shall not increase the malady. This they are credulous enough to imagine he is constantly on the watch to do, and would carry his inveteracy to a fatal length if they did not thus charm him.

I could not discover that they make use of any other religious ceremonies than those I have described; indeed, on the appearance of the new moon they dance and sing; but it is not evident that they pay that planet any adoration; they only seem to rejoice at the return of a luminary that makes the night cheerful, and which serves to light them on their way when they travel during the absence of the sun.

Notwithstanding Mr. Adair has asserted that the nations among whom he resided, observe with very little variation all the rites appointed by the Mosaic Law, I own I could never discover among those tribes that lie but a few degrees to the north-west, the least traces of the Jewish religion, except it be admitted that one particular female custom and their division into tribes, carry with them proofs sufficient to establish this assertion.

The Jesuits and French missionaries have also pretended that the Indians had, when they first travelled into America, some notions, though these were dark and confused, of the christian institution; that they have been greatly agitated at the sight of a cross, and given proofs, by the impressions made on them, that they were not entirely unacquainted with the sacred mysteries of Christianity. I need not say that these are too glaring absurdities to be credited, and could only receive their existence from the zeal of those fathers, who endeavoured at once to give the public a better opinion of the success of their missions, and to add support to the cause they were engaged in.

The Indians appear to be in their religious principles, rude and uninstructed. The doctrines they hold are few and simple, and such as have been generally impressed on the human mind, by some means or other, in the most ignorant ages. They however have not deviated, as many other uncivilized nations, and too many civilized ones have done, into idolatrous modes of worship; they venerate indeed, and make offerings to the wonderful parts of the creation, as I have before observed; but whether these rites are performed on account of the impression such extraordinary appearances make on them, or whether they consider them as the peculiar charge, or the usual places of residence of the invisible spirits they acknowledge, I cannot positively determine.

The human mind in its uncultivated state is apt to ascribe the extraordinary occurrences of nature, such as earthquakes, thunder, or hurricanes, to the interposition of unseen beings; the troubles and disasters also that are annexed to a savage life, the apprehensions attendant on a precarious subsistence and those numberless inconveniencies which man in his improved state has found means to remedy, are supposed to proceed from the interposition of evil spirits; the savage consequently lives in continual apprehensions of their unkind attacks, and to avert them has recourse to charms, to the fantastic ceremonies of his priest, or the powerful influence of his Manitous. Fear has of course a greater share in his devotions than gratitude, and he pays more attention to deprecating the wrath of the evil than to securing the favour of the good beings.

The Indians, however, entertain these absurdities in common with those of every part of the globe who have not been illumined by that religion which only can disperse the clouds of superstition and ignorance, and they are as free from error as a people can be that has not been favoured with its instructive doctrines.

CHAPTER. XIV.

Of their DISEASES, *&c.*

THE Indians in general are healthy, and subject but to few diseases, many of those that afflict civilized nations, and are the immediate consequences of luxury or sloth, being not known among them; however, the hardships and fatigues which they endure in hunting or war, the inclemency of the seasons to which they are continually exposed, but above all the extremes of hunger, and that voraciousness their long excursions consequently subject them to, cannot fail of impairing the constitution, and bringing on disorders.

Pains

Pains and weaknesses in the stomach and breast are sometimes the result of their long fasting, and consumptions of the excessive fatigue and violent exercises they expose themselves to from their infancy, before they have strength sufficient to support them. But the disorder to which they are most subject, is the pleurisy; for the removal of which, they apply their grand remedy and preservative against the generality of their complaints, sweating.

The manner in which they construct their stoves for this purpose is as follows: They fix several small poles in the ground, the tops of which they twist together, so as to form a rotunda: this frame they cover with skins or blankets; and they lay them on with so much nicety, that the air is kept from entering through any crevice; a small space being only left, just sufficient to creep in at, which is immediately after closed. In the middle of this confined building they place red hot stones, on which they pour water till a steam arises that produces a great degree of heat.

This causes an instantenous perspiration, which they increase as they please. Having continued in it for some time, they immediately hasten to the nearest stream, and plunge into the water; and, after bathing therein for about half a minute, they put on their cloaths, sit down and smoak with great composure, thoroughly persuaded that the remedy will prove efficacious. They often make use of this sudoriferous method to refresh themselves, or to prepare their minds for the management of any business that requires uncommon deliberation and sagacity.

They are likewise afflicted with the dropsy and paralytic complaints, which, however, are but very seldom known among them. As a remedy for these as well as for fevers they make use of lotions and decoctions, composed of herbs, which the physicians know perfectly well how to compound and apply. But they never trust to medicines alone; they always have recourse likewise to some superstitious ceremonies, without which their patients would not think the physical preparations sufficiently powerful.

With equal judgment they make use of simples for the cure of wounds, fractures, or bruises; and are able to extract by these, without incision, splinters, iron, or any sort of matter by which the wound is caused. In cures of this kind they are extremely dextrous, and complete them in much less time than might be expected from their mode of proceeding.

With the skin of a snake, which those reptiles annually shed, thy will also extract splinters. It is amazing to see the sudden efficacy of this application, notwithstanding there does not appear to be the least moisture remaining in it.

It has long been a subject of dispute, on what continent the venereal disease first received its destructive power. This dreadful malady is supposed to have originated in America, but the literary contest still remains undecided; to give some elucidation

tion to it I shall remark, that as I could not discover the least traces among the Naudowessies, with whom I resided so long, and was also informed that it was yet unknown among the more western nations, I think I may venture to pronounce that it had not its origin in North America. Those nations that have any communication with the Europeans, or the southern tribes, are greatly afflicted with it; but they have all of them acquired a knowledge of such certain and expeditious remedies, that the communication is not attended with any dangerous consequences.

Soon after I set out on my travels, one of the traders whom I accompanied, complained of a violent gonorrhœa, with all its alarming symptoms: this increased to such a degree, that by the time we had reached the town of the Winnebagoes, he was unable to travel. Having made his complaint known to one of the chiefs of that tribe, he told him not to be uneasy, for he would engage that by following his advice, he should be able in a few days to pursue his journey, and in a little longer time be entirely free from his disorder.

The chief had no sooner said this than he prepared for him a decoction of the bark of the roots of the prickly ash, a tree scarcely known in England, but which grows in great plenty throughout North America; by the use of which, in a few days he was greatly recovered, and having received directions how to prepare it, in a fortnight after his departure from this place perceived that he was radically cured.

If from excessive excercise, or the extremes of heat or cold, they are affected with pains in their limbs or joints, they scarify the parts affected. Those nations who have no commerce with Europeans do this with a sharp flint; and it is surprizing to see how fine a point they have the dexterity to bring them; a lancet can scarcely exceed in sharpness the instruments they make use of this unmalleable substance.

They never can be convinced a person is ill, whilst he has an appetite; but when he rejects all kind of nourishment, they consider the disease as dangerous, and pay great attention to it; and during the continuance of the disorder, the physician refuses his patient no sort of food that he is desirous of.

Their doctors are not only supposed to be skilled in the physical treatment of diseases; but the common people believe that by the ceremony of the Chichicoué usually made use of, as before described, they are able to gain intelligence from the spirits of the cause of the complaints with which they are afflicted, and are thereby the better enabled to find remedies for them. They discover something supernatural in all their diseases, and the physick administered must invariably be aided by these superstitions.

Sometimes a sick person fancies that his disorder arises from witchcraft; in this case the physician or juggler is consulted, who, after the usual preparations, gives his opinion on the state of the disease, and frequently finds some means for his cure.

But

But notwithstanding the Indian physicians always annex these superstitious ceremonies to their prescriptions, it is very certain, as I have already observed, that they exercise their art by principles which are founded on the knowledge of simples, and on experience which they acquire by an indefatigable attention to their operations.

The following story, which I received from a person of undoubted credit, proves that the Indians are not only able to reason with great acuteness on the causes and symptoms of many of the disorders which are attendant on human nature, but to apply with equal judgment proper remedies.

In Penobscot, a settlement in the province of Main, in the north-east parts of New-England, the wife of a soldier was taken in labour, and notwithstanding every necessary assistance was given her, could not be delivered. In this situation she remained for two or three days, the persons around her expecting that the next pang would put an end to her existence.

An Indian woman, who accidentally passed by, heard the groans of the unhappy sufferer, and enquired from whence they proceeded. Being made acquainted with the desperate circumstances attending the case, she told the informant, that if she might be permitted to see the person, she did not doubt but that she could be of great service to her.

The surgeon that had attended, and the midwife who was then present, having given up every hope of preserving their patient, the Indian woman was allowed to make use of any methods she thought proper. She accordingly took a handkerchief, and bound it tight over the nose and mouth of the woman: this immediately brought on a suffocation; and from the struggles that consequently ensued she was in a few seconds delivered. The moment this was atchieved, and time enough to prevent any fatal effect, the handkerchief was taken off. The long suffering patient thus happily relieved from her pains, soon after perfectly recovered, to the astonishment of all those who had been witness to her desperate situation.

The reason given by the Indian for this hazardous method of proceeding was, that desperate disorders require desperate remedies; that as she observed the exertions of nature were not sufficiently forcible to effect the desired consequence, she thought it necessary to augment their force, which could only be done by some mode that was violent in the extreme.

CHAP.

CHAPTER XV.

Of the Manner in which they treat their DEAD.

AN Indian meets death when it approaches him in his hut, with the same resolution he has often faced him in the field. His indifference relative to this important article, which is the source of so many apprehensions to almost every other nation, is truly admirable. When his fate is pronounced by the physician, and it remains no longer uncertain, he harangues those about him with the greatest composure.

If he is a chief and has a family, he makes a kind of funeral oration, which he concludes by giving to his children such advice for the regulation of their conduct as he thinks necessary. He then takes leave of his friends, and issues out orders for the preparation of a feast, which is designed to regale those of his tribe that come to pronounce his eulogium.

After the breath is departed, the body is dressed in the same attire it usually wore whilst living, his face is painted, and he seated in an erect posture, on a mat or skin, placed in the middle of the hut, with his weapons by his side. His relations being seated round, each harangues in turn the deceased; and if he has been a great warrior, recounts his heroic actions nearly to the following purport, which in the Indian language is extremely poetical and pleasing:

"You still sit among us, Brother, your person retains its
"usual resemblance, and continues similar to ours, without any
"visible deficiency, except that it has lost the power of action.
"But whither is that breath flown, which a few hours ago sent
"up smoke to the Great Spirit? Why are those lips silent, that
"lately delivered to us expressive and pleasing language? why
"are those feet motionless, that a short time ago were fleeter
"than the deer on yonder mountains? why useless hang those
"arms that could climb the tallest tree, or draw the toughest
"bow? Alas! every part of that frame which we lately beheld
"with admiration and wonder, is now become as inanimate as
"it was three hundred winters ago. We will not, however,
"bemoan thee as if thou wast for ever lost to us, or that thy
"name would be buried in oblivion; thy soul yet lives in the
"great Country of Spirits, with those of thy nation that are
"gone before thee; and though we are left behind to perpe-
"tuate thy fame, we shall one day join thee. Actuated by the
"respect

"respect we bore thee whilst living, we now come to tender
"to thee the last act of kindness it is in our power to bestow:
"that thy body might not lie neglected on the plain, and be-
"come a prey to the beasts of the field, or the fowls of the
"air, we will take care to lay it with those of thy predecessors
"who are gone before thee; hoping at the same time, that thy
"spirit will feed with their spirits, and be ready to receive
"ours, when we also shall arrive at the great Country of Souls."

In short speeches somewhat similar to this does every chief speak the praises of his departed friend. When they have so done, if they happen to be at a great distance from the place of interment, appropriated to their tribe, and the person dies during the winter season, they wrap the body in skins, and lay it on a high stage built for this purpose, or on the branches of a large tree, till the spring arrives. They then, after the manner described in my journal, carry it, together with all those belonging to the same nation, to the general burial place, where it is interred with some other ceremonies that I could not discover.

When the Naudowessies brought their dead for interment to the great cave, I attempted to get an insight into the remaining burial rites; but whether it was on account of the stench which arose from so many bodies, the weather being then hot, or whether they chose to keep this part of their customs secret from me, I could not discover; I found, however, that they considered my curiosity as ill-timed, and therefore I withdrew.

After the interment, the band to which the person belongs, take care to fix near the place such hieroglyphicks as shall show to future ages his merit and accomplishments. If any of these people die in the summer at a distance from the burying-ground, and they find it impossible to remove the body before it putrefies, they burn the flesh from the bones, and preserving the latter, bury them in the manner described.

As the Indians believe that the souls of the deceased employ themselves in the same manner in the country of spirits, as they did on earth, that they acquire their food by hunting, and have there, also, enemies to contend with, they take care that they do not enter those regions defenceless and unprovided: they consequently bury with them their bows, their arrows, and all the other weapons used either in hunting or war. As they doubt not but they will likewise have occasion both for the necessaries of life, and those things they esteem as ornaments, they usually deposit in their tombs such skins or stuffs as they commonly made their garments of, domestic utensils, and paint for ornamenting their persons.

The near relations of the deceased lament his loss with an appearance of great sorrow and anguish; they weep and howl, and make use of many contortions, as they sit in the hut or tent around the body, when the intervals between the praises of the chiefs will permit.

One formality in mourning for the dead among the Naudowessies is very different from any mode I observed in the other nations through which I passed. The men, to show how great their sorrow is, pierce the flesh of their arms, above the elbows, with arrows; the scars of which I could perceive on those of every rank, in a greater or less degree; and the women cut and gash their legs with sharp broken flints, till the blood flows very plentifully.

Whilst I remained among them, a couple whose tent was adjacent to mine, lost a son of about four years of age. The parents were so much affected at the death of their favourite child, that they pursued the usual testimonies of grief with such uncommon rigour, as through the weight of sorrow and loss of blood, to occasion the death of the father. The woman, who had hitherto been inconsolable, no sooner saw her husband expire, than she dried up her tears, and appeared cheerful and resigned.

As I knew not how to account for so extraordinary a transition, I took an opportunity to ask her the reason of it; telling her at the same time, that I should have imagined the loss of her husband would rather have occasioned an increase of grief, than such a sudden diminution of it.

She informed me, that as the child was so young when it died, and unable to support itself in the country of spirits, both she and her husband had been apprehensive that its situation would be far from happy; but no sooner did she behold its father depart for the same place, who not only loved the child with the tenderest affection, but was a good hunter, and would be able to provide plentifully for its support, than she ceased to mourn. She added, that she now saw no reason to continue her tears, as the child on whom she doated, was happy under the care and protection of a fond father, and she had only one wish that remained ungratified, which was that of being herself with them.

Expressions so replete with unaffected tenderness, and sentiments that would have done honour to a Roman matron, made an impression on my mind greatly in favour of the people to whom she belonged, and tended not a little to counteract the prejudices I had hitherto entertained, in common with every other traveller, of Indian insensibility and want of parental tenderness.

Her subsequent conduct confirmed the favourable opinion I had just imbibed; and convinced me, that, notwithstanding this apparent suspension of her grief, some particles of that reluctance, to be separated from a beloved relation, which is implanted either by nature or custom in every human heart, still lurked in hers. I observed that she went almost every evening to the foot of the tree, on a branch of which the bodies of her husband and child were laid, and after cutting off a lock of " r-hair, and throwing it on the ground, in a plaintive melancholy

choly song bemoaned its fate. A recapitulation of the actions he might have performed, had his life been spared, appeared to be her favourite theme; and whilst she foretold the fame that would have attended an imitation of his father's virtues, her grief seemed to be suspended:———

"If thou hadst continued with us, my dear Son," would she cry, "how well would the bow have become thy hand, and "and how fatal would thy arrows have proved to the enemies "of our bands. Thou wouldst often have drank their blood, and "eaten their flesh, and numerous slaves would have rewarded "thy toils. With a nervous arm wouldst thou have seized the "wounded buffaloe, or have combated the fury of the enraged "bear. Thou wouldst have overtaken the flying elk, and have "kept pace on the mountain's brow with the fleetest deer. "What feats mightest thou not have performed, hadst thou "staid among us till age had given thee strength, and thy father "had instructed thee in every Indian accomplishment!" In terms like these did this untutored savage bewail the loss of her son, and frequently would she pass the greatest part of the night in the affectionate employ.

The Indians in general are very strict in the observance of their laws relative to mourning for their dead. In some nations they cut off their hair, blacken their faces, and sit in an erect posture, with their heads closely covered, and depriving themselves of every pleasure. This severity is continued for several months, and with some relaxations the appearance is sometimes kept up for several years. I was told that when the Naudowessies recollected any incidents of the lives of their deceased relations, even after an interval of ten years, they would howl so as to be heard at a great distance. They would sometimes continue this proof of respect and affection for several hours; and if it happened that the thought occurred, and the noise was begun towards the evening, those of their tribe, who are at hand would join with them.

CHAPTER XVI.

A concise CHARACTER *of the* INDIANS.

THE character of the Indians, like that of other uncivilized nations, is composed of a mixture of ferocity and gentleness. They are at once guided by passions and appetites, which they hold in common with the fiercest beasts that inhabit their woods, and are possessed of virtues which do honour to human nature.

In the following estimate I shall endeavour to forget on the one hand the prejudices of Europeans, who usually annex to the word Indian epithets that are disgraceful to human nature, and who view them in no other light than as savages and cannibals; whilst with equal care I avoid any partiality towards them, as some must naturally arise from the favourable reception I met with during my stay among them.

At the same time I shall confine my remarks to the nations inhabiting only the western regions, such as the Naudowessies, the Ottaguamies, the Chipéways, the Winnebagoes, and the Saukies; for as throughout that diversity of climates, the extensive continent of America is composed of, there are people of different dispositions and various characters, it would be incompatible with my present undertaking to treat of all these, and to give a general view of them as a conjunctive body.

That the Indians are of a cruel, revengeful, inexorable disposition, that they will watch whole days unmindful of the calls of nature, and make their way through pathless, and almost unbounded woods, subsisting only on the scanty produce of them, to pursue and revenge themselves of an enemy; that they hear unmoved the piercing cries of such as unhappily fall into their hands, and receive a diabolical pleasure from the tortures they inflict on their prisoners, I readily grant; but let us look on the reverse of this terrifying picture, and we shall find them temperate both in their diet and potations (it must be remembered that I speak of those tribes who have little communication with Europeans) that they with-stand, with unexampled patience, the attacks of hunger, or the inclemency of the seasons, and esteem the gratification of their appetites but as a secondary consideration.

We shall likewise see them social and humane to those whom they consider as their friends, and even to their adopted enemies; and ready to partake with them of the last morsel, or to risk their lives in their defence.

In contradiction to the report of many other travellers, all of which have been tinctured with prejudice, I can assert, that notwithstanding the apparent indifference with which an Indian meets his wife and children after a long absence, an indifference proceeding rather from custom than insensibility, he is not unmindful of the claims either of connubial or parental tenderness; the little story I have introduced in the preceeding chapter, of the Naudowessie woman lamenting her child, and the immature death of the father, will elucidate this point, and enforce the assertion much better than the most studied arguments I can make use of.

Accustomed from their youth to innumerable hardships, they soon become superior to a sense of danger, or the dread of death; and their fortitude, implanted by nature, and nurtured by example, by precept and accident, never experiences a moment's allay.

Though

Though flothful and inactive whilst their store of provision remains unexhausted, and their foes are at a distance, they are indefatigable and persevering in pursuit of their game, or in circumventing their enemies.

If they are artful and designing, and ready to take every advantage, if they are cool and deliberate in their councils, and cautious in the extreme either of discovering their sentiments, or of revealing a secret, they might at the same time boast of possessing qualifications of a more animated nature, of the sagacity of a hound, the penetrating sight of a lynx, the cunning of the fox, the agility of a bounding roe, and the unconquerable fierceness of the tyger.

In their public characters, as forming part of a community, they possess an attachment for that band to which they belong, unknown to the inhabitants of any other country. They combine, as if the were actuated only by one soul, against the enemies of their nation, and banish from their minds every consideration opposed to this.

They consult without unnecessary opposition, or without giving way to the excitements of envy or ambition, on the measures necessary to be pursued for the destruction of those who have drawn on themselves their displeasure. No selfish views ever influence their advice, or obstruct their consultations. Nor is it in the power of bribes or threats to diminish the love they bear their country.

The honour of their tribe, and the welfare of their nation, is the first and most predominat emotion of their hearts; and from hence proceed in a great measure all their virtues and their vices. Actuated by by this, they brave every danger, endure the most exquisite torments, and expire triumphing in their fortitude, not as a personal qualification, but as a national characteristic.

From these also flow that insatiable revenge towards those with whom they are at war, and all the consequent horrors that disgrace their name. Their uncultivated mind, being incapable of judging of the propriety of an action, in opposition to their passions, which are totally insensible to the controuls of reason or humanity, they know not how to keep their fury within any bounds, and consequently that courage and resolution, which would otherwise do them honour, degenerates into a savage ferocity.

But this short dissertation must suffice; the limits of my work will not permit me to treat the subject more copiously, or to pursue it with a logical regularity. The observations already made by my readers on the preceeding pages, will, I trust, render it unnecessary; as by them they will be enabled to form a tolerably just idea of the people I have been describing. Experience teaches, that anecdotes, and relations of particular events, however trifling they might appear, enable us to form a truer judgment of the manners and customs of a people, and are

much

much declaratory of their real state, than the most studied and elaborate disquisition, without these aids.

CHAPTER XVII.

Of their LANGUAGE, HIEROGLY-PHICKS, &c.

THE principal languages of the natives of North America may be divided into four classes, as they consist of such as are made use of by the nations of the Iroquois towards the eastern parts of it, the Chipéways or Algonkins to the north-west, the Naudowessies to the west, and the Cherokees, Chickasaws, &c. to the south. One or other of these four are used by all the Indians who inhabit the parts that lie between the coast of Labradore north, the Florida south, the Atlantic ocean east, and, as far as we can judge from the discoveries hitherto made, the Pacific Ocean on the west.

But of all these, the Chipéway tongue appears to be the most prevailing; it being held in such esteem, that the chiefs of every tribe, dwelling about the great lakes, or to the westward of these on the banks of the Mississippi, with those as far south as the Ohio, and as far north as Hudson's Bay, consisting of more than thirty different tribes, speak this language alone in their councils, notwithstanding each has a peculiar one of their own.

It will probably in time become universal among all the Indian nations, as none of them attempt to make excursions to any great distance, or are considered as qualified to carry on any negociation with a distant band, unless they have acquired the Chipéway tongue.

At present, besides the Chipéways, to whom it is natural, the Ottawaws, the Saukies, the Ottagaumies, the Killistinoes, the Nipegons, the bands about Lake Le Pleuve, and the remains of the Algonkins, or Gens de Terre, all converse in it, with some little variation of dialect; but whether it be natural to these nations, or acquired, I was not able to discover. I am however of opinion that the barbarous and uncouth dialect of the Winnebagoes, the Menomonies, and many other tribes, will become in time totally extinct, and this be adopted in its stead.

The Chipéway tongue is not incumbered with any unnecessary tones or accents, neither are there any words in it that are superfluous; it is also easy to pronounce, and much more copious than any other Indian language.

As the Indians are unacquainted with the polite arts, or with the sciences, and as they are also strangers to ceremony, or compliment,

pliment, they neither have nor need an infinity of words wherewith to embellish their discourse. Plain and unpolished in their manners, they only make use of such as serve to denominate the necessaries or conveniences of life, and to express their wants, which in a state of nature can be but few.

I have annexed hereto a short vocabulary of the Chipéway language, and another of that of the Naudoweffies, but am not able to reduce them to the rules of grammar.

The latter is spoken in a soft accent, without any guttural sounds, so that it may be learnt with facility, and is not difficult either to be pronounced or written. It is nearly as copious and expressive as the Chipéway tongue, and is the most prevailing language of any on the western banks of the Missisippi; being in use, according to their account, among all the nations that lie to the north of the Messorie, and extend as far west as the shores of the Pacific Ocean.

As the Indians are not acquainted with letters, it is very difficult to convey with precision the exact sound of their words; I have however endeavoured to write them as near to the manner in which they expressed, as such an uncertain mode will admit of.

Although the Indians cannot communicate their ideas by writing, yet they form certain hieroglyphicks, which, in some measure, serve to perpetuate any extraordinary transaction, or uncommon event. Thus when they are on their excursions, and either intend to proceed, or have been on any remarkable enterprize, they peel the bark from the trees which lie in their way, to give intelligence to those parties that happen to be at a distance, of the path they must pursue to overtake them.

The following instance will convey a more perfect idea of the methods they make use of on this occasion, than any expressions I can frame.

When I left the Missisippi, and proceeded up the Chipéway River, in my way to Lake Superior, as related in my Journal, my guide, who was a chief of the Chipéways that dwell on the Ottawaw Lake, near the heads of the river we had just entered, fearing that some parties of the Naudoweffies, with whom his nation are perpetually at war, might accidentally fall in with us, and before they were apprized of my being in company, do us some mischief, he took the following steps:

He peeled the bark from a large tree, near the entrance of a river, and with wood-coal, mixed with bear's greafe, their usual substitute for ink, made in an uncouth, but expressive manner, the figure of the town of the Ottagaumies. He then formed to the left a man dressed in skins, by which he intended to represent a Naudoweffie, with a line drawn from his mouth to that of a deer, the symbol of the Chipéways. After this he depictured still farther to the left a canoe as proceeding up the river, in which he placed a man sitting with a hat on; this figure was designed to represent an Englishman, or myself, and my Frenchman

man was drawn with a handkerchief tied round his head, and rowing the canoe; to these he added several other significant emblems, among which the Pipe of Peace appeared painted on the prow of the canoe.

The meaning he intended to convey to the Naudowessies, and which I doubt not appeared perfectly intelligible to them, was, that one of the Chipéway chiefs had received a speech from some Naudowessie chiefs, at the town of the Ottagaumies, desiring him to conduct the Englishman, who had lately been among them, up the Chipéway river; and that they thereby required, that the Chipéway, notwithstanding he was an avowed enemy, should not be molested by them on his passage, as he had the care of a person whom they esteemed as one of their nation.

Some authors have pretended that the Indians have armorial bearings, which they blazon with great exactness, and which distinguish one nation from another; but I never could observe any other arms among them than the symbols already described.

A short VOCABULARY of the Chipéway Language.

N. B. This people do not make use either of the consonants *F* or *V*.

A

Above	*Spimink*
Abandon	*Packiton*
Admirable	*Pilawah*
Afterwards	*Mipidach*
All	*Kokinum*
Always	*Kokali*
Amiss	*Napitch*
Arrive	*Takouchin*
Ax	*Agacwet*
Ashes	*Pingoe*
Assist	*Mawinewáh*

B

Ball	*Alewin*
Bag, or tobacco-pouch	*Caspetawgan*
Barrel	*Owentowgan*
Beat	*Pakhite*
Bear,	*Mackwah*
Bear, a young one	*Makon*
Beaver	*Amik*
Beaver's skin	*Apiminiqué*
Be, or to be	*Tapaié*
Beard	*Mischiton*
Because	*Mewinch*
Believe	*Tilerimah*
Belly	*Misbemout*
Black	*Markaute*
Blood	*Miskow*
Body	*Yoe*

Bottle

[173]

Bottle	Shishego
Brother	Neconnis
Brandy or Rum	Scuttawawbah
Bread	Paboushigan
Breech	Mischousah
Breeches	Kipokitis Kousah
Buck	Wasketch

C

Canoe	Cheman
Call	Teshenekaw
Chief, a	Okemaw
Carry	Petou
Child or Children	Bobeloskin
Coat	Capotewian
Cold, I am	Kekalch
Come on	Moppa
Come to	Pemotcka
Comrade	Neechee
Concerned	Tallemissi
Corn	Melomin
Covering, or a Blanket	Wawberion
Country	Endawkawkeen
Courage	Tagwawmissi
Cup	Olawgan

D

Dance	Nemeh
Dart	Sheshikwea
Die, to	Nip
Dish	Mackoan
Dog	Alim
Dead	Neepoo
Devil or evil Spirit	Matche-Manitou
Dog, a little one	Alemon
Done, it is done	Shiah
Do	Tashiton
Doubtless	Ontclateubah
Dress the kettle	Poutwea
Drink	Minikwah
Drunken	Ouisquiba
Duck	Chickhip

E

Earth	Aukwin
Eat	Owissué
Each	Papégik
English	Sagaunosh
Enough	Mimilic
Equal, or alike	Tawbiscouch
Esteem	Nawpetelimaw
Eyes	Wiskinkhie

F

Fast	Waliebic
Fall	Ponkissin
Far off	Watsew
Fat	Pinmitee
Friend	Niconnis
Father	Noosah
Few, or little	Maungis
Fatigued	Taukwissi
Field sown	Kittegaumic
Fire	Scutta
Fire, to strike	Scutecke
Find	Nantounawaw
Fish	Kicken
Fork	Nassewokwot
Formerly	Pirwego
Fort	Wakaigon
Forward	Nopawink
French	Neclaegoosh
Freeze, to	Kissin
Freezes hard	Kissin Magat
Full	Moushinet
Fuzee or Gun	Paskessigan

G

God, or the Great Spirit	Kitcai Manitou
Go by water	Pimmiscaw
Girl	Jeckwassin
Give	Millaw
Glass, a mirror	Wawbemo
Good	Cawlatch
Good for nothing	Malatal
Govern	Tibarimaw

General,

[174]

General, or Commander in Chief	*Kitchi Okimaw Simáuganish*	Knife that is crooked	*Cootawgan*
Grapes	*Shoamin*	Know	*Thickeremaw*
Great	*Manatou*		
Greedy	*Sawsúwkiſſi*		
Guts	*Oláwbiſh*		

L

H

		Lake	*Kitchigawmink*
		Laugh	*Pawpi*
		Lazy	*Kittimi*
		Lame	*Kikekate*
Hare	*Wawpoos*	Leave	*Pockitan*
Heart	*Michewah*	Letter	*Mawsignaugon*
Hate	*Shingaurimaw*	Life	*Nauchinowin*
Half	*Nawbal*	Love	*Saukie*
Hair, human	*Liſſis*	Long since	*Shawsbia*
Hair of beasts	*Pewal*	Land Carriage	*Cappatawgon*
Handsome	*Canoginne*	Lose	*Packilaugué*
Have	*Tandaulaw*	Lie down	*Weipemaw*
Head	*Ouſtecouan*	Little	*Waubesbeen*
Heaven	*Speminkakwin*		
Herb	*Mejaſk*		
Here	*Aconda*	**M**	
Hidden	*Keinouch*		
Home	*Entayent*	Meat	*Weas*
Honour	*Mackawalaw*	Much	*Nibbilaw*
Hot	*Akeſbotta*	Man	*Alliſſinape*
How	*Tawné*	March, to go	*Pimmouſſie*
How many	*Tawnemilik*	Marry	*Weewin*
Hunt	*Kewaſſa*	Medicine	*Maſkikic*
Hut, or House	*Wig-Waum*	Merchandize	*Alokochigon*
		Moon	*Debicot*
		Mortar to pound in	*Poutawgon*
I		Male	*Nape*
		Mistress	*Neremousin*
Indians	*Iſhinawbah*		
Iron	*Pewawbick*	**N**	
Island	*Minis*		
Immediately	*Webatch*	Needle	*Shawbonkin*
Indian Corn	*Mittawmin*	Near	*Pewitch*
Intirely	*Nawpitch*	Nation	*Irinee*
Impostor	*Mawlawtiſſie*	Never	*Cawikkaw*
It might be so	*Tawneendo*	Night	*Debicot*
		No	*Kaw*
		Nose	*Yoch*
K		Nothing	*Kakezo*
		Not yet	*Kawmiſchi*
Kettle	*Ackikons*	Not at all	*Kagutch*
King, or Chief	*Okemaw*	Nought, good for nothing	*Malatat*
Keep	*Ganwerimaw*		
Knife	*Mockoman*		

[175]

O

Old	Kauweshine
Otter	Nikkik
Other	Coutack

P

Pipe	Poagan
Part, what part	Tawnapee
Play	Packeigo
Powder, gun, or duſt	Pingo
Peace, to make	Pecacotiche
Pray	Tawlaimia
Proper	Sawſega
Preſently	Webatch
Peninſula	Minniſſin

Q

Quick	Kegotch

R

Regard	Wawbema
Red	Miſcow
Reſolve	Tibelindon
Relation	Towwemaw
Reſpect	Tawbawnica
Rain	Kimmewan
Robe	Ockolaw
River	Sippim
Run, to	Pitchebot

S

Sad	Talimiſſie
Sail	Pemiſcaw
Sack, or Bag	Maſkimot
Sea, or large Lake	Agankitchigawmink
Shoes	Maukiſſin
Ship, or large Canoe	Kitchi Chemaan
Sorry	Niſcottiſſie
Spirit	Manitou
Spoon	Mickwon

Star	Alank
Steal	Kemautia
Stockings	Mittaus
Strong	Maſhkauwaſh
Sturgeon	Lawmack
Sun	Kiſſis
Sword	Simaugan
Surprizing	Etwah, Etwah
See	Wawbemo
Since	Mapedoh
Shirt	Papawkwéan
Slave	Wackan
Sleep	Nippee
Sit down	Mintepin

T

Take	Emaundah
Teeth	Tibbit
That	Mawbah
There	Watſaudebi
This	Maundah
Truly	Kikit
Together	Mawmawwee
Tobacco	Semau
Tongue	Outon
Tired	Tawkonſie
Too little	Oſauminangis
Too much	Oſſauné
Thank you	Megwatch
To-morrow	Wawbunk
To-morrow the day after	Ouſwawburk

W

Warriors	Semauganauſh
Water	Nebbi
War	Nantaubqulaw
Way	Mickon
Well then!	Tauneendah!
What is that?	Wawwewin?
What now?	Quagonie?
Whence	Taunippi
Where	Tah
White	Waubé
Who is there?	Quagonie Maubah?
Wind	Loutin
Winter	

[176]

Winter	Pepoun		Y
Woman	Ickwee	Yesterday	Petchilawgo
Wood	Mittie	Yet	Minnewatch
Wolf	Mawhingen	Young	Wisconekissi
		Yellow	Wazzo.

The Numerical Terms of the Chipeways.

One	Pásbik	Fifty	Naran Mittawnaw
Two	Ninch	Sixty	Ningoutwassou Mittawnaw
Three	Nissou	Seventy	Ninchowasseu Mittawnaw
Four	Neau	Eighty	Nissowassou Mittawnaw
Five	Naran	Ninety	Shongassou Mittawnaw
Six	Ningoutwassou	Hundred	Mittaussou Mittawnaw
Seven	Ninchowassou	Thousand	Mittaussou Mittaussou Mittawnaw.
Eight	Nissowassou		
Nine	Shongassou		
Ten	Mittaussou		
Eleven	Mittaussou Pásbik		
Twenty	Ninchtawnaw		
Thirty	Nissou Mittawnaw		
Forty	Neau Mittawnaw		

A Short VOCABULARY of the Naudowessie Language.

	A	Child, a Male	Wecheakseh
Axe	Ashpaw	Child, a Female	Whacheekseh
		Come here	Accooyouiyore
	B		**D**
Beaver	Chawbah	Dead	Negush
Buffalo	Tawtongo	Deer	Tohinjoh
Bad	Shejah	Dog	Shungush
Broach	Muzahootoo		
Bear, a	Wahkonshejah		**E**
	C	Eat	Echawmenaw
		Ears	Nookah
Canoe	Waahtoh	Eyes	Eshtike
Cold	Mechustah	Evil	Shejah

Fire

F

Fire	*Paahtah*
Father	*Otah*
Frenchman	*Neehteegush*
Falls of Water	*Owah Menah*
Friend	*Kitchiwah*

G

Good	*Woshtch*
Give	*Accooyeh*
Go away	*Accowab*
God, or the Great Spirit }	*Wakon*
Gun	*Muzah Wakon*
Great	*Tongo*
Gold	*Muzaham*

H

Hear	*Nookishon*
Horse	*Shuetongo*
Home, or domestic }	*Shuah*
House	*Teebee*
Heaven	*Woshta Tebee*

I

Iron	*Muzah*
I, or me	*Meoh*

K

King, or Chief	*Otah*
Kill	*Negushraugaw*

L

Little	*Jestin*
Long	*Tongoom*
Lake	*Tongo Meneh*
Love	*Ehwahmeah*

M

Much	*Otah*
More	*Otenaw*

Moon	*Oweeh*
Mouth	*Eeh*
Medal	*Muzah Otah*
Mine	*Meyah*
Milk	*Etsawboh*

N

No	*Heyah*
Near	*Jeestinaw*

O

Oh!	*Hopiniyahie!*

P

Pipe	*Shanuapaw*
Pipe of Peace	*Shanuapaw Wakon*

R

Rain	*Owah Meneh*
Ring	*Muzamchupah*
Round	*Chupeh*

S

Smoke	*Shaweah*
Salt Water	*Menus Queah*
See, to	*Eshtaw*
Sleep	*Eshteemo*
Snake	*Omlisocaw*
Sun	*Paahtah*
Spirit	*Wakon*
Spirituous Liquors }	*Meneh Wakon*
Snow	*Sinnee*
Surprizing	*Hopiniayare*
Silver	*Muzaham*

T

Tobacco	*Shawsassaw*
Talk	*Owehchin*
Tree	*Ochaw*
There	*Daché*

Woman

W		Y	
Woman	*Winnokejah*	You	*Chee*
Wonderful	*Hopiniyare*	Young	*Hawpawnaw*
Water	*Meneh*	You are good	*Washtah Chee*
What	*Tawgo*	You are a Spirit	*Wakon Chee*
Who is there?	*Tewgodaché?*	You are my good Friend	*Washtah Kitchiwah Chee*
Wicked	*Heyahatchta*	No Good	*Heyah Washtah.*

The Numerical Terms of the Naudowessies.

One	*Wonchaw*	Forty	*Wegochunganong Toboh*
Two	*Noompaw*		
Three	*Tawmcnee*	Fifty	*Wegochunganong Sawbuttee*
Four	*Toboh*		
Five	*Sawbuttee*	Sixty	*Wegochunganong Shawco*
Six	*Shawco*		
Seven	*Shawcopee*	Seventy	*Wegochunganong Shawcopee*
Eight	*Shahindohin*		
Nine	*Nebochunganong*	Eighty	*Wegochunganong Shahindohin*
Ten	*Wegochunganong*		
Eleven	*Wegochunganong Wonchaw*	Ninety	*Wegochunganong Nebochunganong*
Twenty	*Wegochunganong Noompaw*	Hundred	*Opohng*
Thirty	*Wegochunganong Tawmonee*	Thousand	*Wegochudganong Opohng*

To this short vocabulary of the Naudowessie language, I shall adjoin a specimen of the manner in which they unite their words. I have chosen for this purpose a short song, which they sing, with some kind of melody, though not with any appearance of poetical measure, when they set out on their hunting expeditions: and have given as near a translation as the difference of the idioms will permit.

Meoh accoowah eshtaw paatah negushtawgaw shojah menah. Tongo Wakon meoh washta, paatah accoowah. Hopiniyahie owech accooyec meoh, woshta patah otoh tohirsoh mesh tcebee.

I will rise before the sun, and ascend yonder hill, to see the new light chase away the vapours, and disperse the clouds. Great Spirit give me success. And when the sun is gone, lend me, oh moon, light sufficient to guide me with safety back to my tent loaden with deer!

CHAPTER

frightful look. There is a bunch on his ba[...]
the haunches, and increafing gradually t[...]
on to the neck. Both this excrefc[...]
covered with long hair, or rath[...]
[...], which is exceeding [...] E R   XVIII.
[...] body

Of the BEASTS, BIRDS, FISHES, REPTILES, and INSECTS, which are found in the interior Parts of North America.

OF thefe I fhall, in the firft place, give a catalogue, and afterwards a defcription of fuch only as are either peculiar to this country, or which differ in fome material point from thofe that are to be met with in other realms.

OF THE BEASTS.

The Tyger, the Bear, Wolves, Foxes, Dogs, the Cat of the Mountain, the Wild Cat, the Buffalo, the Deer, the Elk, the Moofe, the Carraboa, the Carcajou, the Skunk, the Porcupine, the Hedge-hog, the Wood-chuck, the Raccoon, the Marten, the Fifher, the Muskquaw, Squirrels, Hares, Rabbits, the Mole, the Weezel, the Moufe, the Dormoufe, the Beaver, the Otter, the Mink, and Bats.

The TYGER. The Tyger of America refembles in fhape thofe of Africa and Afia, but is confiderably fmaller. Nor does it appear to be fo fierce and ravenous as they are. The colour of it is a darkifh fallow, and it is entirely free from fpots. I faw one on an ifland in the Chipéway River, of which I had a very good view, as it was at no great diftance from me. It fat up on its hinder parts like a dog; and did not feem either to be apprehenfive of our approach, or to difcover any ravenous inclinations. It is however very feldom to be met with in this part of the world.

The BEAR. Bears are very numerous on this continent, but more particularly fo in the northern parts of it, and contribute to furnifh both food and beds for almoft every Indian nation. Thofe of America differ in many refpects from thofe either of Greenland or Ruffia, they being not only fomewhat fmaller, but timorous and inoffenfive, unlefs they are pinched by hunger, or fmarting from a wound. The fight of a man terrifies them; and a dog will put feveral to flight. They are extremely fond of grapes, and will climb to the top of the higheft trees in queft of them. This kind of food renders their flefh exceffively rich and finely flavoured; and it is confequently preferred

ferred by the Indians.
The fat is very white, and is poffeffed of one valuable quality. The inhabitants of thefe cloys. The inhabitants of the felves with it, and to its efficacy there a Spirit their agility. The feafon for hunting the ————— during the winter; when they take up their abode in hollow trees, or make themfelves dens in the roots of thofe that are blown down, the entrance of which they ftop up with branches of fir that lie fcattered about. From thefe retreats it is faid they ftir not whilft the weather continues fevere, and as it is well known that they do not provide themfelves with food, they are fuppofed to be enabled by nature to fubfift for fome months without, and during this time to continue of the fame bulk.

	Y
You	*Chee*
Young	*Hawpawnaw*
You are good	*Wafhtah Chee*
a Spirit	*Wakon Che*

The W O L F. The wolves of North America are much lefs than thofe which are met with in other parts of the world. They have, however, in common with the reft of their fpecies, a wildnefs in their looks, and a fiercenefs in their eyes; notwithftanding which, they are far from being fo ravenous as the European wolves, nor will they ever attack a man, except they have accidentally fed on the flefh of thofe flain in battle. When they herd together, as they often do in the winter, they make a hideous and terrible noife. In thefe parts there are two kinds; one of which is of a fallow colour, the other of a dun, inclining to a black.

The F O X. There are two forts of foxes in North America, which differ only in their colour, one being of a reddifh brown, the other of a grey; thofe of the latter kind that are found near the river Miffiffippi, are extremely beautiful, their hair being of a fine filver grey.

D O G S. The dogs employed by the Indians in hunting appear to be all of the fame fpecies; they carry their ears erect, and greatly refemble a wolf about the head. They are exceedingly ufeful to them in their hunting excurfions, and will attack the fierceft of the game they are in purfuit of. They are alfo remarkable for their fidelity to their mafters; but being ill fed by them, are very troublefome in their huts or tents.

The C A T of the Mountain. This creature is in fhape like a cat, only much larger. The hair or fur refembles alfo the skin of that domeftic animal; the colour however differs, for the former is of a reddifh or orange caft, but grows lighter near the belly. The whole skin is beautified with black fpots of different figures, of which thofe on the back are long, and thofe on the lower parts round. On the ears there are black ftripes. This creature is nearly as fierce as a leopard, but will feldom attack a man.

The B U F F A L O. This beaft, of which there are amazing numbers in thefe parts, is larger than an ox, has fhort black horns, with a large beard under his chin, and his head is fo full of hair, that it falls over his eyes, and gives him a
frightful

frightful look. There is a bunch on his back which begins at the haunches, and increafing gradually to the fhoulders, reaches on to the neck. Both this excrefcence and its whole body are covered with long hair, or rather wool, of a dun or moufe colóur, which is exceedingly valuable, efpecially that on the fore part of the body. Its head is larger than a bull's, with a very fhort neck; the breaft is broad, and the body decreafes towards the buttocks. Thefe creatures will run away at the fight of a man, and a whole herd will make off when they perceive a fingle dog. The flefh of the buffalo is excellent food, its hide extremely ufeful, and the hair very proper for the manufacture of various articles.

The D E E R. There is but one fpecies of deer in North America, and thefe are higher and of a flimmer make than thofe in Europe. Their fhape is nearly the fame as the European, their colour of a deep fallow, and their horns very large and branching. This beaft is the fwifteft on the American plains, and they herd together as they do in other countries.

The E L K greatly exceeds the deer in fize, being in bulk equal to a horfe. Its body is fhaped like that of a deer, only its tail is remarkably fhort, being not more than three inches long. The colour of its hair, which is grey, and not unlike that of a camel, but of a more reddifh caft, is nearly three inches in length, and as coarfe as that of a horfe. The horns of this creature grow to a prodigious fize, extending fo wide that two or three perfons might fit between them at the fame time. They are not forked like thofe of a deer, but have all their teeth or branches on the outer edge. Nor does the form of thofe of the elk refemble a deer's, the former being flat, and eight or ten inches broad, whereas the latter are round and confiderably narrower. They fhed their horns every year in the month of February, and by Auguft the new ones are nearly arrived at their full growth. Notwithftanding their fize, and the means of defence nature has furnifhed them with, they are as timorous as a deer. Their skin is very ufeful, and will drefs as well as that of a buck. They feed on grafs in the fummer, and on mofs or buds in the winter.

The MOOSE is nearly about the fize of the elk, and the horns of it are almoft as enormous as that animal's; the ftem of them however are not quite fo wide, and they branch on both fides like thofe of a deer. This creature alfo fheds them every year. Though its hinder parts are very broad, its tail is not above an inch long. It has feet and legs like a camel; its head is about two feet long, its upper lip much larger than the under, and the noftrils of it are fo wide that a man might thruft his hand into them a confiderable way. The hair of the moofe is light grey, mixed with a blackifh red. It is very elaftic, for though it be beaten ever fo long, it will retain its original fhape. The flefh is exceeding good food, eafy of digeftion, and very nourifhing. The nofe, or upper lip, which is large

and

and loose from the gums, is esteemed a great delicacy, being of a firm consistence, between marrow and gristle, and when properly dressed, affords a rich and luscious dish. Its hide is very proper for leather, being thick and strong, yet soft and pliable. The pace of this creature is always a trot, which is so expeditious, that it is exceeded in swiftness but by few of its fellow inhabitants of these woods. It is generally found in the forests, where it feeds on moss and buds. Though this creature is of the deer kind, it never herds as those do. Most authors confound it with the elk, deer, or carrabou, but it is a species totally different, as might be discovered by attending to the description I have given of each.

The **CARRABOU**. This beast is not near so tall as the moose, however it is something like it in shape, only rather more heavy, and inclining to the form of the ass. The horns of it are not flat as those of the elk are, but round like those of the deer; they also meet nearer together at the extremities, and bend more over the face, than either those of the elk or moose. It partakes of the swiftness of the deer, and is with difficulty overtaken by its pursuers. The flesh of it likewise is equally as good, the tongue particularly is in high esteem. The skin being smooth and free from veins, is as valuable as shamoy.

The **CARCAJOU**. This creature, which is of the cat kind, is a terrible enemy to the preceding four species of beasts. He either comes upon them from some concealment unperceived, or climbs up into a tree, and taking his station on some of the branches, waits till one of them, driven by an extreme of heat or cold, takes shelter under it; when he fastens upon his neck, and opening the jugular vein, soon brings his prey to the ground. This he is enabled to do by his long tail, with which he encircles the body of his adversary; and the only means they have to shun their fate, is by flying immediately to the water; by this method, as the carcajou has a great dislike to that element, he is sometimes got rid of before he can effect his purpose.

The **SKUNK**. This is the most extraordinary animal that the American woods produce. It is rather less than a pole-cat, and of the same species; it is therefore often mistaken for that creature, but it is very different from it in many points. Its hair is long and shining, variegated with large black and white spots, the former mostly on the shoulders and rump; its tail is very bushy, like that of the fox, part black, and part white, like its body; it lives chiefly in the woods and hedges; but its extraordinary powers are only shewn when it is pursued. As soon as he finds himself in danger he ejects, to a great distance from behind, a small stream of water, of so subtile a nature, and at the same time of so powerful a smell, that the air is tainted with it for half a mile in circumference; and his pursuers, whether men or dogs, being almost suffocated with the stench, are obliged to give over the pursuit. On this account he is called by the French, Enfant du Diable, the Child of the Devil;

or Béte Puante, the Stinking Beast. It is almost impossible to describe the noisome effects of the liquid with which this creature is supplied by nature for its defence. If a drop of it falls on your cloaths, they are rendered so disagreeable that it is impossible ever after to wear them; or if any of it enters your eyelids, the pain becomes intolerable for a long time, and perhaps at last you lose your sight. The smell of the skunk, though thus to be dreaded, is not like that of a putrid carcase, but a strong fœtid effluvia of musk, which displeases rather from its penetrating power than from its nauseousness. It is notwithstanding considered as conducive to clear the head, and to raise the spirits. This water is supposed by naturalists to be its urine; but I have dissected many of them that I have shot, and have found within their bodies, near the urinal vessel, a small receptacle of water, totally distinct from the bladder which contained the urine, and from which alone I am satisfied the horrid stench proceeds. After having taken out with great care the bag wherein this water is lodged, I have frequently fed on them, and have found them very sweet and good; but one drop emitted taints not only the carcase, but the whole house, and renders every kind of provisions, that are in it, unfit for use. With great justice therefore do the French give it such a diabolical name.

The PORCUPINE. The body of an American porcupine is in bulk about the size of a small dog, but it is both shorter in length, and not so high from the ground. It varies very much from those of other countries both in its shape and the length of its quills. The former is like that of a fox, except the head, which is not so sharp and long, but resembles more that of a rabbit. Its body is covered with hair of a dark brown, about four inches long, great part of which are the thickness of a straw, and are termed its quills. These are white, with black points, hollow, and very strong, especially those that grow on the back. The quills serve this creature for offensive and defensive weapons, which he darts at his enemies, and if they pierce the flesh in the least degree, they will sink quite into it, and are not to be extracted without incision. The Indians use them for boring their ears and noses, to insert their pendants, and also by way of ornament to their stockings, hair, &c. besides which they greatly esteem the flesh.

The WOOD-CHUCK is a ground animal of the fur kind, about the size of a martin, being nearly fifteen inches long; its body however is rounder, and his legs shorter; the fore-paws of it are broad, and constructed for the purpose of digging holes in the ground, where it burrows like a rabit; its fur is of a grey colour, on the reddish cast, and its flesh tolerable food.

The RACOON is somewhat less in size than a beaver, and its feet and legs are like those of that creature, but short in proportion to its body, which resembles that of a badger. The shape of its head is much like a fox's, only the ears are shorter,
more

more round and naked; and its hair is also similar to that animal's, being thick, long, soft, and black at the ends. On its face there is a broad stripe that runs across it, and includes the eyes, which are large. Its muzzle is black, and at the end roundish like that of a dog; the teeth are also similar to those of a dog in number and shape; the tail is long and round, with annular stripes on it like those of a cat; the feet have five long slender toes, armed with sharp claws, by which it is enabled to climb up trees like a monkey, and to run to the very extremities of the boughs. It makes use of its fore feet, in the manner of hands, and feeds itself with them. The flesh of this creature is very good in the months of September and October, when fruit and nuts, on which it likes to feed, are plenty.

The MARTIN is rather larger than a squirrel, and somewhat of the same make; its legs and claws however are considerably shorter. Its ears are short, broad, and roundish, and its eyes shine in the night like those of a cat. The whole body is covered with fur of a brownish fallow colour, and there are some in the more northern parts which are black; the skins of the latter are of much greater value than the others. The tail is covered with long hair, which makes it appear thicker than it really is. Its flesh is sometimes eaten, but is not in any great esteem.

The MUSQUASH, or MUSK-RAT, is so termed for the exquisite musk which it affords. It appears to be a diminutive of the beaver, being endowed with all the properties of that sagacious animal, and wants nothing but size and strength, being not much bigger than a large rat of the Norway breed, to rival the creature it so much resembles. Was it not for its tail, which is exactly the same as that of an European rat, the structure of their bodies is so much alike, especially the head, that it might be taken for a small beaver. Like that creature it builds itself a cabbin, but of a less perfect construction, and takes up its abode near the side of some piece of water. In the spring they leave their retreats, and in pairs subsist on leaves and roots till the summer comes on, when they feed on strawberries, rasberries, and such other fruits as they can reach. At the approach of winter they separate, when each takes up its lodging apart by itself in some hollow of a tree, where they remain quite unprovided with food, and there is the greatest reason to believe, subsist without any till the return of spring.

SQUIRRELS. There are five sorts of squirrels in America; the red, the grey, the black, the variegated, and the flying. The two former are exactly the same as those of Europe; the black are somewhat larger, and differ from them only in colour; the variegated also resemble them in shape and figure, but are very beautiful, being finely striped with white or grey, and sometimes with red and black. The American flying squirrel is much less than the European, being not above five inches long, and of a russet grey or ash-colour on the back, and white on the

under

under parts. It has black prominent eyes, like those of the mouse, with a long flat broad tail. By a membrane on each side which reaches from its fore to its hind legs, this creature is enabled to leap from one tree to another, even if they stand a considerable distance apart; this loose skin, which it is enabled to stretch out like a sail, and by which it is buoyed up, is about two inches broad, and is covered with a fine hair or down. It feeds upon the same provisions as the others, and is easily tamed.

The BEAVER. This creature has been so often treated of, and his uncommon abilities so minutely described, that any further account of it will appear unnecessary; however for the benefit of those of my readers who are not so well acquainted with the form and properties of this sagacious and useful animal, I shall give a concise description of it. The beaver is an amphibious quadruped, which cannot live for any long time in the water, and it is said is even able to exist entirely without it, provided it has the convenience of sometimes bathing itself. The largest beavers are nearly four feet in length, and about fourteen or fifteen inches in breadth over the haunches; they weigh about sixty pounds. Its head is like that of the otter, but larger; its snout is pretty long, the eyes small, the ears short, round, hairy on the outside, and smooth within, and its teeth very long; the under teeth stand out of their mouths about the breadth of three fingers, and the upper half a finger, all of which are broad, crooked, strong and sharp; besides those teeth called the incisors, which grow double, are set very deep in their jaws, and bend like the edge of an axe, they have sixteen grinders, eight on each side, four above and four below, directly opposite to each other. With the former they are able to cut down trees of a considerable size, with the latter to break the hardest substances. Its legs are short, particularly the fore legs, which are only four or five inches long, and not unlike those of a badger; the toes of the fore-feet are separate, the nails placed obliquely, and are hollow like quills; but the hind feet are quite different, and furnished with membranes between the toes. By this means it can walk, though but slowly, and is able to swim with as much ease as any other aquatic animal. The tail has somewhat in it that resembles a fish, and seems to have no manner of relation to the rest of the body, except the hind feet, all the other parts being similar to those of land animals. The tail is covered with a skin furnished with scales, that are joined together by a pellicle; these scales are about the thickness of parchment, nearly a line and a half in length, and generally of a hexagonical figure, having six corners; it is about eleven or twelve inches in length, and broader in the middle, where it is four inches over, than either at the root or the extremity. It is about two inches thick near the body, where it is almost round, and grows gradually thinner and flatter to the end. The colour of the beaver is different according to the different climates

mates in which it is found. In the moſt northern parts they are generally quite black; in more temperate, brown; their colour becoming lighter and lighter as they approach towards the ſouth. The fur is of two ſorts all over the body, except at the feet, where it is very ſhort; that which is the longeſt is generally in length about an inch, but on the back it ſometimes extends to two inches, gradually diminiſhing towards the head and tail. This part of the fur is harſh, coarſe, and ſhining, and of little uſe; the other part conſiſts of a very thick and fine down, ſo ſoft that it feels almoſt like ſilk, about three quarters of an inch in length, and is what is commonly manufactured. Caſtor, which is uſeful in medicine, is produced from the body of this creature; it was formerly believed to be its teſticles, but later diſcoveries have ſhown that it is contained in four bags, ſituated in the lower belly. Two of which, that are called the ſuperior, from their being more elevated than the others, are filled with a ſoft reſinous, adheſive matter, mixed with ſmall fibres, greyiſh without, and yellow within, of a ſtrong, diſagreeable, and penetrating ſcent, and very inflammable. This is the true caſtoreum; it hardens in the air, and becomes brown, brittle, and friable. The inferior bags contain an unctuous liquor like honey; the colour of which is a pale yellow, and its odour ſomewhat different from the other, being rather weaker and more diſagreeable; it however thickens as it grows older, and at length becomes about the conſiſtence of tallow. This has alſo its particular uſe in medicine; but it is not ſo valuable as the true caſtoreum.

The ingenuity of theſe creatures in building their cabins, and in providing for their ſubſiſtence, is truly wonderful. When they are about to chuſe themſelves a habitation, they aſſemble in companies ſometimes of two or three hundred, and after mature deliberation fix on a place where plenty of proviſions, and all neceſſaries are to be found. Their houſes are always ſituated in the water, and when they can find neither lake nor pond adjacent, they endeavour to ſupply the defect by ſtopping the current of ſome brook or ſmall river, by means of a cauſeway or dam. For this purpoſe they ſet about felling of trees, and they take care to chuſe out thoſe that grow above the place where they intend to build, that they might ſwim down with the current. Having fixed on thoſe that are proper, three or four beavers placing themſelves round a large one, find means with their ſtrong teeth to bring it down. They alſo prudently contrive that it ſhall fall towards the water, that they may have the leſs way to carry it. After they have by a continuance of the ſame labour and induſtry, cut it into proper lengths, they roll theſe into the water, and navigate them towards the place where they are to be employed. Without entering more minutely into the meaſures they purſue in the conſtruction of their dams, I ſhall only remark, that having prepared a kind of mortar with their feet, and laid it on with their tails, which they had before

made

made ufe of to tranfport it to the place where it is requifite; they conftruct them with as much folidity and regularty as the moft experienced workman could do. The formation of their cabins is no lefs amazing. Thefe are either built on piles in the middle of the fmall lakes they have thus formed, on the bank of a river, or at the extremity of fome point of land that advances into a lake. The figure of them is round or oval, and they are fafhioned with an ingenuity equal to their dams. Two thirds of the edifice ftands above the water, and this part is fufficiently capacious to contain eight or ten inhabitants. Each beaver has his place affigned him, the floor of which he curioufly ftrews with leaves, or fmall branches of the pine tree, fo as to render it clean and comfortable; and their cabins are all fituated fo contiguous to each other, as to allow of an eafy communication. The winter never furprizes thefe animals before their bufinefs is completed; for by the latter end of September their houfes are finifhed, and their ftock of provifions are generally laid in. Thefe confift of fmall pieces of wood whofe texture is foft, fuch as the poplar, the afpin, or willow, &c. which they lay up in piles, and difpofe of in fuch manner as to preferve their moifture. Was I to enumerate every inftance of fagacity that is to be difcovered in thefe animals, they would fill a volume, and prove not only entertaining but inftructive.

The OTTER. This creature alfo is amphibious, and greatly refembles a beaver, but is very different from it in many refpects. Its body is nearly as long as a beaver's, but confiderably lefs in all its parts. The muzzle, eyes, and the form of the head are nearly the fame, but the teeth are very unlike, for the otter wants the large incifors or nippers that a beaver has; inftead of thefe, all his teeth, without any diftinction, are fhaped like thofe of a dog or wolf. The hair alfo of the former is not half fo long as that belonging to the latter, nor is the colour of it exactly the fame, for the hair of an otter under the neck, ftomach, and belly, is more greyifh than that of a beaver, and in many other refpects it likewife varies. This animal, which is met with in moft parts of the world, but in much greater numbers in North America, is very mifchievous, and when he is clofely purfued, will not only attack dogs but men.

It generally feeds upon fifh, efpecially in the fummer, but in the winter is contented with the bark of trees, or the produce of the fields. Its flefh both taftes and fmells of fifh, and is not wholefome food, though it is fometimes eaten through neceffity.

The MINK is of the otter kind, and fubfifts in the fame manner. In fhape and fize it refembles a pole-cat, being equally long and flender. Its skin is blacker than that of an otter, or almoft any other creature; " as black as a mink," being a proverbial expreffion in America; it is not however fo valuable, though this greatly depends on the feafon in which it is taken.

en. Its tail is round like that of a snake, but growing flattish towards the end, and is entirely without hair. An agreeable musky scent exhales from its body; and it is met with near the sources of rivers, on whose banks it chiefly lives.

OF THE BIRDS.

The Eagle, the Hawk, the Night Hawk, the Fish Hawk, the Whipperwill, the Raven, the Crow, the Owl, Parrots, the Pelican, the Crane, the Stork, the Cormorant, the Heron, the Swan, the Goose, Ducks, Teal, the Loon, the Water-Hen, the Turkey, the Heath Cock, the Partridge, the Quail, Pigeons, the Snipe, Larks, the Woodpecker, the Cuckoo, the Blue Jay, the Swallow, the Wakon Bird, the Black Bird, the Red Bird, the Thrush, the Whetsaw, the Nightingale, the King Bird, the Robin, the Wren, and the Humming Bird.

The EAGLE. There are only two sorts of eagles in these parts, the bald and the grey, which are much the same in size, and similar to the shape of those of other countries.

The NIGHT HAWK. This Bird is of the hawk species, its bill being crooked, its wings formed for swiftness, and its shape nearly like that of the common hawk; but in size it is considerably less, and in colour rather darker. It is scarcely ever seen but in the evening, when, at the approach of twilight, it flies about, and darts itself in wanton gambols at the head of the belated traveller. Before a thunder-shower these birds are seen at an amazing height in the air assembled together in great numbers, as swallows are observed to do on the same occasion.

The WHIPPERWILL, or, as it is termed by the Indians, the Muckawiss. This extraordinary bird is somewhat like the last-mentioned in its shape and colour, only it has some whitish stripes across the wings, and like that is seldom ever seen till after sun-set. It also is never met with but during the spring and summer months. As soon as the Indians are informed by its notes of its return, they conclude that the frost is entirely gone, in which they are seldom deceived; and on receiving this assurance of milder weather, begin to sow their corn. It acquires its name by the noise it makes, which to the people of the colonies sounds like the name they give it, Whipper-will; to an Indian ear Muck-a-wiss. The words, it is true, are not alike, but in this manner they strike the imagination of each; and the circumstance is a proof that the same sounds, if they are not rendered certain by being reduced to the rules of orthography,

phy, might convey different ideas to different people. As foon as night comes on, these birds will place themselves on the fences, stumps, or stones that lie near some house, and repeat their melancholy notes without any variation till midnight. The Indians, and some of the inhabitants of the back settlements, think if this bird perches upon any house, that it betokens some mishap to the inhabitants of it.

The FISH HAWK greatly resembles the latter in its shape, and receives his name from his food, which is generally fish; it skims over the lakes and rivers, and sometimes seems to lie expanded on the water, as he hovers so close to it, and having by some attractive power drawn the fish within its reach, darts suddenly upon them. The charm it makes use of is supposed to be an oil contained in a small bag in the body, and which nature has by some means or other supplied him with the power of using for this purpose; it is however very certain that any bait touched with a drop of the oil collected from this bird is an irresistible lure for all sorts of fish, and insures the angler great success.

The OWL. The only sort of owls that is found on the banks of the Missisippi is extremely beautiful in its plumage, being of a fine deep yellow or gold colour, pleasingly shaded and spotted.

The CRANE. There is a kind of crane in these parts, which is called by Father Hennepin a pelican, that is about the size of the European crane, of a greyish colour, and with long legs; but this species differs from all others in its bill, which is about twelve inches long, and one inch and half broad, of which breadth it continues to the end, where it is blunted, and round like a paddle; its tongue is of the same length.

DUCKS. Among a variety of wild ducks, the different species of which amount to upwards of twenty, I shall confine my description to one sort, that is, the wood duck, or, as the French term it, Canard branchus. This fowl receives its name from its frequenting the woods, and perching on the branches of trees, which no other kind of water fowl (a characteristic that this still preserves) is known to do. It is nearly of a size with other ducks; its plumage is beautifully variegated, and very brilliant. The flesh of it also, as it feeds but little on fish, is finely flavoured, and much superior to any other sort.

The TEAL. I have already remarked in my Journal, that the teal found on the Fox River, and the head branches of the Missisippi, are perhaps not to be equalled for the fatness and delicacy of their flesh by any other in the world. In colour, shape, and size they are very little different from those found in other countries.

The LOON is a water fowl, somewhat less than a teal, and is a species of the dobchick. Its wings are short, and its legs and feet large in proportion to the body; the colour of it is a dark brown, nearly approaching to black; and as it feeds only on fish, the flesh of it is very ill-flavoured. These birds are
exceed-

exceedingly nimble and expert at diving, so that it is almost impossible for one person to shoot them, as they will dextrously avoid the shot by diving before they reach them; so that it requires three persons to kill one of them, and this can only be done the moment it raises his head out of the water as it returns to the surface after diving. It however only repays the trouble taken to obtain it, by the excellent sport it affords.

The PARTRIDGE. There are three sorts of partridges here, the brown, the red, and the black, the first of which are most esteemed. They are all much larger than the European partridges, being nearly the size of a hen pheasant; their head and eyes are also like that bird, and they have all long tails, which they spread like a fan, but not erect; but contrary to the custom of those in other countries, they will perch on the branches of the poplar and black birch, on the buds of which they feed early in the morning and in the twilight of the evening during the winter months, when they are easily shot.

The WOOD PIGEON, is nearly the same as ours, and there is such prodigious quantities of them on the banks of the Missisippi, that they will sometimes darken the sun for several minutes.

The WOODPECKER. This is a very beautiful bird; there is one sort whose feathers are a mixture of various colours; and another that is brown all over the body, except the head and neck, which are of a fine red. As this bird is supposed to make a greater noise than ordinary at particular times, it is conjectured his cries then denote rain.

The BLUE JAY. This bird is shaped nearly like the European jay, only that its tail is longer. On the top of its head is a crest of blue feathers, which is raised or let down at pleasure. The lower part of the neck behind, and the back, are of a purplish colour, and the upper sides of the wings and tail, as well as the lower part of the back and rump, are of a fine blue; the extremities of the wings are blackish, faintly tinctured with dark blue on the edges, whilst the other parts of the wing are barred across with black in an elegant manner. Upon the whole this bird can scarcely be exceeded in beauty by any of the winged inhabitants of this or other climates. It has the same jetting motion that jays generally have, and its cry is far more pleasing.

The WAKON BIRD, as it is termed by the Indians, appears to be of the same species as the birds of paradise. The name they have given it is expressive of its superior excellence, and the veneration they have for it; the wakon bird being in their language the bird of the Great Spirit. It is nearly the size of a swallow, of a brown colour, shaded about the neck with a bright green; the wings are of a darker brown than the body; its tail is composed of four or five feathers, which are three times as long as its body, and which are beautifully shaded with green and purple. It carries this fine length of plumage in the same

same manner as a peacock does, but it is not known whether it ever raises it into the erect position that bird sometimes does. I never saw any of these birds in the colonies, but the Naudoweſſie Indians caught several of them when I was in their country, and seemed to treat them as if they were of a superior rank to any other of the feathered race.

The BLACK BIRD. There are three sorts of birds in North America that bear this name; the first is the common, or as it is there termed, the crow blackbird, which is quite black, and of the same size and shape of those in Europe, but it has not that melody in its notes which they have. In the month of September this sort fly in large flights, and do great mischief to the Indian corn, which is at that time just ripe. The second sort is the red-wing, which is rather smaller than the first species, but like that it is black all over its body, except on the lower rim of the wings, where it is of a fine bright full scarlet. It builds its nest, and chiefly resorts among the small bushes that grow in meadows and low swampy places. It whistles a few notes, but is not equal in its song to the European blackbird. The third sort is of the same size as the latter, and is jet black like that, but all the upper part of the wing, just below the back, is of a fine clear white; as if nature intended to diversify the species, and to atone for the want of a melodious pipe by the beauty of its plumage; for this also is deficient in its musical powers. The beaks of every sort are of a full yellow, and the females of each of a rusty black like the European.

The RED BIRD is about the size of a sparrow, but with a long tail, and is all over of a bright vermilion colour. I saw many of them about the Ottawaw Lakes, but I could not learn that they sung. I also observed in some other parts, a bird of much the same make, that was entirely of a fine yellow.

The WHETSAW is of the cuckoo kind, being like that, a solitary bird, and scarcely ever seen. In the summer months it is heard in the groves, where it makes a noise like the filing of a saw; from which it receives its name.

The KING BIRD is like a swallow, and seems to be of the same species as the black martin or swift. It is called the King Bird because it is able to master almost every bird that flies. I have often seen it bring down a hawk.

The HUMMING BIRD. This beautiful bird, which is the smallest of the feathered inhabitants of the air, is about the third part the size of a wren, and is shaped extremely like it. Its legs, which are about an inch long, appear like two small needles, and its body is proportionable to them. But its plumage exceeds description. On its head it has a small tuft of a jetty shining black; the breast of it is red, the belly white, the back, wings, and tail of the finest pale green; and small specks of gold are scattered with inexpressible grace over the whole: besides this, an almost imperceptible down softens the colours, and produces the most pleasing shades. With its bill, which is of the same diminutive size as the other parts of its body, it extracts from the flowers a moisture which is its nourishment; over these it hovers like a bee, but never lights on them, moving at the same time its wings with such velocity that the motion of them is imperceptible; notwithstanding which they make a humming noise, from whence it receives its name.

Of the FISHES *which are found in the waters of the Miſſiſſippi.*

I have already given a description of those that are taken in the great lakes.

The Sturgeon, the Pout or Cat Fish, the Pike, the Carp, and the Chub.

The STURGEON. The fresh water sturgeon is shaped in no other respect like those taken near the sea, except in the formation of its head and tail; which are fashioned in the same manner, but the body is not so angulated, nor are there so many horny scales about it as on the latter. Its length is generally about two feet and a half or three feet long, but in circumference not proportionable, being a slender fish. The flesh is exceedingly delicate and finely flavoured; I caught some in the head waters of the river St. Croix that far exceeded trout. The manner of taking them is by watching them as they lie under the banks in a clear stream, and darting at them with a fish-spear; for they will not take a bait. There is also in the Miſſiſſippi, and there only, another sort than the species I have described, which is similar to it in every respect, except that the upper jaw extends fourteen or fifteen inches beyond the under; this extensive jaw, which is of a gristly substance, is three inches and a half broad, and continues of that breadth, somewhat in the shape of an oar, to the end, which is flat. The flesh of this fish, however, is not to be compared with the other sort, and is not so much esteemed even by the Indians.

The CAT FISH. This fish is about eighteen inches long; of a brownish colour and without scales. It has a large round head, from whence it receives its name, on different parts of which grow three or four strong sharp horns about two inches long. Its fins are also very bony and strong, and without great care will pierce the hands of those who take them. It weighs commonly

commonly about five or six pounds; the flesh of it is excessively fat and luscious, and greatly resembles that of an eel in its flavour.

The CARP and CHUB are much the same as those in England, and nearly about the same in size.

OF SERPENTS.

The Rattle Snake, the Long Black Snake, the Wall or House Adder, the Striped or Garter Snake, the Water Snake, the Hissing Snake, the Green Snake, the Thorn-tail Snake, the Speckled Snake, the Ring Snake, the Two-headed Snake.

The RATTLE SNAKE. There appears to be two species of this reptile; one of which is commonly termed the Black, and the other the yellow; and of these the latter is generally considered as the largest. At their full growth they are upwards of five feet long, and the middle part of the body, at which it is of the greatest bulk, measures about nine inches round. From that part it gradually decreases both towards the head and the tail. The neck is proportionably very small, and the head broad and depressed. These are of a light brown colour, the iris of the eye red, and all the upper part of the body brown, mixed with a ruddy yellow, and chequered with many regular lines of a deep black, gradually shading towards a gold colour. In short the whole of this dangerous reptile is very beautiful, and could it be viewed with less terror, such a variegated arrangement of colours would be extremely pleasing. But these are only to be seen in their highest perfection at the time this creature is animated by resentment; then every tint rushes from its subcutaneous recess, and gives the surface of the skin a deeper stain. The belly is of a palish blue, which grows fuller as it approaches the sides, and is at length intermixed with the colour of the upper part. The rattle at its tail, from which it receives its name, is composed of a firm, dry, callous, or horny substance of a light brown, and consists of a number of cells which articulate one within another, like joints; and which increase every year, and make known the age of the creature. These articulations being very loose, the included points strike against the inner surface of the concave parts or rings into which they are admitted, and as the snake vibrates, or shakes its tail, makes a rattling noise. This alarm it always gives when it is apprehensive of danger; and in an instant after forms itself into a spiral wreath, in the centre of which appears the head erect, and breathing forth vengeance against either man or beast that shall

shall dare to come near it. In this attitude he awaits the approach of his enemies, rattling his tail as he sees or hears them coming on. By this timely intimation, which heaven seems to have provided as a means to counteract the mischief this venomous reptile would otherwise be perpetrator of, the unwary traveller is apprized of his danger, and has an opportunity of avoiding it. It is however to be observed, that it never acts offensively; it neither pursues or flies from any thing that approaches it, but lies in the position described, rattling his tail as if reluctant to hurt. The teeth with which this serpent effects his poisonous purposes are not those he makes use of on ordinary occasions, they are only two in number, very small and sharp pointed, and fixed in a sinewy substance that lies near the extremity of the upper jaw, resembling the claws of a cat; at the root of each of these, which might be extended, contracted, or entirely hidden, as need requires, are two small bladders which nature has so constructed, that at the same instant an incision is made by the teeth, a drop of a greenish poisonous liquid enters the wound, and taints with its destructive quality the whole mass of blood. In a moment the unfortunate victim of its wrath feels a chilly tremor run through all his frame; a swelling immediately begins on the spot where the teeth had entered, which spreads by degrees over the whole body, and produces on every part of the skin the variegated hue of the snake. The bite of this reptile is more or less venemous, according to the season of the year in which it is given. In the dog-days it often proves instantly mortal, and especially if the wound is made among the sinews situated in the back part of the leg, above the heel; but in the spring, in autumn, or during a cool day which might happen in the summer, its bad effects are to be prevented by the immediate application of proper remedies; and there Providence has bounteously supplied, by causing the Rattle Snake Plantain, an approved antidote to the poison of this creature, to grow in great profusion where-ever they are to be met with. There are likewise several other remedies besides this, for the venom of its bite. A decoction made of the buds or bark of the white ash, taken internally, prevents its pernicious effects. Salt is a newly discovered remedy, and if applied immediately to the part, or the wound be washed with brine, a cure might be assured. The fat of the reptile also rubbed on it is frequently found to be very efficacious. But though the lives of the persons who have been bitten might be preserved by these, and their health in some degree restored, yet they annually experience a slight return of the dreadful symptoms about the time they received the instillation. However remarkable it may appear it is certain, that though the venom of this creature affects in a greater or less degree all animated nature, the hog is an exception to the rule, as that animal will readily destroy them without dreading their poisonous fangs, and fatten on their flesh. It has been often observed, and I

can

can confirm the obfervation, that fix inches long, and has four with any harmonious founds, whofe blue, is prettily ftriped with have many times feen them, even whe end of the tail is totally place themfelves into a liftening pofture; an inftant it is out of ably attentive and fufceptible of delight all their quickeft eye; has lafted. I fhould have remarked, that when the Rattle Snake bites, it drops its under jaw, and holding the upper jaw erect, throws itfelf in a curve line, with great force, and as quick as lightning, on the object of its refentment. In a moment after, it returns again to its defenfive pofture, having difengaged its teeth from the wound with great celerity, by means of the pofition in which it had placed its head when it made the attack. It never extends itfelf to a greater diftance than half its length will reach, and though it fometimes repeats the blow two or three times, it as often returns, with a fudden rebound to its former ftate. The Black Rattle Snake differs in no other refpect from the yellow, than in being rather fmaller, and in the variegation of its colours, which are exactly reverfed: one is black where the other is yellow, and vice verfa. They are equally venomous. It is not known how thefe creatures engender; I have often found the eggs of feveral other fpecies of the fnake, but notwithftanding no one has taken more pains to acquire a perfect knowledge of every property of thefe reptiles than myfelf, I never could difcover the manner in which they bring forth their young. I once killed a female that had feventy young ones in its belly, but thefe were perfectly formed, and I faw them juft before retire to the mouth of their mother, as a place of fecurity, on my approach. The gall of this ferpent, mixed with chalk, are formed into little balls, and exported from America, for medicinal purpofes. They are of the nature of Gafcoign's powders, and are an excellent remedy for complaints incident to children. The flefh of the fnake alfo dried, and made into broth, is much more nutritive than that of vipers, and very efficacious againft confumptions.

The LONG BLACK SNAKE. Thefe are alfo of two forts, both of which are exactly fimilar in fhape and fize, only the belly of one is a light red, the other a faint blue; all the upper parts of their bodies are black and fcaly. They are generally from fix to eight feet in length, and carry their heads, as they crawl along, about a foot and an half from the ground. They eafily climb the higheft tree, in purfuit of birds and fquirrels, which are their chief food; and thefe, it is faid, they charm by their looks, and render incapable of efcaping from them. Their appearance carries terror with it to thofe who are unacquainted with their inability to hurt, but they are perfectly inoffenfive and free from venom.

The STRIPED or GARTER SNAKE is exactly the fame as that fpecies found in other climates.

The WATER SNAKE is much like the Rattle Snake in fhape and fize, but is not endowed with the fame venomous powers, being quite harmlefs. The

shall dare to come near it. I have already particularly described, proach of his enemies, rattli... ial, of Lake Erie. coming on. By this timely... is about a foot and an half long, and have provided as a m... to grass and herbs, that it cannot be discovered... lies on the ground; happily however it is free from venom, otherwise it would do an infinite deal of mischief, as those who pass through the meadows, not being able to perceive it, are deprived of the power of avoiding it.

The THORN-TAIL SNAKE. This reptile is found in many parts of America, but it is very seldom to be seen. It is of a middle size, and receives its name from a thorn-like dart in its tail, with which it is said to inflict a mortal wound.

The SPECKLED SNAKE is an aqueous reptile about two feet and an half in length, but without venom. Its skin, which is brown and white with some spots of yellow in it, is used by the Americans as a cover for the handles of whips, and it renders them very pleasing to the sight.

The RING SNAKE is about twelve inches long; the body of it is entirely black, except a yellow ring which it has about its neck, and which appears like a narrow piece of ribband tied around it. This odd reptile is frequently found in the bark of trees, and among old logs.

The TWO-HEADED SNAKE. The only snake of this kind that was ever seen in America, was found about the year 1762, near Lake Champlain, by Mr. Park, a gentleman of New England, and made a present to Lord Amherst. It was about a foot long, and in shape like the common snake, but it was furnished with two heads exactly similar, which united at the neck. Whether this was a distinct species of snakes, and was able to propagate its likeness, or whether it was an accidental formation, I know not.

The TORTOISE or LAND TURTLE. The shape of this creature is so well known that it is unnecessary to describe it. There are seven or eight sorts of them in America, some of which are beautifully variegated, even beyond description. The shells of many have spots of red, green, and yellow in them, and the chequer work is composed of small squares, curiously disposed. The most beautiful sort of these creatures are the smallest, and the bite of them is said to be venomous.

LIZARDS, &c.

Though there are numerous kinds of this class of the animal creation, in the country I treat of, I shall only take notice of two of them; which are termed the Swift and the slow Lizard.

The

The SWIFT LIZARD is about six inches long, and has four legs and a tail. Its body, which is blue, is prettily striped with dark lines shaded with yellow; but the end of the tail is totally blue. It is so remarkably agile, that in an instant it is out of sight, nor can its movement be perceived by the quickest eye: so that it might more justly be said to vanish, than to run away. This species are supposed to poison those they bite, but are not dangerous, as they never attack persons that approach them, chusing rather to get suddenly out of their reach.

The SLOW LIZARD is of the same shape as the Swift, but its colour is brown; it is moreover of an opposite disposition, being altogether as slow in its movements as the other is swift. It is remarkable that these lizards are extremely brittle, and will break off near the tail as easily as an icicle.

Among the reptiles of North America, there is a species of the toad termed the TREE TOAD, which is nearly of the same shape as the common sort, but smaller and with longer claws. It is usually found on trees, sticking close to the bark, or lying in the crevices of it; and so nearly does it resemble the colour of the tree to which it cleaves, that it is with difficulty distinguished from it. These creatures are only heard during the twilight of the morning and evening, or just before and after a shower of rain, when they make a croaking noise somewhat shriller than that of a frog, which might be heard to a great distance. They infest the woods in such numbers, that their responsive notes at these times make the air resound. It is only a summer animal, and never to be found during the winter.

INSECTS.

The interior parts of North America abound with nearly the same insects as are met with in the same parallels of latitude; and the species of them are so numerous and diversified that even a succinct description of the whole of them would fill a volume; I shall therefore confine myself to a few, which I believe are almost peculiar to this country; the Silk Worm, the Tobacco Worm, the Bee, the Lightning Bug, the Water Bug, and the Horned Bug.

The SILK WORM is nearly the same as those of France and Italy, but will not produce the same quantity of silk.

The TOBACCO WORM is a catterpiller of the size and figure of a silk worm, it is of a fine sea-green colour, on its rump it has a sting or horn near a quarter of an inch long.

The BEES, in America, principally lodge their honey in the earth to secure it from the ravages of the bears, who are remarkably fond of it.

The

The LIGHTNING BUG or FIRE FLY is about the size of a bee, but it is of the beetle kind, having like that insect two pair of wings the upper of which are of a firm texture, to defend it from danger. When it flies, and the wings are expanded, there is under these a kind of coat, constructed also like wings, which is luminous; and as the insect passes on, causes all the hinder part of its body to appear like a bright fiery coal. Having placed one of them on your hand, the under part only shines, and throws the light on the space beneath; but as soon as it spreads its upper wings to fly away, the whole body which lies behind them appears illuminated all around. The light it gives is not constantly of the same magnitude, even when it flies; but seems to depend on the expansion or contraction of the luminous coat or wings, and is very different from that emitted in a dark night by dry wood or some kinds of fish, it having much more the appearance of real fire. They seem to be sensible of the power they are possessed of, and to know the most suitable time for exerting it, as in a very dark night they are much more numerous than at any other time. They are only seen during the summer months of June, July, and August, and then at no other time but in the night. Whether from their colour, which is a dusky brown, they are not then discernible, or from their retiring to holes and crevices, I know not, but they are never to be discovered in the day. They chiefly are seen in low swampy land, and appear like innumerable transient gleams of light. In dark nights when there is much lightning, without rain, they seem as if they wished either to imitate or assist the flashes; for during the intervals, they are uncommonly agile, and endeavour to throw out every ray they can collect. Notwithstanding this effulgent appearance, these insects are perfectly harmless; you may permit them to crawl upon your hand, when five or six, if they freely exhibit their glow together, will enable you to read almost the smallest print.

The WATER BUG is of a brown colour, about the size of a pea, and in shape nearly oval: it has many legs, by means of which it passes over the surface of the water with such incredible swiftness, that it seems to slide or dart itself along.

The HORNED BUG, or, as it is sometimes termed, the STAG BEETLE, is of a dusky brown colour nearly approaching to black, about an inch and an half long, and half an inch broad. It has two large horns, which grow on each side of the head, and meet horizontally, and with these it pinches very hard; they are branched like those of a stag, from whence it receives its name. They fly about in the evening, and prove very troublesome to those who are in the fields at that time.

I must not omit that the LOCUST is a septennial insect, as they are only seen, a small number of stragglers excepted, every seven years, when they infest these parts, and the interior colonies in large swarms, and do a great deal of mischief. The years when they thus arrive are denominated the locust years.

CHAP.

CHAPTER XIX.

Of the TREES, SHRUBS, ROOTS, HERBS, FLOWERS, &c.

I SHALL here observe the same method that I have pursued in the preceding chapter, and having given a list of the trees, &c. which are natives of the interior parts of North America, particularize such only as differ from the produce of other countries, or, being little known, have not been described.

OF TREES.

The Oak, the Pine Tree, the Maple, the Ash, the Hemlock, the Bass or White Wood, the Cedar, the Elm, the Birch, the Fir, the Locust Tree, the Poplar, the Wickopick or Suckwick, the Spruce, the Hornbeam, and the Button Wood Tree.

The OAK. There are several sorts of oaks in these parts; the black, the white, the red, the yellow, the grey, the swamp oak, and the chesnut oak: the five former vary but little in their external appearance, the shape of the leaves, and the colour of the bark being so much alike, that they are scarcely distinguishable; but the body of the tree when sawed discovers the variation, which chiefly consists in the colour of the wood, they being all very hard and proper for building. The swamp oak differs materially from the others both in the shape of the leaf, which is smaller, and in the bark, which is smoother; and likewise as it grows only in a moist gravelly soil. It is esteemed the toughest of all woods, being so strong yet pliable, that it is often made use of instead of whalebone, and is equally serviceable. The chesnut oak also is greatly different from the others, particularly in the shape of the leaf, which much resembles that of a chesnut-tree, and for this reason is so denominated. It is neither so strong as the former species, or so tough as the latter, but is of a nature proper to be split into rails for fences, in which state it will endure a considerable time.

The PINE TREE. That species of the pine tree peculiar to this part of the continent is the white, the quality of which I need not describe, as the timber of it is so well known under the name of deals. It grows here in great plenty, to an amazing height and size, and yields an excellent turpentine, though not in such quantities as those in the northern parts of Europe.

The MAPLE. Of this tree there are two sorts, the hard and the soft, both of which yield a luscious juice, from which the Indians, by boiling, make very good sugar. The sap of the former is much richer and sweeter than the latter, but the soft produces a greater quantity. The wood of the hard maple is very beautifully veined and curled, and when wrought into cabinets, tables, gunstocks, &c. is greatly valued. That of the soft sort differs in its texture, wanting the variegated grain of the hard; it also grows more strait and free from branches, and is more easily split. It likewise may be distinguished from the hard, as this grows in meadows and low-lands, that on the hills and up-lands. The leaves are shaped alike, but those of the soft maple are much the largest, and of a deeper green.

The ASH. There are several sorts of this tree in these parts, but that to which I shall confine my description, is the yellow ash, which is only found near the head branches of the Mississippi. This tree grows to an amazing height, and the body of it is so firm and sound, that the French traders who go into that country from Louisiana, to purchase furs, make of them periaguays; this they do by excavating them by fire, and when they are compleated, convey in them the produce of their trade to New Orleans, where they find a good market both for their vessels and cargoes. The wood of this tree greatly resembles that of the common ash; but it might be distinguished from any other tree by its bark; the ross or outside bark being near eight inches thick, and indented with furrows more than six inches deep, which make those that are arrived to a great bulk appear uncommonly rough; and by this peculiarity they may be readily known. The rind or inside bark is of the same thickness as that of other trees, but its colour is a fine bright yellow, insomuch that if it is but slightly handled, it will leave a stain on the fingers, which cannot easily be washed away; and if in the spring you peel off the bark, and touch the sap, which then rises between that and the body of the tree, it will leave so deep a tincture that it will require three or four days to wear it off. Many useful qualities belonging to this tree I doubt not will be discovered in time, besides it proving a valuable acquisition to the dyer.

The HEMLOCK TREE grows in every part of America, in a greater or less degree. It is an ever-green of a very large growth, and has leaves somewhat like that of the yew; it is however quite useless, and only an incumbrance to the ground, the wood being of a very coarse grain, and full of wind-shakes or cracks.

The BASS or WHITE WOOD is a tree of a middling size, and the whitest and softest wood that grows; when quite dry it swims on the water like a cork; in the settlements the turners

make

make of it bowls, trenchers, and dishes, which wear smooth, and will laſt a long time; but when applied to any other purpoſe it is far from durable.

The WICKOPICK or SUCKWICK appears to be a ſpecies of the white wood, and is diſtinguiſhed from it by a peculiar quality in the bark, which when pounded and moiſtened with a little water, inſtantly becomes a matter of the conſiſtence and nature of ſize. With this the Indians pay their canoes, and it greatly exceeds pitch, or any other material uſually appropriated to that purpoſe; for beſides its adheſive quality, it is of ſo oily a nature, that the water cannot penetrate through it, and its repelling power abates not for a conſiderable time.

The BUTTON WOOD is a tree of the largeſt ſize, and might be diſtinguiſhed by its bark, which is quite ſmooth and prettily mottled. The wood is very proper for the uſe of cabinet-makers. It is covered with ſmall hard burs, which ſpring from the branches, that appear not unlike buttons, and from theſe, I believe, it receives its name.

NUT TREES.

The Butter or Oil Nut, the Walnut, the Hazle Nut, the Beech Nut, the Pecan Nut, the Cheſnut, the Hickory.

The BUTTER or OIL NUT. As no mention has been made by any authors of this nut, I ſhall be the more particular in my account of it. The tree grows in meadows where the ſoil is rich and warm. The body of it ſeldom exceeds a yard in circumference, is full of branches, the twigs of which are ſhort and blunt, and its leaves reſemble thoſe of the walnut. The nut has a ſhell like that fruit, which when ripe is more furrowed, and more eaſily craked; it is alſo much longer and larger than a walnut, and contains a greater quantity of kernel, which is very oily, and of a rich agreeable flavour. I am perſuaded that a much purer oil than that of olives might be extracted from this nut. The inſide bark of this tree dyes a good purple; and it is ſaid, varies in its ſhade, being either darker or lighter, according to the month in which it is gathered.

The BEECH NUT. Though this tree grows exactly like that of the ſame name in Europe, yet it produces nuts equally as good as cheſnuts; on which bears, martins, ſquirrels, partridges, turkies, and many other beaſts and birds feed. The nut is contained, whilſt growing, in an outſide caſe, like that of a cheſnut, but not ſo prickly; and the coat of the inſide ſhell is alſo ſmooth like that; only its form is nearly triangular. Vaſt quantities of them lie ſcattered about in the woods, and ſupply with food great numbers of the creatures juſt mentioned.

The leaves, which are white, continue on the trees during the whole winter. A decoction made of them is a certain and expeditious cure for wounds which arise from burning or scalding, as well as a restorative for those members that are nipped by the frost.

The PECAN NUT is somewhat of the walnut kind, but rather smaller than a walnut, being about the size of a middling acorn, and of an oval form; the shell is easily cracked, and the kernel shaped like that of a walnut. This tree grows chiefly near the Illinois river.

The HICKORY is also of the walnut kind, and bears a fruit nearly like that tree. There are several sorts of them, which vary only in the colour of the wood. Being of a very tough nature, the wood is generally used for the handles of axes, &c. It is also very good fire-wood, and as it burns an excellent sugar distils from it.

FRUIT TREES.

I need not to observe that these are all the spontaneous productions of nature, which have never received the advantages of ingrafting, transplanting, or manuring.

The Vine, the Mulberry Tree, the Crab Apple Tree, the Plum Tree, the Cherry Tree, and the Sweet Gum Tree.

The VINE is very common here, and of three kinds; the first sort hardly deserves the name of a grape; the second much resembles the Burgundy grape, and if exposed to the sun a good wine might be made from them. The third sort resembles Zant currants, which are so frequently used in cakes, &c. in England, and if proper care was taken of them, would be equal, if not superior, to those of that country.

The MULBERRY TREE is of two kinds, red and white, and nearly of the same size of those of France and Italy, and grow in such plenty, as to feed any quantity of silk worms.

The CRAB APPLE TREE bears a fruit that is much larger and better flavoured than those of Europe.

The PLUM TREE. There are two sorts of plums in this country, one a large sort of a purple cast on one side, and red on the reverse, the second totally green, and much smaller. Both these are of a good flavour, and are greatly esteemed by the Indians, whose taste is not refined, but who are satisfied with the productions of nature in their unimproved state.

The CHERRY TREE. There are three sorts of cherries in this country; the black, the red, and the sand cherry; the two latter may with more propriety be ranked among the shrubs,

as

as the bush that bears the sand cherries almost creeps along the ground, and the other rises not above eight or ten feet in height; however I shall give an account of them all in this place. The black cherries are about the size of a currant, and hang in clusters like grapes; the trees which bear them being very fruitful, they are generally loaded, but the fruit is not good to eat, however they give an agreeable flavour to brandy, and turn it to the colour of claret. The red cherries grow in the greatest profusion, and hang in bunches, like the black sort just described; so that the bushes which bear them appear at a distance like solid bodies of red matter. Some people admire this fruit, but they partake of the nature and taste of alum, leaving a disagreeable roughness in the throat, and being very astringent. As I have already described the sand cherries, which greatly exceed the two other sorts, both in flavour and size, I shall give no further description of them. The wood of the black cherry tree is very useful, and works well into cabinet ware.

The SWEET GUM TREE or LIQUID AMBER (Copalm) is not only extremely common, but it affords a balm, the virtues of which are infinite. Its bark is black and hard, and its wood so tender and souple, that when the tree is felled, you may draw from the middle of it rods of five or six feet in length. It cannot be employed in building or furniture, as it warps continually. Its leaf is indented with five points, like a star. This balm is reckoned by the Indians to be an excellent febrifuge, and it cures wounds in two or three days.

SHRUBS.

The Willow, Shin Wood, Shumack, Saffafras, the Prickly Ash, Moose Wood, Spoon Wood, Large Elder, Dwarf Elder, Poisonous Elder, Juniper, Shrub Oak, Sweet Fern, the Laurel, the Witch Hazle, the Myrtle Wax tree, Winter Green, the Fever Bush, the Cranberry Bush, the Goosberry Bush, the Currant Bush, the Whirtle Berry, the Rasberry, the Black Berry, and the Choak Berry.

The WILLOW. There are several species of the willow, the most remarkable of which is a small sort that grows on the banks of the Mississippi, and some other places adjacent. The bark of this shrub supplies the beaver with its winter food; and where the water has washed the soil from its roots, they appear to consist of fibres interwoven together like thread, the colour of which is of an inexpressible fine scarlet; with this the Indians tinge many of the ornamental parts of their dress.

SHIN WOOD. This extraordinary shrub grows in the forests, and rising like a vine, runs near the ground for six or eight feet,

feet, and then takes root again; in the fame manner taking root, and fpringing up fucceffively, one ftalk covers a large fpace; this proves very troublefome to the hafty traveller, by ftriking againft his fhins, and entangling his legs; from which it has acquired its name.

The SASSAFRAS is a wood well known for its medicinal qualities. It might with equal propriety be term'd a tree as a fhrub, as it fometimes grows thirty feet high; but in general it does not reach higher than thofe of the fhrub kind. The leaves, which yield an agreeable fragrance, are large, and nearly feparated into three divifions. It bears a reddifh brown berry, of the fize and fhape of Pimento, and which is fometimes ufed in the colonies as a fubftitute for that fpice. The bark or roots of this tree is infinitely fuperior to the wood for its ufe in medicine, and I am furprized it is fo feldom to be met with, as its efficacy is fo much greater.

The PRICKLY ASH is a fhrub that fometimes grows to the height of ten or fifteen feet, and has a leaf exactly refembling that of an afh, but it receives the epithet to its name from the abundance of fhort thorns with which every branch is covered, and which renders it very troublefome to thofe who pafs through the fpot where they grow thick. It alfo bears a fcarlet berry, which, when ripe, has a fiery tafte, like pepper. The bark of this tree, particularly the bark of the roots, is highly efteemed by the natives for its medicinal qualities. I have already mentioned one inftance of its efficacy, and there is no doubt but that the decoction of it will expeditioufly and radically remove all impurities of the blood.

The MOOSE WOOD grows about four feet high, and is very full of branches; but what renders it worth notice is its bark, which is of fo ftrong and pliable a texture, that being peeled off at any feafon, and twifted, makes equally as good cordage as hemp.

The SPOON WOOD is a fpecies of the laurel, and the wood when fawed refembles box wood.

The ELDER, commonly termed the poifonous elder, nearly refembles the other forts in its leaves and branches, but it grows much ftraiter, and is only found in fwamps and moift foils. This fhrub is endowed with a very extraordinary quality, that renders it poifonous to fome conftitutions, which it effects if the perfon only approaches within a few yards of it, whilft others may even chew the leaves or the rind without receiving the leaft detriment from them: the poifon however is not mortal, though it operates very violently on the infected perfon, whofe body and head fwell to an amazing fize, and are covered with eruptions, that at their height refemble the confluent fmall-pox. As it grows alfo in many of the provinces, the inhabitants cure its venom by drinking faffron tea, and anointing the external parts with a mixture compofed of cream and marfh mallows.

The

The SHRUB OAK is exactly similar to the oak tree, both in its wood and leaves, and like that it bears an acorn, but it never rises from the ground above four or five feet, growing crooked and knotty. It is found chiefly on a dry gravelly soil.

The WITCH HAZLE grows very bushy, about ten feet high, and is covered early in May with numerous white blossoms. When this shrub is in bloom, the Indians esteem it a further indication that the frost is entirely gone, and that they might sow their corn. It has been said, that it is possessed of the power of attracting gold or silver, and that twigs of it are made use of to discover where the veins of these metals lie hid; but I am apprehensive that this is only a fallacious story, and not to be depended on; however that supposition has given it the name of Witch Hazle.

The MYRTLE WAX TREE is a shrub about four or five feet high, the leaves of which are larger than those of the common myrtle, but they smell exactly alike. It bears its fruit in bunches, like a nosegay, rising from the same place in various stalks, about two inches long: at the end of each of these is a little nut containing a kernel, which is wholly covered with a gluey substance, which being boiled in water, swims on the surface of it, and becomes a kind of green wax; this is more valuable than bees-wax, being of a more brittle nature, but mixed with it makes a good candle, which, as it burns, sends forth an agreeable scent.

WINTER GREEN. This is an ever-green, of the species of the myrtle, and is found on dry heaths; the flowers of it are white, and in the form of a rose, but not larger than a silver penny; in the winter it is full of red berries, about the size of a sloe, which are smooth and round; these are preserved during the severe season by the snow, and are at that time in the highest perfection. The Indians eat these berries, esteeming them very balsamic, and invigorating to the stomach. The people inhabiting the interior colonies steep both sprigs and berries in beer, and use it as a diet drink for cleansing the blood from scorbutic disorders.

The FEVER BUSH grows about five or six feet high; its leaf is like that of a lilach, and it bears a reddish berry of a spicy flavour. The stalks of it are excessively brittle. A decoction of the buds or wood is an excellent febrifuge, and from this valuable property it receives its name. It is an ancient Indian remedy for all inflammatory complaints, and likewise much esteemed on the same account, by the inhabitants of the interior parts of the colonies.

The CRANBERRY BUSH. Though the fruit of this bush greatly resembles in size and appearance that of the common sort, which grows on a small vine, in morasses and bogs, yet the bush runs to the height of ten or twelve feet; but it is very rarely to be met with. As the meadow cranberry, being of a local growth, and flourishing only in morasses, cannot be
transplanted

transplanted or cultivated, the former, if removed at a proper season, would be a valuable acquisition to the garden, and with proper nurture prove equally as good, if not better.

The CHOAK BERRY. The shrub thus termed by the natives grows about five or six feet high, and bears a berry about the size of a sloe, of a jet black, which contains several small seeds within the pulp. The juice of this fruit, though not of a disagreeable flavour, is extremely tart, and leaves a roughness in the mouth and throat when eaten, that has gained it the name of choak berry.

ROOTS and PLANTS.

Elecampagne, Spikenard, Angelica, Sarsaparilla, Ginsang, Ground Nuts, Wild Potatoes, Liquorice, Snake Root, Gold Thread, Solomon's Seal, Devil's Bit, Blood Root, Onions, Garlick, Wild Parsnips, Mandrakes, Hellebore White and Black.

SPIKENARD, vulgarly called in the colonies Petty-Morrel. This plant appears to be exactly the same as the Asiatick spikenard, so much valued by the ancients. It grows near the sides of brooks, in rocky places, and its stem, which is about the size of a goose quill, springs up like that of angelica, reaching about a foot and an half from the ground. It bears bunches of berries in all respects like those of the elder, only rather larger. These are of such a balsamic nature, that when infused in spirits, they make a most palatable and reviving cordial.

SARSAPARILLA. The root of this plant, which is the most estimable part of it, is about the size of a goose quill, and runs in different directions, twined and crooked to a great length in the ground; from the principal stem of it spring many smaller fibres, all of which are though and flexible. From the root immediately shoots a stalk about a foot and an half long, which at the top branches into three stems; each of these has three leaves, much of the shape and size of a walnut leaf; and from the fork of each of the three stems grows a bunch of bluish white flowers, resembling those of the spikenard. The bark of the roots, which alone should be used in medicine, is of a bitterish flavour, but aromatic. It is deservedly esteemed for its medicinal virtues, being a gentle sudorific, and very powerful in attenuating the blood when impeded by gross humours.

GINSANG is a root that was once supposed to grow only in Korea, from whence it was usually exported to Japan, and by that means found its way to Europe; but it has been lately discovered to be also a native of North America, where it grows to as great perfection, and is equally valuable. Its root is like a small carot, but not so taper at the end; it it sometimes

divided

divided into two or more branches, in all other respects it resembles sarsaparilla in its growth. The taste of the root is bitterish. In the eastern parts of Asia it bears a great price, being there considered as a panacea, and is the last refuge of the inhabitants in all disorders. When chewed it certainly is a great strengthener of the stomach.

GOLD THREAD. This is a plant of the small vine kind, which grows in swampy places, and lies on the ground. The roots spread themselves just under the surface of the morass, and are easily drawn up by handfuls. They resemble a large entangled skain of thread, of a fine bright gold colour; and I am persuaded would yield a beautiful and permanent yellow dye. It is also greatly esteemed both by the Indians and colonists as a remedy for any soreness in the mouth, but the taste of it is exquisitely bitter.

SOLOMON's SEAL is a plant that grows on the sides of rivers, and in rich meadow land. It rises in the whole to about three feet high, the stalks being two feet, when the leaves begin to spread themselves and reach a foot further. A part in every root has an impression upon it about the size of a sixpence, which appears as if it was made by a seal, and from these it receives its name. It is greatly valued on account of its being a fine purifier of the blood.

DEVIL's BIT is another wild plant, which grows in the fields, and receives its name from a print that seems to be made by teeth in the roots. The Indians say that this was once an universal remedy for every disorder that human nature is incident to; but some of the evil spirits envying mankind in the possession of so efficacious a medicine gave the root a bite, which deprived it of a great part of its virtue.

BLOOD ROOT. A sort of plantain that springs out of the ground in six or seven long rough leaves, the veins of which are red; the root of it is like a small carrot, both in colour and appearance; when broken, the inside of it is of a deeper colour than the outside, and distils several drops of juice that look like blood. This is a strong emetic, but a very dangerous one.

HERBS.

Balm, Nettles, Cinque Foil, Eyebright, Sanicle, Plantain, Rattle Snake Plantain, Poor Robin's Plantain, Toad Plantain, Maiden Hair, Wild Dock, Rock Liverwort, Noble Liverwort, Bloodwort, Wild Beans, Ground Ivy, Water Cresses, Yarrow, May Weed, Gargit, Skunk Cabbage or Poke, Wake Robin, Betony, Scabious, Mullen, Wild Pease, Mouse Ear, Wild Indigo, Tobacco, and Cat Mint.

SANICLE

SANICLE has a root which is thick towards the upper part, and full of small fibres below; the leaves of it are broad, roundish, hard, smooth, and of a fine shining green; a stalk rises from these to the height of a foot, which is quite smooth and free from knots, and on the top of it are several small flowers of a reddish white, shaped like a wild rose. A tea made of the root is vulnerary and balsamic.

RATTLE SNAKE PLANTAIN. This useful herb is of the plantain kind, and its leaves, which spread themselves on the ground, are about one inch and an half wide, and five inches long; from the centre of these arises a small stalk, nearly six inches long, which bears a little white flower; the root is about the size of a goose quill, and much bent and divided into several branches. The leaves of this herb are more efficacious than any other part of it for the bite of the reptile from which it receives its name; and being chewed and applied immediately to the wound, and some of the juice swallowed, seldom fails of averting every dangerous symptom. So convinced are the Indians of the power of this infallible antidote, that for a trifling bribe of spirituous liquor, they will at any time permit a rattle snake to drive his fangs into their flesh. It is to be remarked that during those months in which the bite of these creatures is most venomous, that this remedy for it is in its greatest perfection, and most luxuriant in its growth.

POOR ROBIN's PLANTAIN is of the same species as the last, but more diminutive in every respect; it receives its name from its size, and the poor land on which it grows. It is a good medicinal herb, and often administered with success in fevers and internal weaknesses.

TOAD PLANTAIN resembles the common plaintain, only it grows much ranker, and is thus denominated because toads love to harbour under it.

ROCK LIVERWORT is a sort of Liverwort that grows on rocks, and is of the nature of kelp or moss. It is esteemed as an excellent remedy against declines.

GARGIT or SKOKE is a large kind of weed, the leaves of which are about six inches long, and two inches and an half broad; they resemble those of spinage in their colour and texture, but not in shape. The root is very large, from which spring different stalks that run eight or ten feet high, and are full of red berries; these hang in clusters in the month of September, and are generally called pigeon berries, as those birds then feed on them. When the leaves first spring from the ground, after being boiled, they are a nutritious and wholesome vegetable, but when they are grown nearly to their full size, they acquire a poisonous quality. The roots applied to the hands or feet of a person afflicted with a fever, prove a very powerful absorbent.

SKUNK CABBAGE or POKE is an herb that grows in moist and swampy places. The leaves of it are about a foot long, and

and six inches broad, nearly oval, but rather pointed. The roots are composed of great numbers of fibres, a lotion of which is made use of by the people in the colonies for the cure of the itch. There issues a strong musky smell from this herb, something like the animal of the same name before described, and on that account it is so termed.

WAKE ROBIN is an herb that grows in swampy lands; its root resembles a small turnip, and, if tasted will greatly inflame the tongue, and immediately convert it from its natural shape into a round hard substance; in which state it will continue for some time, and during this no other part of the mouth will be affected. But when dried, it loses its astringent quality, and becomes beneficial to mankind, for if grated into cold water, and taken internally, it is very good for all complaints of the bowels.

WILD INDIGO is an herb of the same species as that from whence indigo is made in the southern colonies. It grows in one stalk to the height of five or six inches from the ground, when it divides into many branches, from which issue a great number of small hard bluish leaves that spread to a great breadth, and among these it bears a yellow flower; the juice of it has a very disagreeable scent.

CAT MINT has a woody root, divided into several branches, and it sends forth a stalk about three feet high; the leaves are like those of the nettle or betony, and they have a strong smell of mint, with a biting acrid taste; the flowers grow on the tops of the branches, and are of a faint purple or whitish colour. It is called cat mint, because it is said that cats have an antipathy to it, and will not let it grow. It has nearly the virtues of common mint, *

FLOWERS.

Heart's Ease, Lilies red and yellow, Pond Lilies, Cowslips, May Flowers, Jessamine, Honeysuckles, Rock Honeysuckles, Roses red and white, Wild Hollyhock, Wild Pinks, Golden Rod.

I shall not enter into a minute description of the flowers above recited, but only just observe, that they much resemble those of the same name which grow in Europe, and are as beautiful in colour, and as perfect in odour, as they can be supposed to be in their wild uncultivated state.

* For an account of Tobacco, see a treatise I have published on the culture of that plant.

FARINACEOUS and LEGUMINOUS ROOTS, &c.

Maize or Indian Corn, Wild Rice, Beans, the Squash, &c.

MAIZE or INDIAN CORN grows from six to ten feet high, on a stalk full of joints, which is stiff and solid, and when green, abounding with a sweet juice. The leaves are like those of the reed, about two feet in length, and three or four inches broad. The flowers which are produced at some distance from the fruit on the same plant, grow like the ears of oats, and are sometimes white, yellow, or of a purple colour. The seeds are as large as peas, and like them quite naked and smooth, but of a roundish surface, rather compressed. One spike generally consists of about six hundred grains, which are placed closely together in rows to the number of eight or ten, and sometimes twelve. This corn is very wholesome, easy of digestion, and yields as good nourishment as any other sort. After the Indians have reduced it into meal by pounding it, they make cakes of it, and bake them before the fire. I have already mentioned that some nations eat it in cakes before it is ripe, in which state it is very agreeable to the palate, and extremely nutritive.

WILD RICE. This grain, which grows in the greatest plenty throughout the interior parts of North America, is the most valuable of all the spontaneous productions of that country. Exclusive of its utility, as a supply of food for those of the human species, who inhabit this part of the continent, and obtained without any other trouble than that of gathering it in, the sweetness and nutritious quality of it attracts an infinite number of wild fowl of every kind, which flock from distant climes, to enjoy this rare repast; and by it become inexpressibly fat and delicious. In future periods it will be of great service to the infant colonies, as it will afford them a present support, until in the course of cultivation other supplies may be produced; whereas in those realms which are not furnished with this bounteous gift of nature, even if the climate is temperate and the soil good, the first settlers are often exposed to great hardships from the want of an immediate resource for necessary food. This useful grain grows in the water where it is about two feet deep, and where it finds a rich muddy soil. The stalks of it, and the branches or ears that bear the seed, resemble oats both in their appearance and manner of growing. The stalks are full of joints, and rise more than eight feet above the water. The natives gather the grain in the following manner: nearly about the time that it begins to turn from its milky state and to ripen, they run their canoes into the midst of it, and tying bunches of it together, just below the ears with bark, leave it in this situation three or four weeks longer, till it is perfectly ripe. About the latter end of of September they return to the river, when each family having its separate allotment, and being able to diſtinguiſh their own property by the manner of faſtening the ſheaves, gather in the portion that belongs to them. This they do by placing their canoes cloſe to the bunches of rice, in ſuch poſition as to receive the grain when it falls, and then beat it out, with pieces of wood formed for that purpoſe. Having done this, they dry it with ſmoke, and afterwards tread or rub off the outſide huſk; when it is fit for uſe they put it into the ſkins of fawns, or young buffaloes, taken off nearly whole for this purpoſe, and ſewed into a ſort of ſack, wherein they preſerve it till the return of their harveſt. It has been the ſubject of much ſpeculation, why this ſpontaneous grain is not found in any other regions of America, or in thoſe countries ſituated in the ſame parallels of latitude, where the waters are as apparently adapted for its growth as in the climates I treat of. As for inſtance, none of the countries that lie to the ſouth and eaſt of the great lakes, even from the provinces north of the Carolinas, to the extremities of Labradore, produce any of this grain. It is true I found great quantities of it in the watered lands near Detroit, between Lake Huron and Lake Erie, but on enquiry I learned that it never arrived nearer to maturity than juſt to bloſſom; after which it appeared blighted, and died away. This convinces me that the north-weſt wind, as I have before hinted, is much more powerful in theſe than in the interior parts; and that it is more inimical to the fruits of the earth, after it has paſſed over the lakes, and become united with the wind which joins it from the frozen regions of the north, than it is farther to the weſtward.

BEANS. Theſe are nearly of the ſame ſhape as the European beans, but are not much larger than the ſmalleſt ſize of them. They are boiled, by the Indians, and eaten chiefly with bear's fleſh.

The SQUASH. They have alſo ſeveral ſpecies of the MELON or PUMPKIN, which by ſome are called ſquaſhes, and which ſerve many nations partly as a ſubſtitute for bread. Of theſe there is the round, the crane-neck, the ſmall flat, and the large oblong ſquaſh. The ſmaller ſorts being boiled, are eaten during the ſummer as vegetables; and are all of a pleaſing flavour. The crane-neck, which greatly excels all the others, are uſually hung up for a winter's ſtore, and in this manner might be preſerved for ſeveral months.

APPENDIX.

APPENDIX.

THE countries that lie between the great lakes and River Miſſiſſippi, and from thence ſouthward to Weſt Florida, although in the midſt of a large continent, and at a great diſtance from the ſea, are ſo ſituated, that a communication between them and other realms might conveniently be opened; by which means thoſe empires or colonies that may hereafter be founded or planted therein, will be rendered commercial ones. The great River Miſſiſſippi, which runs through the whole of them, will enable their inhabitants to eſtabliſh an intercourſe with foreign climes, equally as well as the Euphrates, the Nile, the Danube, or the Wolga do thoſe people which dwell on their banks, and who have no other convenience for exporting the produce of their own country, or for importing thoſe of others, than boats and veſſels of light burden: notwithſtanding which they have become powerful and opulent ſtates.

The Miſſiſſippi, as I have before obſerved, runs from north to ſouth, and paſſes through the moſt fertile and temperate part of North America, excluding only the extremities of it, which verge both on the torrid and frigid zones. Thus favourably ſituated, when once it's banks are covered with inhabitants, they need not long be at a loſs for means to eſtabliſh an extenſive and profitable commerce. They will find the country towards the ſouth almoſt ſpontaneouſly producing ſilk, cotton, indigo, and tobacco; and the more northern parts, wine, oil, beef, tallow, ſkins, buffalo-wool, and furs; with lead, copper, iron, coals, lumber, corn, rice, and fruits, beſides earth and barks for dying.

Theſe articles, with which it abounds even to profuſion, may be tranſported to the ocean through this river without greater difficulty than that which attends the conveyance of merchandize down ſome of thoſe I have juſt mentioned. It is true that the Miſſiſſippi being the boundary between the Engliſh and Spaniſh ſettlements, and the Spaniards in poſſeſſion of the mouth of it, they may obſtruct the paſſage of it, and greatly diſhearten thoſe who make the firſt attempts; yet when the advantages that will certainly ariſe to ſettlers are known, multitudes of adventurers, allured by the proſpect of ſuch abundant riches, will flock to it, and eſtabliſh themſelves, though at the expence of rivers of blood.

But ſhould the nation that happens to be in poſſeſſion of New Orleans prove unfriendly to the internal ſettlers, they may find a way into the Gulph of Mexico, by the River Iberville, which empties itſelf from the Miſſiſſippi, after paſſing through Lake Maurepas, into Lake Ponchartrain; which has a communication

tion with the sea within the borders of West-Florida. The River Iberville branches off from the Mississippi about eighty miles above New Orleans, and though it is at present choaked up in some parts, it might at an inconsiderable expence be made navigable, so as to answer all the purposes proposed.

Although the English have acquired since the last peace a more extensive knowledge of the interior parts than were ever obtained before, even by the French, yet many of their productions still remain unknown. And though I was not deficient either in assiduity or attention during the short time I remained in them, yet I must acknowledge that the intelligence I gained was not so perfect as I could wish, and that it requires further researches to make the world thoroughly acquainted with the real value of these long hidden realms.

The parts of the Mississippi of which no survey have hitherto been taken, amount to upwards of eight hundred miles, following the course of the stream, that is, from the Illinois to the Ouisconsin Rivers. Plans of such as reach from the Mississippi to the Gulph of Mexico, have been delineated by several hands, and I have the pleasure to find that an actual survey of the intermediate parts of the Mississippi, between the Illinois River and the sea, with the Ohio, Cherokee, and Ouabache Rivers, taken on the spot by a very ingenious Gentleman*, is now published. I flatter myself that the observations therein contained, which have been made by one whose knowledge of the parts therein described was acquired by a personal investigation, aided by a solid judgment, will confirm the remarks I have made, and promote the plan I am here recommending.

I shall also here give a concise description of each, beginning, according to the rule of geographers, with that which lies most to the north.

It is however necessary to observe, that before these settlements can be established, grants must be procured in the manner customary on such occasions, and the lands be purchased of those who have acquired a right to them by a long possession; but no greater difficulty will attend the completion of this point, than the original founders of every colony on the continent met with to obstruct their intentions; and the number of Indians who inhabit these tracts being greatly inadequate to their extent, it is not to be doubted, but they will readily give up for a reasonable consideration, territories that are of little use to them, or remove for the accommodation of their new neighbours, to lands at a greater distance from the Mississippi, the navigation of which is not essential to the welfare of their communities.

No. I. The country within these lines, from its situation, is colder than any of the others; yet I am convinced that the air is much more temperate than in those provinces that lie in the

---

* Thomas Hutchins, Esq; Captain in his Majesty's 60th, or Royal American Regiment of Foot.

the same degree of latitude to the east of it. The soil is excellent, and there is a great deal of land that is free from woods in the parts adjoining to the Missisippi; whilst on the contrary the north-eastern borders of it are well wooded. Towards the heads of the River Saint Croix, rice grows in great plenty, and there is abundance of copper. Though the falls of Saint Anthony are situated at the south-east corner of this division, yet that impediment will not totally obstruct the navigation, as the River Saint Croix, which runs through a great part of the southern side of it, enters the Missisippi just below the Falls, and flows with so gentle a current, that it affords a convenient navigation for boats. This tract is about one hundred miles from north-west to south-east, and one hundred and twenty miles from north-east to south-west.

No. II. This tract, as I have already described it in my Journals, exceeds the highest encomiums I can give it; notwithstanding which it is entirely uninhabited, and the profusion of blessings that nature has showered on this heavenly spot, return unenjoyed to the lap from whence they sprung. Lake Pepin, as I have termed it after the French, lies within these bounds; but the lake to which that name properly belongs is a little above the River St. Croix; however, as all the traders call the lower lake by that name, I have so denominated it, contrary to the information I received from the Indians. This colony lying in unequal angles, the dimensions of it cannot be exactly given, but it appears to be on an average about one hundred and ten miles long, and eighty broad.

No. III. The greatest part of this division is situated on the River Ouisconsin, which is navigable for boats about one hundred and eighty miles, till it reaches the carrying place that divides it from the Fox River. The land which is contained within its limits, is in some parts mountainous, and in others consists of fertile meadows and fine pasturage. It is furnished also with a great deal of good timber, and, as is generally the case on the banks of the Missisippi and its branches, has much fine, open, clear land, proper for cultivation. To these are added an inexhaustible fund of riches, in a number of lead mines which lie at a little distance from the Ouisconsin towards the south, and appear to be uncommonly full of ore. Although the Saukies and Ottagaumies inhabit a part of this tract, the whole of the lands under their cultivation does not exceed three hundred acres. It is in length from east to west about one hundred and fifty miles, and about eighty from north to south.

No. IV. This colony consists of lands of various denominations, some of which are very good, and others very bad. The best is situated on the borders of the Green Bay and the Fox River, where there are innumerable acres covered with fine grass, most part of which grows to an astonishing height. This river will afford a good navigation for boats throughout the whole of its course, which is about one hundred and eighty miles

miles, except between the Winnebago Lake, and the Green Bay; where there are several carrying-places in the space of thirty miles. The Fox River is rendered remarkable by the abundance of rice that grows on its shores, and the almost infinite numbers of wild fowl that frequent its banks. The land which lies near it appears to be very fertile, and promises to produce a sufficient supply of all the necessaries of life for any number of inhabitants. A communication might be opened by those who shall settle here, either through the Green Bay, Lake Michigan, Lake Huron, Lake Erie, and Lake Ontario with Canada, or by way of the Ouisconsin into the Mississippi. This division is about one hundred and sixty miles long from north to south, and one hundred and forty broad.

No. V. This is an excellent tract of land, and, considering its interior situation, has greater advantages than could be expected; for having the Mississippi on its western borders, and the Illinois on its south-east, it has as free a navigation as most of the others. The northern parts of it are somewhat mountainous, but it contains a great deal of clear land, the soil of which is excellent, with many fine fertile meadows, and not a few rich mines. It is upwards of two hundred miles from north to south, and one hundred and fifty from east to west.

No. VI. This colony being situated upon the heads of the Rivers Illinois and Ouabache, the former of which empties itself immediately into the Mississippi, and the latter into the same river by means of the Ohio, will readily find a communication with the sea through these. Having also the River Miamis passing through it, which runs into Lake Erie, an intercourse might be established with Canada also by way of the lakes, as before pointed out. It contains a great deal of rich fertile land, and though more inland than any of the others, will be as valuable an acquisition as the best of them. From north to south it is about one hundred and sixty miles, from east to west one hundred and eighty.

No. VII. This division is not inferior to any of the foregoing. Its northern borders lying adjacent to the Illinois river, and its western to the Mississippi, the situation of it for establishing a commercial intercourse with foreign nations is very commodious. It abounds with all the necessaries of life, and is about one hundred and fifty miles from north to south, and sixty miles from east to west; but the confines of it being more irregular than the others, I cannot exactly ascertain the dimensions of it.

No. VIII. This colony having the River Ouabache running through the centre of it, and the Ohio for its southern boundary, will enjoy the advantages of a free navigation. It extends about one hundred and forty miles from north to south, and one hundred and thirty from east to west.

No. IX. X. and XI. being similar in situation, and furnished with nearly the same conveniencies as all the others, I shall only ly give their dimensions. No. IX. is about eighty miles each way, but not exactly square. No. X. is nearly in the same form, and about the same extent. No. XI. is much larger, being at least one hundred and fifty miles from north to south, and one hundred and forty from east to west, as nearly as from its irregularity it is possible to calculate.

After the description of this delightful country I have already given, I need not repeat that all the spots I have thus pointed out as proper for colonization, abound not only with the necessaries of life, being well stored with rice, deer, buffalos, bears, &c. but produce in equal abundance such as may be termed luxuries, or at least those articles of commerce before recited, which the inhabitants of it will have an opportunity of exchanging for the needful productions of other countries.

The discovery of a north-west passage to India has been the subject of innumerable disquisitions. Many efforts likewise have been made by way of Hudson's Bay, to penetrate into the Pacific Ocean, though without success. I shall not therefore trouble myself to enumerate the advantages that would result from this much wished-for discovery, its utility being already too well known to the commercial world to need any elucidation; I shall only confine myself to the methods that appear most probable to ensure success to future adventurers.

The many attempts that have hitherto been made for this purpose, but which have all been rendered abortive, seem to have turned the spirit of making useful researches into another channel, and this most interesting one has almost been given up as impracticable; but, in my opinion, their failure rather proceeds from their being begun at an improper place, than from their impracticability.

All navigators that have hitherto gone in search of this passage, have first entered Hudson's Bay; the consequence of which has been, that having spent the season during which only those seas are navigable, in exploring many of the numerous inlets lying therein, and this without discovering any opening, terrified at the approach of winter, they have hastened back for fear of being frozen up, and consequently of being obliged to continue till the return of summer in those bleak and dreary realms. Even such as have perceived the coasts to enfold themselves, and who have of course entertained hopes of succeeding, have been deterred from prosecuting their voyage, lest the winter should set in before they could reach a more temperate climate.

These apprehensions have discouraged the boldest adventurers, from completing the expeditions in which they have engaged, and frustrated every attempt. But as it has been discovered by such as have sailed into the northern parts of the Pacific Ocean, that there are many inlets which verge towards Hudson's Bay, it is not to be doubted but that a passage might be made out from that quarter, if it be sought for at a proper season. And should these expectations be disappointed, the explorers would
not

not be in the same hazardous situation with those who set out from Hudson's Bay, for they will always be sure of a safe retreat, through an open sea, to warmer regions, even after repeated disappointments. And this confidence will enable them to proceed with greater resolution, and probably be the means of effecting what too much circumspection or timidity has prevented.

These reasons for altering the plan of enquiry after this convenient passage, carry with them such conviction, that in the year 1774 Richard Whitworth, Esq; member of parliament for Stafford, a gentleman of an extensive knowledge in geography, of an active enterprising disposition, and whose benevolent mind is ever ready to promote the happiness of individuals, or the welfare of the public, from the representations made to him of the expediency of it by myself and others, intended to travel across the continent of America, that he might attempt to carry a scheme of this kind into execution.

He designed to have pursued nearly the same route that I did; and after having built a fort at Lake Pepin, to have proceeded up the River St. Pierre, and from thence up a branch of the River Messorie, till having discovered the source of the Oregan or River of the West, on the other side the summit of the lands that divide the waters which run into the Gulph of Mexico from those that fall into the Pacific Ocean, he would have sailed down that river to the place where it is said to empty itself near the Straights of Annian.

Having there established another settlement on some spot that appeared best calculated for the support of his people, in the neighbourhood of some of the inlets which tend towards the north-east, he would from thence have begun his researches. This gentleman was to have been attended in the expedition by Colonel Rogers, myself, and others, and to have taken out with him a sufficient number of artificers and mariners for building the forts and vessels necessary on the occasion, and for navigating the latter; in all not less than fifty or sixty men. The grants and other requisites for this purpose were even nearly completed, when the present troubles in America began, which put a stop to an enterprize that promised to be of inconceivable advantage to the British dominions.

F I N I S.

www.ingramcontent.com/pod-product-compliance
Lightning Source LLC
Chambersburg PA
CBHW031832230426
43669CB00009B/1314